TABLE OF CONTENTS

Secret Key #1 - Time is Your Greatest Enemy

Pace Yourself

Wear a watch. At the beginning of the test, check the time (or start a chronometer on your watch to count the minutes), and check the time after every few questions to make sure you are "on schedule."

If you are forced to speed up, do it efficiently. Usually one or more answer choices can be eliminated without too much difficulty. Above all, don't panic. Don't speed up and just begin guessing at random choices. By pacing yourself, and continually monitoring your progress against your watch, you will always know exactly how far ahead or behind you are with your available time. If you find that you are one minute behind on the test, don't skip one question without spending any time on it, just to catch back up. Take 15 fewer seconds on the next four questions, and after four questions you'll have caught back up. Once you catch back up, you can continue working each problem at your normal pace.

Furthermore, don't dwell on the problems that you were rushed on. If a problem was taking up too much time and you made a hurried guess, it must be difficult. The difficult questions are the ones you are most likely to miss anyway, so it isn't a big loss. It is better to end with more time than you need than to run out of time.

Lastly, sometimes it is beneficial to slow down if you are constantly getting ahead of time. You are always more likely to catch a careless mistake by working more slowly than quickly, and among very high-scoring test takers (those who are likely to have lots of time left over), careless errors affect the score more than mastery of material.

Secret Key #2 - Guessing is not Guesswork

You probably know that guessing is a good idea - unlike other standardized tests, there is no penalty for getting a wrong answer. Even if you have no idea about a question, you still have a 20-25% chance of getting it right.

Most test takers do not understand the impact that proper guessing can have on their score. Unless you score extremely high, guessing will significantly contribute to your final score.

Monkeys Take the Test

What most test takers don't realize is that to insure that 20-25% chance, you have to guess randomly. If you put 20 monkeys in a room to take this test, assuming they answered once per question and behaved themselves, on average they would get 20-25% of the questions correct. Put 20 test takers in the room, and the average will be much lower among guessed questions. Why?

1. The test writers intentionally write deceptive answer choices that "look" right. A test taker has no idea about a question, so picks the "best looking" answer, which is often wrong. The monkey has no idea what looks good and what doesn't, so will consistently be lucky about 20-25% of the time.
2. Test takers will eliminate answer choices from the guessing pool based on a hunch or intuition. Simple but correct answers often get excluded, leaving a 0% chance of being correct. The monkey has no clue, and often gets lucky with the best choice.

This is why the process of elimination endorsed by most test courses is flawed and detrimental to your performance- test takers don't guess, they make an ignorant stab in the dark that is usually worse than random.

$5 Challenge

Let me introduce one of the most valuable ideas of this course- the $5 challenge:

You only mark your "best guess" if you are willing to bet $5 on it.
You only eliminate choices from guessing if you are willing to bet $5 on it.

Why $5? Five dollars is an amount of money that is small yet not insignificant, and can really add up fast (20 questions could cost you $100). Likewise, each answer choice on one question of the test will have a small impact on your overall score, but it can really add up to a lot of points in the end.

The process of elimination IS valuable. The following shows your chance of guessing it right:

If you eliminate wrong answer choices until only this many remain:	Chance of getting it correct:
1	100%
2	50%
3	33%

However, if you accidentally eliminate the right answer or go on a hunch for an incorrect answer, your chances drop dramatically: to 0%. By guessing among all the answer choices, you are GUARANTEED to have a shot at the right answer.

That's why the $5 test is so valuable- if you give up the advantage and safety of a pure guess, it had better be worth the risk.
What we still haven't covered is how to be sure that whatever guess you make is truly random. Here's the easiest way:

Always pick the first answer choice among those remaining.

Such a technique means that you have decided, **before you see a single test question**, exactly how you are going to guess- and since the order of choices tells you nothing about which one is correct, this guessing technique is perfectly random.

This section is not meant to scare you away from making educated guesses or eliminating choices- you just need to define when a choice is worth eliminating. The $5 test, along with a pre-defined random guessing strategy, is the best way to make sure you reap all of the benefits of guessing.

Secret Key #3 - Practice Smarter, Not Harder

Many test takers delay the test preparation process because they dread the awful amounts of practice time they think necessary to succeed on the test. We have refined an effective method that will take you only a fraction of the time.

There are a number of "obstacles" in your way to succeed. Among these are answering questions, finishing in time, and mastering test-taking strategies. All must be executed on the day of the test at peak performance, or your score will suffer. The test is a mental marathon that has a large impact on your future.

Just like a marathon runner, it is important to work your way up to the full challenge. So first you just worry about questions, and then time, and finally strategy:

Success Strategy

1. Find a good source for practice tests.
2. If you are willing to make a larger time investment, consider using more than one study guide- often the different approaches of multiple authors will help you "get" difficult concepts.
3. Take a practice test with no time constraints, with all study helps "open book." Take your time with questions and focus on applying strategies.
4. Take a practice test with time constraints, with all guides "open book."
5. Take a final practice test with no open material and time limits

If you have time to take more practice tests, just repeat step 5. By gradually exposing yourself to the full rigors of the test environment, you will condition your mind to the stress of test day and maximize your success.

Secret Key #4 - Prepare, Don't Procrastinate

Let me state an obvious fact: if you take the test three times, you will get three different scores. This is due to the way you feel on test day, the level of preparedness you have, and, despite the test writers' claims to the contrary, some tests WILL be easier for you than others.

Since your future depends so much on your score, you should maximize your chances of success. In order to maximize the likelihood of success, you've got to prepare in advance. This means taking practice tests and spending time learning the information and test taking strategies you will need to succeed.

Never take the test as a "practice" test, expecting that you can just take it again if you need to. Feel free to take sample tests on your own, but when you go to take the official test, be prepared, be focused, and do your best the first time!

Secret Key #5 - Test Yourself

Everyone knows that time is money. There is no need to spend too much of your time or too little of your time preparing for the test. You should only spend as much of your precious time preparing as is necessary for you to get the score you need.

Once you have taken a practice test under real conditions of time constraints, then you will know if you are ready for the test or not.

If you have scored extremely high the first time that you take the practice test, then there is not much point in spending countless hours studying. You are already there.

Benchmark your abilities by retaking practice tests and seeing how much you have improved. Once you score high enough to guarantee success, then you are ready.

If you have scored well below where you need, then knuckle down and begin studying in earnest. Check your improvement regularly through the use of practice tests under real conditions. Above all, don't worry, panic, or give up. The key is perseverance!

Then, when you go to take the test, remain confident and remember how well you did on the practice tests. If you can score high enough on a practice test, then you can do the same on the real thing.

General Strategies

The most important thing you can do is to ignore your fears and jump into the test immediately- do not be overwhelmed by any strange-sounding terms. You have to jump into the test like jumping into a pool- all at once is the easiest way.

Make Predictions

As you read and understand the question, try to guess what the answer will be. Remember that several of the answer choices are wrong, and once you begin reading them, your mind will immediately become cluttered with answer choices designed to throw you off. Your mind is typically the most focused immediately after you have read the question and digested its contents. If you can, try to predict what the correct answer will be. You may be surprised at what you can predict.

Quickly scan the choices and see if your prediction is in the listed answer choices. If it is, then you can be quite confident that you have the right answer. It still won't hurt to check the other answer choices, but most of the time, you've got it!

Answer the Question

It may seem obvious to only pick answer choices that answer the question, but the test writers can create some excellent answer choices that are wrong. Don't pick an answer just because it sounds right, or you believe it to be true. It MUST answer the question. Once you've made your selection, always go back and check it against the question and make sure that you didn't misread the question, and the answer choice does answer the question posed.

Benchmark

After you read the first answer choice, decide if you think it sounds correct or not. If it doesn't, move on to the next answer choice. If it does, mentally mark that answer choice. This doesn't mean that you've definitely selected it as your answer choice, it just means that it's the best you've seen thus far. Go ahead and read the next choice. If the next choice is worse than the one you've already selected, keep going to the next answer choice. If the next choice is better than the choice you've already selected, mentally mark the new answer choice as your best guess.

The first answer choice that you select becomes your standard. Every other answer choice must be benchmarked against that standard. That choice is correct until proven otherwise by another answer choice beating it out. Once you've decided that no other answer choice seems as good, do one final check to ensure that your answer choice answers the question posed.

Valid Information

Don't discount any of the information provided in the question. Every piece of information may be necessary to determine the correct answer. None of the information in the question is there to throw you off (while the answer choices will certainly have information to throw you off). If two seemingly unrelated topics are discussed, don't ignore either. You can be confident there is a relationship, or it wouldn't be included in the question, and you are probably going to have to determine what is that relationship to find the answer.

Avoid "Fact Traps"

Don't get distracted by a choice that is factually true. Your search is for the answer that answers the question. Stay focused and don't fall for an answer that is true but incorrect. Always go back to the question and make sure you're choosing an answer that actually answers the question and is not just a true statement. An answer can be factually correct, but it MUST answer the question asked. Additionally, two answers can both be seemingly correct, so be sure to read all of the answer choices, and make sure that you get the one that BEST answers the question.

Milk the Question

Some of the questions may throw you completely off. They might deal with a subject you have not been exposed to, or one that you haven't reviewed in years. While your lack of knowledge about the subject will be a hindrance, the question itself can give you many clues that will help you find the correct answer. Read the question carefully and look for clues. Watch particularly for adjectives and nouns describing difficult terms or words that you don't recognize. Regardless of if you completely understand a word or not, replacing it with a synonym either provided or one you more familiar with may help you to understand what the questions are asking. Rather than wracking your mind about specific detailed information concerning a difficult term or word, try to use mental substitutes that are easier to understand.

The Trap of Familiarity

Don't just choose a word because you recognize it. On difficult questions, you may not recognize a number of words in the answer choices. The test writers don't put "make-believe" words on the test; so don't think that just because you only recognize all the words in one answer choice means that answer choice must be correct. If you only recognize words in one answer choice, then focus on that one. Is it correct? Try your best to determine if it is correct. If it is, that is great, but if it doesn't, eliminate it. Each word and answer choice you eliminate increases your chances of getting the question correct, even if you then have to guess among the unfamiliar choices.

Eliminate Answers

Eliminate choices as soon as you realize they are wrong. But be careful! Make sure you consider all of the possible answer choices. Just because one appears right, doesn't mean that the next one won't be even better! The test writers will usually put more than one good answer choice for every question, so read all of them. Don't worry if you are stuck between two that seem right. By getting down to just two remaining possible choices, your odds are now 50/50. Rather than wasting too much time, play the odds. You are guessing, but guessing wisely, because you've been able to knock out some of the answer choices that you know are wrong. If you are eliminating choices and realize that the last answer choice you are left with is also obviously wrong, don't panic. Start over and consider each choice again. There may easily be something that you missed the first time and will realize on the second pass.

Tough Questions

If you are stumped on a problem or it appears too hard or too difficult, don't waste time. Move on! Remember though, if you can quickly check for obviously incorrect answer choices, your chances of guessing correctly are greatly improved. Before you completely give up, at least try to knock out a couple of possible answers. Eliminate what you can and then guess at the remaining answer choices before moving on.

Brainstorm

If you get stuck on a difficult question, spend a few seconds quickly brainstorming. Run through the complete list of possible answer choices. Look at each choice and ask yourself, "Could this answer the question satisfactorily?" Go through each answer choice and consider it independently of the other. By systematically going through all possibilities, you may find something that you would otherwise overlook. Remember that when you get stuck, it's important to try to keep moving.

Read Carefully

Understand the problem. Read the question and answer choices carefully. Don't miss the question because you misread the terms. You have plenty of time to read each question thoroughly and make sure you understand what is being asked. Yet a happy medium must be attained, so don't waste too much time. You must read carefully, but efficiently.

Face Value

When in doubt, use common sense. Always accept the situation in the problem at face value. Don't read too much into it. These problems will not require you to make huge leaps of logic. The test writers aren't trying to throw you off with a cheap trick. If you have to go beyond creativity and make a leap of logic in order to have an answer choice answer the question, then you should look at the other answer choices. Don't overcomplicate the problem by creating theoretical relationships or explanations that will warp time or space. These are normal problems rooted in reality. It's just that the applicable relationship or explanation may not be readily apparent and you have to figure things out. Use your common sense to interpret anything that isn't clear.

Prefixes

If you're having trouble with a word in the question or answer choices, try dissecting it. Take advantage of every clue that the word might include. Prefixes and suffixes can be a huge help. Usually they allow you to determine a basic meaning. Pre- means before, post- means after, pro - is positive, de- is negative. From these prefixes and suffixes, you can get an idea of the general meaning of the word and try to put it into context. Beware though of any traps. Just because con is the opposite of pro, doesn't necessarily mean congress is the opposite of progress!

Hedge Phrases

Watch out for critical "hedge" phrases, such as likely, may, can, will often, sometimes, often, almost, mostly, usually, generally, rarely, sometimes. Question writers insert these hedge phrases to cover every possibility. Often an answer choice will be wrong simply because it leaves no room for exception. Avoid answer choices that have definitive words like "exactly," and "always".

Switchback Words

Stay alert for "switchbacks". These are the words and phrases frequently used to alert you to shifts in thought. The most common switchback word is "but". Others include although, however, nevertheless, on the other hand, even though, while, in spite of, despite, regardless of.

New Information

Correct answer choices will rarely have completely new information included. Answer choices typically are straightforward reflections of the material asked about and will directly relate to the question. If a new piece of information is included in an answer choice that doesn't even seem to relate to the topic being asked about, then that answer choice is likely incorrect. All of the information needed to answer the question is usually provided for you, and so you should not have to make guesses that are unsupported or choose answer choices that require unknown information that cannot be reasoned on its own.

Time Management

On technical questions, don't get lost on the technical terms. Don't spend too much time on any one question. If you don't know what a term means, then since you don't have a dictionary, odds are you aren't going to get much further. You should immediately recognize terms as whether or not you know them. If you don't, work with the other clues that you have, the other answer choices and terms provided, but don't waste too much time trying to figure out a difficult term.

Contextual Clues

Look for contextual clues. An answer can be right but not correct. The contextual clues will help you find the answer that is most right and is correct. Understand the context in which a phrase or statement is made. This will help you make important distinctions.

Don't Panic

Panicking will not answer any questions for you. Therefore, it isn't helpful. When you first see the question, if your mind goes blank, take a deep breath. Force yourself to mechanically go through the steps of solving the problem and using the strategies you've learned.

Pace Yourself

Don't get clock fever. It's easy to be overwhelmed when you're looking at a page full of questions, your mind is full of random thoughts and feeling confused, and the clock is ticking down faster than you would like. Calm down and maintain the pace that you have set for yourself. As long as you are on track by monitoring your pace, you are guaranteed to have enough time for yourself. When you get to the last few minutes of the test, it may seem like you won't have enough time left, but if you only have as many questions as you should have left at that point, then you're right on track!

Answer Selection

The best way to pick an answer choice is to eliminate all of those that are wrong, until only one is left and confirm that is the correct answer. Sometimes though, an answer choice may immediately look right. Be careful! Take a second to make sure that the other choices are not equally obvious. Don't make a hasty mistake. There are only two times that you should stop before checking other answers. First is when you are positive that the answer choice you have selected is correct. Second is when time is almost out and you have to make a quick guess!

Check Your Work

Since you will probably not know every term listed and the answer to every question, it is important that you get credit for the ones that you do know. Don't miss any questions through careless mistakes. If at all possible, try to take a second to look back over your answer selection and make sure you've selected the correct answer choice and haven't made a costly careless mistake (such as marking an answer choice that you didn't mean to mark). This quick double check should more than pay for itself in caught mistakes for the time it costs.

Beware of Directly Quoted Answers

Sometimes an answer choice will repeat word for word a portion of the question or reference section. However, beware of such exact duplication – it may be a trap! More than likely, the correct choice will paraphrase or summarize a point, rather than being exactly the same wording.

Slang

Scientific sounding answers are better than slang ones. An answer choice that begins "To compare the outcomes…" is much more likely to be correct than one that begins "Because some people insisted…"

Extreme Statements

Avoid wild answers that throw out highly controversial ideas that are proclaimed as established fact. An answer choice that states the "process should used in certain situations, if…" is much more likely to be correct than one that states the "process should be discontinued completely." The first is a calm rational statement and doesn't even make a definitive, uncompromising stance, using a hedge word "if" to provide wiggle room, whereas the second choice is a radical idea and far more extreme.

Answer Choice Families

When you have two or more answer choices that are direct opposites or parallels, one of them is usually the correct answer. For instance, if one answer choice states "x increases" and another answer choice states "x decreases" or "y increases," then those two or three answer choices are very similar in construction and fall into the same family of answer choices. A family of answer choices is when two or three answer choices are very similar in construction, and yet often have a directly opposite meaning. Usually the correct answer choice will be in that family of answer choices. The "odd man out" or answer choice that doesn't seem to fit the parallel construction of the other answer choices is more likely to be incorrect.

Top 20 Test Taking Tips

1. Carefully follow all the test registration procedures
2. Know the test directions, duration, topics, question types, how many questions
3. Setup a flexible study schedule at least 3-4 weeks before test day
4. Study during the time of day you are most alert, relaxed, and stress free
5. Maximize your learning style; visual learner use visual study aids, auditory learner use auditory study aids
6. Focus on your weakest knowledge base
7. Find a study partner to review with and help clarify questions
8. Practice, practice, practice
9. Get a good night's sleep; don't try to cram the night before the test
10. Eat a well balanced meal
11. Know the exact physical location of the testing site; drive the route to the site prior to test day
12. Bring a set of ear plugs; the testing center could be noisy
13. Wear comfortable, loose fitting, layered clothing to the testing center; prepare for it to be either cold or hot during the test
14. Bring at least 2 current forms of ID to the testing center
15. Arrive to the test early; be prepared to wait and be patient
16. Eliminate the obviously wrong answer choices, then guess the first remaining choice
17. Pace yourself; don't rush, but keep working and move on if you get stuck
18. Maintain a positive attitude even if the test is going poorly
19. Keep your first answer unless you are positive it is wrong
20. Check your work, don't make a careless mistake

United States History

Well-known Native Americans

The following are five well-known Native Americans and their roles in early U.S. history:

- Squanto, an Algonquian, helped early English settlers survive the hard winter by teaching them the native methods of planting corn, squash, and pumpkins.
- Pocahontas, also Algonquian, became famous as a liaison with John Smith's Plymouth colony in 1607.
- Sacagawea, a Shoshone, served a vital role in the Lewis and Clark expedition when the two explorers hired her as their guide in 1805.
- Crazy Horse and Sitting Bull led Sioux and Cheyenne troops in the Battle of the Little Bighorn in 1876, soundly defeating George Armstrong Custer.
- Chief Joseph, a leader of the Nez Perce who supported peaceful interaction with white settlers, attempted to relocate his tribe to Canada rather than move them to a reservation.

Native American groups

The major regional Native American groups and the major traits of each one are as follows:

- The Algonquians in the eastern part of the United States lived in wigwams. The northern tribes subsisted on hunting and gathering, while those who were farther south grew crops such as corn.
- The Iroquois, also an east coast tribe, spoke a different language from the Algonquians, and lived in rectangular longhouses.
- The Plains tribes lived between the Mississippi River and the Rocky Mountains. Nomadic tribes, they lived in teepees and followed the buffalo herds. Plains tribes included the Sioux, Cheyenne, Comanche and Blackfoot.
- Pueblo tribes included the Zuni, Hope, and Acoma. They lived in the Southwest deserts in homes made of stone or adobe. They domesticated animals and cultivated corn and beans.
- On the Pacific coast, tribes such as the Tlingit, Chinook and Salish lived on fish as well as deer, native berries and roots. Their rectangular homes housed large family groups, and they used totem poles.
- In the far north, the Aleuts and Inuit lived in skin tents or igloos. Talented fishermen, they built kayaks and umiaks and also hunted caribou, seals, whales and walrus.

Age of Exploration

The Age of Exploration is also called the Age of Discovery. It is generally considered to have begun in the early fifteenth century, and continued into the seventeenth century. Major developments of the Age of Exploration included technological advances in navigation, mapmaking and shipbuilding. These advances led to expanded European exploration of the rest of the world. Explorers set out from several European countries, including Portuguese, Spain, France and England, seeking new routes to Asia. These efforts led to the discovery of new lands, as well as colonization in India, Asia, Africa, and North America.

Advancements in navigation and seafaring tools

For long ocean journeys, it was important for sailors to be able to find their way home even when their vessels sailed far out to sea, well out of sight of land. A variety of navigational tools enabled them to launch ambitious journeys over long distances. The compass and astrolabe were particularly important advancements. The magnetic compass had been used by Chinese navigators for some time, and knowledge of the astrolabe came to Europe from Arab navigators and traders who had refined designs developed by the ancient Greeks.

The Portuguese developed a ship called a caravel in the 1400s that incorporated navigational advancements with the ability to make long sea journeys. Equipped with this advanced vessel, the Portuguese achieved a major goal of the Age of Exploration by discovering a sea route from Europe to Asia in 1498.

Voyage of Christopher Columbus

In 1492, Columbus, a Genoan explorer, obtained financial backing from King Ferdinand and Queen Isabella of Spain to seek a sea route to Asia. He sought a trade route with the Asian Indies to the west. With three ships, the *Niña*, the *Pinta* and the *Santa Maria*, he eventually landed in the West Indies. While Columbus failed in his effort to discover a western route to Asia, he is credited with the discovery of the Americas.

Colonization of the Americas

The following are the various goals of the French, Spanish, Dutch and British in the colonization of the Americas:

- Initial French colonies were focused on expanding the fur trade. Later, French colonization led to the growth of plantations in Louisiana which brought numerous African slaves to the New World.
- Spanish colonists came to look for wealth, and to converting the natives to Christianity. For some, the desire for gold led to mining in the New World, while others established large ranches.
- The Dutch were also involved in the fur trade, and also imported slaves as the need for laborers increased.
- British colonists arrived with various goals. Some were simply looking for additional income, while others were fleeing Britain to escape religious persecution.

New England colonies
The New England colonies were: New Hampshire, Connecticut, Rhode Island and Massachusetts. The colonies in New England were founded largely to escape religious persecution in England. The beliefs of the Puritans, who migrated to America in the 1600s, significantly influenced the development of these colonies. Situated in the northeast coastal areas of America, the New England colonies featured numerous harbors as well as dense forest. The soil, however, is rocky and, with a very short growing season, was not well suited for agriculture. The economy of New England during the colonial period centered around fishing, shipbuilding and trade along with some small farms and lumber mills. Although some groups congregated in small farms, life centered largely on towns and cities where merchants largely controlled the trade economy. Coastal cities such as Boston grew and thrived.

Middle or Middle Atlantic Colonies
The Middle or Middle Atlantic Colonies were: New York, New Jersey, Pennsylvania and Delaware. Unlike the New England colonies, where most colonists were from England and Scotland, the Middle Colonies founders were from various countries including the Netherlands, Holland and Sweden. Various factors led these colonists to America. More fertile than New England, the Middle Colonies became major producers of crops included rye, oats, potatoes, wheat, and barley. Some particularly wealthy inhabitants owned large farms and/or businesses. Farmers in general were able to produce enough to have a surplus to sell. Tenant farmers also rented land from larger land owners.

Southern Colonies
The Southern Colonies were Maryland, Virginia, North Carolina, South Carolina and Georgia. Of the Southern Colonies, Virginia was the first permanent English colony and Georgia the last. The warm climate and rich soil of the south encouraged agriculture, and the growing season was long. As a result, economy in the south was based largely on labor-intensive plantations. Crops included tobacco, rice and indigo, all of which became valuable cash crops. Most land in the south was controlled by wealthy plantation

owners and farmers. Labor on the farms came in the form of indentured servants and African slaves. The first of these African slaves arrived in Virginia in 1619, starting a long, unpleasant history of slavery in the American colonies.

French and Indian Wars

The British defeat of the Spanish Armada in 1750 led to the decline of Spanish power in Europe. This in turn led the British and French into battle over several wars between 1689 and 1748. These wars were:

- King William's War, or the Nine Years War, 1689-1697. This war was fought largely in Flanders.
- The War of Spanish Succession, or Queen Anne's War, 1702-1713
- War of Austrian Succession, or King George's War, 1740-1748

The fourth and final, the French and Indian War, was fought largely in the North American territory, and resulted in the end of France's reign as a colonial power in North America. Although the French held many advantages, including more cooperative colonists and numerous Indian allies, the strong leadership of William Pitt eventually led the British to victory. Costs incurred during the wars eventually led to discontent in the colonies. This helped spark the American Revolution

Navigation Acts

Enacted in 1651, the Navigation Acts were an attempt by Britain to dominate international trade. Aimed largely at the Dutch, the Acts banned foreign ships from transporting goods to the British colonies, and from transporting goods to Britain from elsewhere in Europe. While the restrictions on trade angered some colonists, these Acts were helpful to other American colonists who, as members of the British Empire, were legally able to provide ships for Britain's growing trade interests and use the ships for their own trading ventures. By the time the French and Indian War had ended, one-third of British merchant ships were built in the American colonies. Many colonists amassed fortunes in the shipbuilding trade.

Higher taxes after the French and Indian War

The French and Indian War created circumstances for which the British desperately needed more revenue. These included:

- The need to pay off the war debt.
- The need for funds to defend the expanding empire
- The need for funds to govern Britain's thirty-three far-flung colonies, including the American colonies

These needs led the British to pass additional laws to increase revenues from the colonies. Because they had spent so much money to defend the American colonies, the British felt it was appropriate to collect considerably higher taxes from them. The colonists felt this was unfair, and many were led to protest the increasing taxes. Eventually, protest led to violence.

Triangular trade

Triangular trade began in the Colonies with ships setting off for Africa carrying rum. In Africa, the rum was traded for gold or slaves. Ships then went from Africa to the West Indies, trading slaves for sugar, molasses, or money. To complete the triangle, the ships returned to the colonies with sugar or molasses to make more rum, as well as stores of gold and silver. This trade triangle violated the Molasses Act of 1733, which required the colonists to pay high duties to Britain on molasses acquired from French, Dutch, and Spanish colonies. The colonists ignored these duties, and the British government adopted a policy of salutary neglect by not enforcing them.

Effects of new laws on British-Colonial relations

While earlier revenue-generating acts such as the Navigation Acts brought money to the colonists, the new laws after 1763 required colonists to pay money back to Britain. The British felt this was fair since the colonists were British subjects and since they had incurred debt protecting the Colonies. The colonists felt it was not only unfair, but illegal.

The development of local government in America had given the colonists a different view of the structure and role of government. This made it difficult for the British to understand colonist's protests against what the British felt was a fair and reasonable solution to the mother country's financial problems.

Increasing discontent in the American colonies

More and more colonists had been born on American soil, decreasing any sense of kinship with the far away British rulers. Their new environment had led to new ideas of government and a strong view of the colonies as a separate entity from Britain. Colonists were allowed to self-govern in domestic issues, but Britain controlled international issues. In fact, the American colonies were largely left to form their own local government bodies, giving them more freedom than any other colonial territory. This gave the colonists a sense of independence which led them to resent control from Britain. Threats during the French and Indian War led the colonists to call for unification in order to protect themselves.

Difference between colonial government and British government

As new towns and other legislative districts developed in America, the colonists began to practice representative government. Colonial legislative bodies were made up of elected representatives chosen by male property owners in the districts. These individuals represented interests of the districts from which they had been elected.

By contrast, in Britain the Parliament represented the entire country. Parliament was not elected to represent individual districts. Instead, they represented specific classes. Because of this drastically different approach to government, the British did not understand the colonists' statement that they had no representation in the British Parliament.

Acts of British Parliament

Four major Acts of British Parliament that occurred after the French and Indian Wars and what they governed are:

- The Quartering Act, 1765. This act required colonists to provide accommodations and supplies for British troops. In addition, colonists were prohibited from settling west of the Appalachians until given permission by Britain.
- The Sugar Act, 1764. This act not only required taxes to be collected on molasses brought into the colonies, but gave British officials the right to search the homes of anyone suspected of violating it.
- The Stamp Act, 1765. The Stamp Act taxed printed materials such as newspapers and legal documents. Protests led the Stamp Act to be repealed in 1766, but the repeal also included the Declaratory Act, which stated that Parliament had the right to govern the colonies.
- The Townshend Acts, 1767. These acts taxed paper, paint, lead and tea that came into the colonies. Colonists led boycotts in protest, and in Massachusetts leaders like Samuel and John Adams began to organize resistance against British rule.

Boston Massacre

With the passage of the Stamp Act, nine colonies met in New York to demand its repeal. Elsewhere, protest arose in New York City,

Philadelphia, Boston and other cities. These protests sometimes escalated into violence, often targeting ruling British officials. The passage of the Townshend Acts in 1767 led to additional tension in the colonies. The British sent troops to New York City and Boston. On March 5, 1770, protesters began to taunt the British troops, throwing snowballs. The soldiers responded by firing into the crowd. This clash between protesters and soldiers led to five deaths and eight injuries, and was christened the Boston Massacre. Shortly thereafter, Britain repealed the majority of the Townshend Acts.

Tea Act and the Boston Tea Party

The majority of the Townshend Acts were repealed after the Boston Massacre in 1770, but Britain kept the tax on tea. In 1773, the Tea Act was passed. This allowed the East India Company to sell tea for much lower prices, and also allowed them to bypass American distributors, selling directly to shopkeepers instead. Colonial tea merchants saw this as a direct assault on their business. In December of 1773, 150 merchants boarded ships in Boston Harbor and dumped 342 chests of tea into the sea in protest of the new laws. This act of protest came to be known as the Boston Tea Party.

Coercive Acts

The Coercive Acts passed by Britain in 1774 were meant to punish Massachusetts for defying British authority. The four Coercive Acts:

- Shut down ports in Boston until the city paid back the value of the tea destroyed during the Boston Tea Party.
- Required that local government officials in Massachusetts be appointed by the governor rather than being elected by the people.
- Allowed trials of British soldiers to be transferred to Britain rather than being held in Massachusetts.
- Required locals to provide lodging for British soldiers any time there was a disturbance, even if lodging required them to stay in private homes.

These Acts led to the assembly of the First Continental Congress in Philadelphia on September 5, 1774. Fifty-five delegates met, representing 12 of the American colonies. They sought compromise with England over England's increasingly harsh efforts to control the colonies.

First Continental Congress

The First Continental Congress met in Philadelphia on September 5, 1774. Their goal was to achieve a peaceful agreement with Britain. Made up of delegates from 12 of the 13 colonies, the Congress affirmed loyalty to Britain and the power of Parliament to dictate foreign affairs in the colonies. However, they demanded that the Intolerable Acts be repealed, and instituted a trade embargo with Britain until this came to pass.

In response, George III of Britain declared that the American colonies must submit or face military action. The British sought to end assemblies opposing their policies. These assemblies gathered weapons and began to form militias. On April 19, 1775, the British military was ordered to disperse a meeting of the Massachusetts Assembly. A battle ensued on Lexington Common as the armed colonists resisted. The resulting battles became the Battle of Lexington and Concord—the first battles of the American Revolution.

Second Continental Congress

The Second Continental Congress met in Philadelphia on May 10, 1775, a month after Lexington and Concord. Their discussions centered on defense of the American colonies and how to conduct the growing war, as well as local government. The delegates also discussed declaring independence from Britain, with many members in favor of this drastic move. They established an army, and on June 15, named George Washington as its commander in chief. By 1776, it was obvious that there was no turning back from full-scale war with Britain. The colonial delegates of the Continental

Congress drafted the Declaration of Independence on July 4, 1776.

Battles of the Revolutionary War

The following are five battles of the Revolutionary War and their significance:

- The Battle of Lexington and Concord (April, 1775) is considered the first engagement of the Revolutionary War.
- The Battle of Bunker Hill, in June of 1775, was one of the bloodiest of the entire war. Although American troops withdrew, about half the British army was lost. The colonists proved they could stand against professional British soldiers. In August, Britain declared that the American colonies were officially in a state of rebellion.
- The first colonial victory occurred in Trenton, New Jersey, when Washington and his troops crossed the Delaware River on Christmas Day, 1776 for a December 26, surprise attack on British and Hessian troops.
- The Battle of Saratoga effectively ended a plan to separate the New England colonies from their Southern counterparts. The surrender of British general John Burgoyne led to France joining the war as allies of the Americans, and is generally considered a turning point of the war.
- On October 19, 1781, General Cornwallis surrendered after a defeat in the Battle of Yorktown, Virginia, ending the Revolutionary War.

Declaration of Independence

Penned by Thomas Jefferson and signed on July 4, 1776, the Declaration of Independence stated that King George III had violated the rights of the colonists and was establishing a tyrannical reign over them. Many of Jefferson's ideas of natural rights and property rights were shaped by seventeenth century philosopher John Locke. Jefferson focused on natural rights, as demonstrated by the assertion of people's rights to "life, liberty and the pursuit of happiness." Locke's comparable idea asserted "life, liberty, and private property." Both felt that the purpose of government was to protect the rights of the people, and that individual rights were more important than individuals' obligations to the state.

Treaty of Paris

The Treaty of Paris was signed on September 3, 1783, bringing an official end to the Revolutionary War. In this document, Britain officially recognized the United States of America as an independent nation. The treaty established the Mississippi River as the country's western border. The treaty also restored Florida to Spain, while France reclaimed African and Caribbean colonies seized by the British in 1763. On November 24, 1783, the last British troops departed from the newly born United States of America.

Articles of Confederation

A precursor to the Constitution, the Articles of Confederation represented the first attempt of the newly independent colonies to establish the basics of independent government. The Continental Congress passed the Articles on November 15, 1777. They went into effect on March 1, 1781, following ratification by the thirteen states.
The Articles prevented a central government from gaining too much power, instead giving power to a Congressional body made up of delegates from all thirteen states. However, the individual states retained final authority.

Without a strong central executive, though, this weak alliance among the new states proved ineffective in settling disputes or enforcing laws. The idea of a weak central government needed to be revised. Recognition of these weaknesses eventually led to the drafting of a new document, the Constitution.

Constitution

Delegates from twelve of the thirteen states (Rhode Island was not represented) met in Philadelphia in May of 1787, initially intending to revise the Articles of Confederation. However, it quickly became apparent that a simple revision would not provide the workable governmental structure the newly formed country needed. After vowing to keep all the proceedings secret until the final document was completed, the delegates set out to draft what would eventually become the Constitution of the United States of America. By keeping the negotiations secret, the delegates were able to present a completed document to the country for ratification, rather than having every small detail hammered out by the general public.

Structure of proposed government

The delegates agreed that the new nation required a strong central government, but that its overall power should be limited. The various branches of the government should have balanced power, so that no one group could control the others. Final power belonged with the citizens who voted officials into office based on who would provide the best representation.

Virginia Plan, New Jersey Plan, and the Great Compromise

Disagreement immediately occurred between delegates from large states and those from smaller states. The governor of Virginia, Edmond Randolph, felt that representation in Congress should be based on state population. This was the Virginia Plan. The New Jersey Plan, presented by William Paterson, from New Jersey, proposed each state have equal representation. Finally, Roger Sherman from Connecticut formulated the Connecticut Compromise, also called the Great Compromise. The result was the familiar structure we have today. Each state has the equal representation of two Senators in the Senate, with the number of representatives in the House of Representatives based on population. This is called a bicameral Congress. Both houses may draft bills, but financial matters must originate in the House of Representatives.

Three-fifths compromise

During debate on the U.S. Constitution, a disagreement arose between the Northern and Southern states involving how slaves should be counted when determining a state's quota of representatives. In the South large numbers of slaves were commonly used to run plantations. Delegates wanted slaves to be counted to determine the number of representatives, but not counted to determine the amount of taxes the states would pay. The Northern states wanted exactly the opposite arrangement. The final decision was to count three-fifths of the slave population both for tax purposes and to determine representation. This was called the three-fifths compromise.

Commerce Compromise

The Commerce Compromise also resulted from a North/South disagreement. In the North the economy was centered on industry and trade. The Southern economy was largely agricultural. The Northern states wanted to give the new government the ability to regulate exports as well as trade between the states. The South opposed this plan. Another compromise was in order. In the end, Congress received regulatory power over all trade, including the ability to collect tariffs on exported goods. In the South, this raised another red flag regarding the slave trade, as they were concerned about the effect on their economy if tariffs were levied on slaves. The final agreement allowed importing slaves to continue for twenty years without government intervention. Import taxes on slaves were limited, and after the year 1808, Congress could decide whether to allow continued imports of slaves.

Objections against the Constitution

Once the Constitution was drafted, it was presented for approval by the states. Nine states needed to approve the document for it to become official. However, debate and discussion continued. Major concerns included:

- The lack of a bill of rights to protect individual freedoms.
- States felt too much power was being handed over to the central government.
- Voters wanted more control over their elected representatives.

Discussion about necessary changes to the Constitution divided roughly into two camps: Federalists and Anti-Federalists. Federalists wanted a strong central government. Anti-Federalists wanted to prevent a tyrannical government from developing if a central government held too much power.

Federalist and Anti-Federalist camps

Major Federalist leaders included Alexander Hamilton, John Jay and James Madison. They wrote a series of letters, called the Federalist Papers, aimed at convincing the states to ratify the Constitution. These were published in New York papers.

Anti-Federalists included Thomas Jefferson and Patrick Henry. They argued against the Constitution as it was originally drafted in arguments called the Anti-Federalist Papers. The final compromise produced a strong central government controlled by checks and balances. A Bill of Rights was also added, becoming the first ten amendments to the Constitution. These amendments protected rights such as freedom of speech, freedom of religion, and other basic rights. Aside from various amendments added throughout the years, the United States Constitution has remained unchanged.

Administration of the new government

The individuals who formed the first administration of the new government are as follows:

- George Washington was elected as the first President of the United States in 1789.
- John Adams, who finished second in the election, became the first Vice President.
- Thomas Jefferson was appointed by Washington as Secretary of State.
- Alexander Hamilton was also appointed Secretary of the Treasury.

Alien and Sedition Acts

When John Adams became president, a war was raging between Britain and France. While Adams and the Federalists backed the British, Thomas Jefferson and the Republican Party supported the French. The United States nearly went to war with France during this time period, while France worked to spread its international standing and influence under the leadership of Napoleon Bonaparte. The Alien and Sedition Acts grew out of this conflict, and made it illegal to speak in a hostile fashion against the existing government. They also allowed the president to deport anyone in the U.S. who was not a citizen and who was suspected of treason or treasonous activity.

When Jefferson became the third president in 1800, he repealed these four laws and pardoned anyone who had been convicted under them.

Political parties

Many in the U.S. were against political parties after seeing the way parties, or factions, functioned in Britain. The factions in Britain were more interested in personal profit than the overall good of the country, and they did not want this to happen in the U.S.

However, the differences of opinion between Thomas Jefferson and Alexander Hamilton led to formation of political parties. Hamilton favored a stronger central government, while Jefferson felt more power should remain with the states. Jefferson was in favor of strict Constitutional interpretation, while Hamilton believed in a more flexible approach. As various others joined the separate camps, Hamilton backers began to term themselves Federalists while those supporting Jefferson became identified as Democratic-Republicans.

Whig Party, Democratic Party, and Republican Party

Thomas Jefferson was elected president in 1800 and again in 1804. The Federalist Party began a decline, and its major figure, Alexander Hamilton, died in a duel with Aaron Burr in 1804. By 1816, the Federalist Party virtually disappeared.

New parties sprang up to take its place. After 1824, the Democratic-Republican Party suffered a split. The Whigs arose, backing John Quincy Adams and industrial growth. The new Democratic Party formed, in opposition to the Whigs, and their candidate, Andrew Jackson, was elected as president in 1828.

By the 1850s, issues regarding slavery led to the formation of the Republican Party, which was anti-slavery, while the Democratic Party of the time, with a larger interest in the South, favored slavery. This Republican/Democrat division formed the basis of today's two-party system.

Marbury v. Madison

The main duty of the Supreme Court today is judicial review. This power was largely established by Marbury v. Madison. When John Adams was voted out of office in 1800, he worked, during his final days in office, to appoint Federalist judges to Supreme Court positions, knowing Jefferson, his replacement, held opposing views. As late as March 3, the day before Jefferson was to take office, Adams made last-minute appointments referred to as "Midnight Judges." One of the late appointments was William Marbury. The next day, March 4, Jefferson ordered his Secretary of State, James Madison, not to deliver Marbury's commission. This decision was backed by Chief Justice Marshall, who determined that the Judiciary Act of 1789, which granted the power to deliver commissions, was illegal in that it gave the Judicial Branch powers not granted in the Constitution. This case set precedent for the Supreme Court to nullify laws it found to be unconstitutional.

McCulloch v Maryland

Judicial review was further exercised by the Supreme Court in McCulloch v Maryland. When Congress chartered a national bank, the Second Bank of the United States, Maryland voted to tax any bank business dealing with banks chartered outside the state, including the federally chartered bank. Andrew McCulloch, an employee of the Second Bank of the US in Baltimore, refused to pay this tax. The resulting lawsuit from the State of Maryland went to the Supreme Court for judgment.

John Marshall, Chief Justice of the Supreme Court, stated that Congress was within its rights to charter a national bank. In addition, the State of Maryland did not have the power to levy a tax on the federal bank or on the federal government in general. In cases where state and federal government collided, precedent was set for the federal government to prevail.

Effects of the Treaty of Paris on Native Americans

After the Revolutionary War, the Treaty of Paris, which outlined the terms of surrender of the British to the Americans, granted large parcels of land to the U.S. that were occupied by Native Americans. The new government attempted to claim the land, treating the natives as a conquered people. This approached proved unenforceable.

Next, the government tried purchasing the land from the Indians via a series of treaties as the country expanded westward. In practice, however, these treaties were not honored, and Native Americans were simply dislocated and forced to move farther and farther west as American expansion continued, often with military action.

Indian Removal Act of 1830 and the Treaty of New

The Indian Removal Act of 1830 gave the new American government power to form treaties with Native Americans. In theory, America would claim land east of the Mississippi in exchange for land west of the Mississippi, to which the natives would relocate voluntarily. In practice, many tribal leaders were forced into signing the treaties, and relocation at times occurred by force.

The Treaty of New Echota was supposedly a treaty between the US government and Cherokee tribes in Georgia. However, the treaty was not signed by tribal leaders, but rather by a small portion of the represented people. The leaders protested by refusing to be removed, but President, Martin Van Buren, enforced the treaty by sending soldiers. During their forced relocation, more than 4,000 Cherokee Indians died on what became known as the Trail of Tears.

Early economic trends by region

In the Northeast, the economy mostly depended on manufacturing, industry and industrial development. This led to a dichotomy between rich business owners and industrial leaders and the much poorer workers who supported their businesses. The South continued to depend on agriculture, especially large-scale farms or plantations worked mostly by slaves and indentured servants. In the West, where new settlement had begun to develop, the land was largely wild. Growing communities were essentially agricultural; growing crops and raising livestock. The differences between regions led each to support different interests both politically and economically.

Louisiana Purchase

With tension still high between France and Britain, Napoleon was in need of money to support his continuing war efforts. To secure necessary funds, he decided to sell the Louisiana Territory to the U.S. At the same time President Thomas Jefferson wanted to buy New Orleans, feeling U.S. trade was made vulnerable to both Spain and France at that port. Instead, Napoleon sold him the entire territory for the bargain price of fifteen million dollars. The Louisiana Territory was larger than all the rest of the United States put together, and it eventually became fifteen additional states.

Federalists in Congress were opposed to the purchase. They feared that the Louisiana Purchase would extend slavery, and that further western growth would weaken the power of the northern states.

Early foreign policy

The three major ideas driving American foreign policy during its early years are described below:

- Isolationism – the early US government did not intend to establish colonies, though they did plan to grow larger within the bounds of North America.
- No entangling alliances – both George Washington and Thomas Jefferson were opposed to forming any permanent alliances with other countries or becoming involved in other countries' internal issues.
- Nationalism – a positive patriotic feeling about the United States blossomed quickly among its citizens, particularly after the War of 1812, when the U.S. once again defeated Britain. The Industrial Revolution also sparked increased nationalism by allowing even the most far-flung areas of the U.S. to communicate with each other via telegraph and the expanding railroad.

War of 1812

The War of 1812 grew out of the continuing tension between France and Great Britain. Napoleon continued to strive to conquer Britain, while the U.S. continued trade with both countries, but favoring France and the French colonies. Because of what Britain saw as an alliance between America and France, they determined to bring an end to trade between the two nations.

With the British preventing U.S. trade with the French and the French preventing trade with the British, James Madison's presidency introduced acts to regulate international trade. If either Britain or France removed their restrictions, America would not trade with the other. Napoleon acted first, and Madison prohibited trade with England. England saw this as the U.S. formally siding with the French, and war ensued in 1812.

The War of 1812 has been called the Second American Revolution. It established the superiority of the U.S. naval forces and reestablished U.S. independence from Britain and Europe.

The British had two major objections to America's continued trade with France. First, they saw the US as helping France's war effort by providing supplies and goods. Second, the United States had grown into a competitor, taking trade and money away from British ships and tradesmen. In its attempts to end American trade with France, the British put into effect the Orders in Council, which made any and all French-owned ports off-limits to American ships. They also began to seize American ships and conscript their crews, a practice greatly offensive to the U.S.

Military events

Two major naval battles, at Lake Erie and Lake Champlain, kept the British from invading the U.S. via Canada. American attempts to conquer Canadian lands were not successful.

In another memorable British attack, the British invaded Washington DC and burned the White House. Legend has it that Dolly Madison, the First Lady, salvaged the American flag from the fire. On Christmas Eve, 1814, the Treaty of Ghent officially ended the war. However, Andrew Jackson, unaware that the war was over, managed another victory at New Orleans on January 8, 1815. This victory upped American morale and led to a new wave of nationalism and national pride known as the "Era of Good Feelings."

Monroe Doctrine

On December 2, 1823, President Monroe delivered a message to Congress in which he introduced the Monroe Doctrine. In this address, he stated that any attempts by European powers to establish new colonies on the North American continent would be considered interference in American politics. The U.S. would stay out of European matters, and expected Europe to offer America the same courtesy. This approach to foreign policy stated in no uncertain terms that America would not tolerate any new European colonies in the New World, and that events occurring in Europe would no longer influence the policies and doctrines of the U.S.

Lewis and Clark Expedition

The purchase of the Louisiana Territory from France in 1803 more than doubled the size of the United States. President Thomas Jefferson wanted to have the area mapped and explored, since much of the territory was wilderness. He chose Meriwether Lewis and William Clark to head an expedition into the Louisiana Territory. After two years, Lewis and Clark returned, having traveled all the way to the Pacific Ocean. They brought maps, detailed journals, and various types of knowledge and information about the wide expanse of land they had traversed. The Lewis and Clark Expedition opened up the west in the Louisiana Territory and beyond for further exploration and settlement.

Manifest Destiny

In the 1800's, many believed America was destined by God to expand west, bringing as much of the North American continent as possible under the umbrella of U.S. government. With the Northwest Ordinance and the Louisiana

Purchase, over half of the continent became American. However, the rapid and relentless expansion brought conflict with the Native Americans, Great Britain, Mexico and Spain. One result of "Manifest Destiny" was the Mexican-American War, which occurred in 1846-1848. By the end of the war, Texas, California and a large portion of what is now the American Southwest joined the growing nation. Conflict also arose over the Oregon country, shared by the US and Britain. In 1846, President James Polk resolved this problem by compromising with Britain, establishing a U.S. boundary south of the 49th parallel.

Mexican-American War

Spain had held colonial interests in America since the 1540s—earlier even than Great Britain. In 1821, Mexico revolted against Spain and became a free nation. Likewise, this was followed by Texas, who after an 1836 revolution declared its independence. In 1844, the Democrats pressed President Tyler to annex Texas. Unlike his predecessor, Andrew Jackson, Tyler agreed to admit Texas into the Union. In 1845, Texas became a state.

During Mexico's war for independence, they had incurred $4.5 million in war debts to the U.S. Polk offered to forgive the debts in return for New Mexico and Upper California, but Mexico refused. In 1846, war was declared in response to a Mexican attack on American troops along the southern border of Texas. Additional conflict arose in Congress over the Wilmot Proviso, which stated that any territory the U.S. acquired from Mexico should be legally open to slavery. The war ended in 1848.

Gadsden Purchase and the 1853 post-war treaty with Mexico

After the Mexican-American war, a second treaty in 1853 determined America's southwest borders, a border which went as far as the West Coast. In 1854, the Gadsden Purchase was finalized, providing even more territory to aid in the building of the transcontinental railroad. This purchase added what would eventually become California, Nevada and Utah, and portions of New Mexico, Wyoming, Colorado and Arizona to the growing nation. The modern outline of the United States was by this time nearly complete.

American System

Spurred by the trade conflicts of the War of 1812, and supported by Henry Clay and others, the American System set up tariffs to help protect American interests from competition with products from overseas. Reducing competition led to growth in employment and an overall increase in American industry. The higher tariffs also provided funds for the government to pay for various improvements. Congress passed high tariffs in 1816 and also chartered a federal bank. The Second Bank of the United States was given the job of regulating America's money supply.

Jacksonian Democracy

Jacksonian Democracy is largely seen as a shift from politics favoring the wealthy to politics favoring the common man. All free white males were given the right to vote, not just property owners, as had been the case previously. Jackson's approach favored the patronage system, Laissez faire economics, and relocation of the Indian tribes from the Southeast portion of the country. Jackson opposed the formation of a federal bank and allowed the Second Band of the United States to collapse by vetoing a bill to renew the charter. Jackson also faced the challenge of the "null and void" or nullification theory when South Carolina claimed that it could ignore or nullify any federal law it considered unconstitutional. Jackson sent troops to the state to enforce the protested tariff laws, and a compromise engineered by Henry Clay in 1833 settled the matter for the time being.

Conflict between North and South

The conflict between North and South coalesced around the issue of slavery, but other elements contributed to the growing disagreement. Though most farmers in the South worked small farms with little or no slave labor, the huge plantations run by the South's rich depended on slaves or indentured servants to remain profitable. They had also become more dependent on cotton, with slave populations growing in concert with the rapid increase in cotton production. In the North, a more diverse agricultural economy and the growth of industry made slaves rarer. The abolitionist movement grew steadily, with Harriet Beecher Stowe's *Uncle Tom's Cabin* giving many an idea to rally around. A collection of anti-slavery organizations formed, with many actively working to free slaves in the South, often bringing them North.

Anti-slavery organizations

Five anti-slavery organizations and their significance are:

- American Colonization Society—protestant churches formed this group, aimed at returning black slaves to Africa. Former slaves subsequently formed Liberia, but the colony did not do well, as the region was not well-suited for agriculture.
- American Anti-Slavery Society—William Lloyd Garrison, a Quaker, was the major force behind this group and its newspaper, *The Liberator.*
- Female Anti-Slavery Society—a women-only group formed by Margaretta Forten because women were not allowed to join the Anti-Slavery Society formed by her father.
- Anti-Slavery Convention of American Women—This group continued meeting even after pro-slavery factions burned down their original meeting place.
- Female Vigilant Society—an organization that raised funds to help the Underground Railroad, as well as slave refugees.

Attitudes toward education

Horace Mann, among others, felt that public schooling could help children become better citizens, keep them away from crime, prevent poverty, and help American society become more unified. His *Common School Journal* brought his ideas of the importance of education into the public consciousness. Increased literacy led to increased awareness of current events, Western expansion, and other major developments of the time period. Public interest and participation in the arts and literature also increased. By the end of the 19th century, all children had access to a free public elementary education.

Transportation

As America expanded its borders, it also developed new technology to travel the rapidly growing country. Roads and railroads traversed the nation, with the Transcontinental Railroad eventually allowing travel from one coast to the other. Canals and steamboats simplified water travel and made shipping easier and less expensive. The Erie Canal (1825) connected the Great Lakes with the Hudson River. Other canals connected other major water ways, further facilitating transportation and the shipment of goods.

With growing numbers of settlers moving into the West, wagon trails developed, including the Oregon Trail, California Trail and the Santa Fe Trail. The most common vehicles seen along these westbound trails were covered wagons, also known as prairie schooners.

Industrial activity and major inventions

During the eighteenth century, goods were often manufactured in houses or small shops. With increased technology allowing for the use of machines, factories began to develop. In factories a large volume of salable goods could be produced in a much shorter amount of time. Many Americans, including increasing numbers of immigrants, found jobs in these factories, which were in constant need of labor. Another major invention was the cotton gin, which significantly decreased the processing time of cotton and was a major factor in the rapid expansion of cotton production in the South.

Labor movements in the 1800s

In 1751, a group of bakers held a protest in which they stopped baking bread. This was technically the first American labor strike. In the 1830s and 1840s, labor movements began in earnest. Boston's masons, carpenters and stoneworkers protested the length of the workday, fighting to reduce it to ten hours. In 1844, a group of women in the textile industry also fought to reduce their workday to ten hours, forming the Lowell Female Labor Reform Association. Many other protests occurred and organizations developed through this time period with the same goal in mind.

Second Great Awakening

Led by Protestant evangelical leaders, the Second Great Awakening occurred between 1800 and 1830. Several missionary groups grew out of the movement, including the American Home Missionary Society, which formed in 1826. The ideas behind the Second Great Awakening focused on personal responsibility, both as an individual and in response to injustice and suffering. The American Bible Society and the American Tract Society provided literature, while various traveling preachers spread the word. New denominations arose, including the Latter Day Saints and Seventh-Day Adventists.

Another movement associated with the Second Great Awakening was the temperance movement, focused on ending the production and use of alcohol. One major organization behind the temperance movement was the Society for the Promotion of Temperance, formed in 1826 in Boston, Massachusetts.

Women's rights movement

The women's rights movement began in the 1840s with leaders including Elizabeth Cady Stanton, Ernestine Rose and Lucretia Mott. Later, in 1869, the National Woman Suffrage Association, fighting for women's right to vote, came into being. It was led by Susan B. Anthony, Ernestine Rose and Elizabeth Cady Stanton.

In 1848 in Seneca Falls, the first women's rights convention was held, with about three hundred attendees. The Seneca Falls Convention brought to the floor the issue that women could not vote or run for office. The convention produced a "Declaration of Sentiments" which outlined a plan for women to attain the rights they deserved. Frederick Douglass supported the women's rights movement, as well as the abolition movement. In fact, women's rights and abolition movements often went hand-in-hand through this time period.

Missouri Compromise

By 1819, the United States had developed a tenuous balance between slave and free states, with exactly twenty-two senators in Congress from each faction. However, Missouri was ready to join the union as a state. As a slave state, it would tip the balance in Congress. To prevent this imbalance, the Missouri Compromise brought the northern part of Massachusetts into the union as Maine, established as a free state. Maine's admission balanced the admission of Missouri as a slave state, maintaining the status quo. In addition, the remaining portion of the Louisiana Purchase was to remain free north of latitude 36° 30′. Since cotton did not grow well this far north, this limitation was acceptable to congressmen representing the slave states.

However, the proposed Missouri constitution presented a problem, as it outlawed immigration of free blacks into the state. Another compromise was in order, this time proposed by Henry Clay. Clay earned his title of the Great Compromiser by stating that the U.S. Constitution overruled Missouri's.

Popular sovereignty and the Compromise of 1850

In addition to the pro-slavery and anti-slavery factions, a third group rose who felt that each individual state should decide whether to allow or permit slavery within its borders. This idea was referred to as popular sovereignty.

When California applied to join the union in 1849, the balance of congressional power was again threatened. The Compromise of 1850 introduced a group of laws meant to bring an end to the conflict.
These laws included:

- California being admitted as a free state.
- Slave trade in Washington, D.C. being outlawed.
- An increase in efforts to capture escaped slaves.
- New Mexico and Utah territories would decide individually whether or not to allow slavery.

In spite of these measures, debate raged each time a new state prepared to enter the union.

Kansas-Nebraska Act

With the creation of the Kansas and Nebraska territories in 1854, another debate began. Congress allowed popular sovereignty in these territories, but slavery opponents argued that the Missouri Compromise had already made slavery illegal in this region. In Kansas, two separate governments arose, one pro- and one anti-slavery. Conflict between the two factions rose to violence, leading Kansas to gain the nickname of "Bleeding Kansas."

Dred Scott Decision

Abolitionist factions coalesced around the case of Dred Scott, using his case to test the country's laws regarding slavery. Scott, a slave, had been taken by his owner from Missouri, which was a slave state. He then traveled to Illinois, a free state, then on to the Minnesota Territory, also free based on the Missouri Compromise. Then, he returned to Missouri. The owner subsequently died. Abolitionists took Scott's case to court, stating that Scott was no longer a slave but free, since he had lived in free territory. The case went to the Supreme Court.

The Supreme Court stated that, because Scott, as a slave, was not a U.S. citizen, his time in free states did not change his status. He also did not have the right to sue. In addition, the Court determined that the Missouri Compromise was unconstitutional, saying Congress had overstepped its bounds by outlawing slavery in the territories.

Harper's Ferry and John Brown

John Brown, an abolitionist, had participated in several anti-slavery actions, including killing five pro-slavery men in retaliation, after Lawrence, Kansas, an anti-slavery town, was sacked. He and other abolitionists also banded together to pool their funds and build a runaway slave colony.
In 1859, Brown seized a federal arsenal in Harper's Ferry, located in what is now West Virginia. Brown intended to seize guns and ammunition and lead a slave rebellion. Robert E. Lee captured Brown and 22 followers, who were subsequently tried and hanged. While Northerners took the executions as an indication that the government supported slavery, Southerners were of the opinion that most of the North supported Brown and were, in general, anti-slavery.

1860 election candidates

The 1860 Presidential candidates represented four different parties, each with a different opinion on slavery.

- John Breckenridge, representing the Southern Democrats, was pro-slavery.
- Abraham Lincoln, of the Republican Party, was anti-slavery.
- Stephen Douglas, of the Northern Democrats, felt that the issue should be determined locally, on a state-by-state basis.

- John Bell, of the Constitutional Union Party, focused primarily on keeping the Union intact.

In the end, Abraham Lincoln won both the popular and electoral election. Southern states, who had sworn to secede from the Union if Lincoln was elected did so, led by South Carolina. Shortly thereafter, the Civil War began when shots were fired on Fort Sumter in Charleston.

Advantages of the North and South in the Civil War

The Northern states had significant advantages, including:

- Larger population. The North consisted of 24 states to the South's 11.
- Better transportation and finances. With railroads primarily in the North, supply chains were much more dependable, as was trade coming from overseas.
- More raw materials. The North held the majority of America's gold, as well as iron, copper and other minerals vital to wartime.

The South's advantages included:

- Better-trained military officers. Many of the Southern officers were West Point trained and had commanded in the Mexican and Indian wars.
- More familiar with weapons. The climate and lifestyle of the South meant most of the people were well versed in both guns and horses. The industrial North had less extensive experience
- Defensive position. The South felt victory was guaranteed, since they were protecting their own lands, while the North would be invading.
- Well-defined goals. The South was fighting an ideological war to be allowed to govern themselves and preserve their way of life.

Emancipation Proclamation

The Emancipation Proclamation, issued by President Lincoln in 1862, freed all slaves in Confederate States that did not return to the Union by the beginning of the year. While the original proclamation did not free any slaves actually under Union control, it did set a precedent for the emancipation of slaves as the war progressed.

The Emancipation Proclamation worked in the Union's favor as many freed slaves and other black troops joined the Union Army. Almost 200,000 blacks fought in the Union army, and over 10,000 served in the navy. By the end of the war, over 4 million slaves had been freed, and in 1865 slavery was banned by Constitutional amendment.

Civil War events

Six major events of the Civil War and their outcomes or significance are as follows:

- The Battle of Bull Run, July 21, 1861. The First Battle of Bull Run, was the first major land battle of the war. Observers, expecting to enjoy an entertaining skirmish, set up picnics nearby. Instead, they found themselves witness to a bloodbath. Union forces were defeated, and the battle set the course of the Civil War as long, bloody and costly.
- The Capture of Fort Henry by Ulysses S. Grant. This battle in February of 1862 marked the Union's first major victory.
- The Battle of Gettysburg, July 1-3, 1863. Often seen as the turning point of the war, Gettysburg also saw the largest number of casualties of the war, with over 50,000 dead. Robert E. Lee was defeated, and the Confederate army, significantly crippled, withdrew.
- The Overland Campaign, 1864. Grant, now in command of all the Union armies, led this high casualty campaign that eventually positioned the Union for victory.

- Sherman's March to the Sea. William Tecumseh Sherman, in May of 1864, conquered Atlanta. He then continued to Savannah, destroying indiscriminately as he went.
- Following Lee's defeat at the Appomattox Courthouse, General Grant accepted Lee's surrender in the home of Wilmer McLean, Appomattox, Virginia on April 9, 1865.

Lincoln's assassination

The Civil War ended with the surrender of the South on April 9, 1865. Five days later, Lincoln and his wife, Mary, attended the play *Our American Cousin* at the Ford Theater. John Wilkes Booth, unaware that the war was over, performed his part in a conspiracy to aid the Confederacy by shooting Lincoln in the back of the head. Booth was tracked down and killed by Union soldiers 12 days later. Lincoln, carried from the theater to a nearby house, died the next morning.

Reconstruction and the Freedmen's Bureau

In the aftermath of the Civil War, the South was left in chaos. From 1865 to 1877, government on all levels worked to help restore order to the South, ensure civil rights to the freed slaves, and bring the Confederate states back into the Union. In 1866, Congress passed the Reconstruction Acts, putting former Confederate states under military rule.

The Freedmen's Bureau was formed to help freedmen and give assistance to whites in the South who needed basic necessities like food and clothing. Many in the South felt the Freedmen's Bureau worked to set freed slaves against their former owners. The Bureau was intended to help former slaves become self-sufficient, and to keep them from falling prey to those who would take advantage of them.

Radical and Moderate Republicans

The Radical Republicans wished to treat the South quite harshly after the war. Thaddeus Stephens, the House Leader, suggested that the Confederate States be treated as if they were territories again, with ten years of military rule and territorial government before they would be readmitted. They also wanted to give all black men the right to vote. Former Confederate soldiers would be required to swear they had not fought against the Union in order to be granted full rights as American citizens.

By contrast, the moderate Republicans wanted only black men who were literate or who had served as Union troops to be able to vote. All Confederate soldiers except troop leaders would also be able to vote. Before his death, Lincoln had favored a more moderate approach to Reconstruction, hoping this approach might bring some states back into the Union before the end of the war.

Black Codes and the Civil Rights bill

The Black Codes were proposed to control freed slaves. They would not be allowed to bear arms, assemble, serve on juries, or testify against whites. Schools would be segregated, and unemployed blacks could be arrested and forced to work.

The Civil Rights bill countered these codes, providing much wider rights for the freed slaves.

Andrew Johnson, who became president after Lincoln's death, supported the Black Codes, and vetoed the Civil Rights bill. Congress overrode his veto and impeached Johnson, the culmination of tensions between Congress and the president. He came within a single vote of being convicted.

Thirteenth, Fourteenth and Fifteenth Amendments

The Thirteenth, Fourteenth and Fifteenth Amendments, all passed shortly after the end of the Civil War, are described below:

- The Thirteenth Amendment was passed on December 18, 1865. This amendment prohibited slavery in the United States.
- The Fourteenth Amendment overturned the Dred Scott decision, and was ratified July 9, 1868. American citizenship was redefined, with all citizens guaranteed equal legal protection by all states. It also guaranteed citizens the right to file a lawsuit or serve on a jury.
- The Fifteenth Amendment was ratified February 3, 1870. It states that no citizen of the United States can be denied the right to vote based on race, color, or previous status as a slave.

Reconstruction

The three phases of Reconstruction are:

- Presidential Reconstruction – largely driven by President Andrew Johnson's policies, the Presidential phase of Reconstruction was lenient on the South and allowed continued discrimination against and control over blacks.
- Congressional Reconstruction – Congress, controlled largely by Radical Republicans, took a different stance, providing a wider range of civil rights for blacks and greater control over Southern government. Congressional Reconstruction is marked by military control of the former Confederate States.
- Redemption – Gradually, the Confederate states were readmitted into the union. During this time, white Democrats took over the government of most of the South. Troops finally departed the South in 1877.

Carpetbaggers and Scalawags

The chaos in the south attracted a number of people seeking to fill the power vacuums and take advantage of the economic disruption. Scalawags were southern Whites who aligned with Freedmen to take over local governments. Many in the South who could have filled political offices refused to take the necessary oath required to grant them the right to vote, leaving many opportunities for Scalawags and others. Carpetbaggers were northerners who traveled to the South for various reasons. Some provided assistance, while others sought to make money or to acquire political power during this chaotic period.

Transcontinental railroad

In 1869, the Union Pacific Railroad completed the first section of a planned transcontinental railroad. This section went from Omaha, Nebraska to Sacramento, California. With the rise of the railroad, products were much more easily transported across country. While this was positive overall for industry throughout the country, it was often damaging to family farmers, who found themselves paying high shipping costs for smaller supply orders while larger companies received major discounts. Ninety percent of the workers constructing the railroad were Chinese, working in very dangerous conditions for very low pay.

Measures taken to limit immigration

In 1870, the Naturalization Act put limits on U.S. citizenship, allowing full citizenship only to whites and those of African descent. The Chinese Exclusion Act of 1882 put limits on Chinese immigration. The Immigration Act of 1882 taxed immigrants, charging fifty cents per person. These funds helped pay administrative costs for regulating immigration. Ellis Island opened in 1892 as a processing center those arriving in New York. 1921 saw the Emergency Quota Act passed, also known as the Johnson Quota Act, which severely limited the number of immigrants allowed into the country.

Nineteenth century changes in agriculture

Technological advancements
During the mid 1800s, irrigation techniques improved significantly. Advances occurred in cultivation and breeding, as well as fertilizer use and crop rotation. In the Great Plains, also

known as the Great American Desert, the dense soil was finally cultivated with steel plows. In 1892, gasoline-powered tractors arrived, and were widely used by 1900. Other advancements in agriculture's tool set included barbed wire fences, combines, silos, deep-water wells, and the cream separator.

Government actions

Four major actions by the government that helped improve agriculture for the U.S. in the nineteenth century are as follows:

- The Department of Agriculture came into being in 1862, working for the interests of farmers and ranchers across the country.
- The Morrill Land-Grant Acts were passed in 1862, allowing land-grant colleges.
- In conjunction with land-grant colleges, the Hatch Act of 1887 brought agriculture experimental stations into the picture, helping discover new farming techniques.
- In 1914, the Smith-Lever Act provided cooperative programs to help educate people about food, home economics, community development and agriculture. Related agriculture extension programs helped farmers increase crop production to feed the rapidly growing nation.

Inventors and inventions

Major inventors from the 1800s and their inventions are:

- Alexander Graham Bell—the telephone
- Orville and Wilbur Wright—the airplane
- Richard Gatling—the machine gun
- Walter Hunt, Elias Howe and Isaac Singer—the sewing machine
- Nikola Tesla—alternating current
- George Eastman—the camera
- Thomas Edison—light bulbs, motion pictures, the phonograph
- Samuel Morse—the telegraph
- Charles Goodyear—vulcanized rubber
- Cyrus McCormick—the reaper
- George Westinghouse—the transformer, the air brake

This was an active period for invention, with about 700,000 patents registered between 1860 and 1900.

Gilded Age

The time period from the end of the Civil War to the beginning of the First World War is often referred to as the Gilded Age or the Second Industrial Revolution. The U.S. was changing from an agriculturally based economy to an industrial economy, with rapid growth accompanying the shift. In addition, the country itself was expanding, spreading into the seemingly unlimited West.

This time period saw the beginning of banks, department stores, chain stores, and trusts—all familiar features of our modern-day landscape. Cities also grew rapidly, and large numbers of immigrants arrived in the country, swelling the urban ranks.

Populist Party

A major recession struck the United States during the 1890s, with crop prices falling dramatically. Drought compounded the problems, leaving many American farmers in crippling debt. The Farmers Alliance formed, drawing the rural poor into a single political entity.

Recession also affected the more industrial parts of the country. The Knights of Labor, formed in 1869 by Uriah Stephens, was able to unite workers into a union to protect their rights. Dissatisfied by views espoused by industrialists, these two groups, the Farmers Alliance and the Knights of Labor, joined to form the Populist Party. Some of the elements of the party's platform included:

- National currency
- Income tax
- Government ownership of railroads, telegraph and telephone systems

- Secret ballot for voting
- Immigration restriction
- Term limits for President and Vice-President

The Populist Party was in favor of decreasing elitism and making the voice of the common man more easily heard in the political process.

Labor movement

The first large, well-organized strike occurred in 1892. Called the Homestead Strike, it occurred when the Amalgamated Association of Iron and Steel Works struck against the Carnegie Steel Company. Gunfire ensued, and Carnegie was able to eliminate the plant's union. In 1864, workers, led by Eugene Debs, initiated the Pullman Strike after the Pullman Palace Car Co. cut their wages by 28 percent. President Grover Cleveland called in troops to break up the strike on the grounds that it interfered with mail delivery. Mary Harris Jones, also known as Mother Jones, organized the Children's Crusade to protest child labor. A protest march proceeded to the home of President Theodore Roosevelt in 1902. Jones also worked with the United Mine Workers of America, and helped found the Industrial Workers of the World.

Panic of 1893

Far from a U.S.-centric event, the Panic of 1893 was an economic crisis that affected most of the globe. As a response to the Panic, President Grover Cleveland repealed the Sherman Silver Purchase Act, afraid it had caused the downturn rather than boosting the economy as intended. The Panic led to bankruptcies, with railroads going under and factory unemployment rising as high as 25 percent. In the end, the Republican Party regained power due to the economic crisis.

Progressive Era

From the 1890s to the end of the First World War, Progressives set forth an ideology that drove many levels of society and politics. The Progressives were in favor of workers' rights and safety, and wanted measures taken against waste and corruption. They felt science could help improve society, and that the government could—and should—provide answers to a variety of social problems. Progressives came from a wide variety of backgrounds, but were united in their desire to improve society.

<u>Muckrakers</u>

"Muckrakers" was a term used to identify aggressive investigative journalists who brought to light scandals, corruption, and many other wrongs being perpetrated in late nineteenth century society. Among these intrepid writers were:

- Ida Tarbell—he exposed the Standard Oil Trust.
- Jacob Riis—a photographer, he helped improve the lot of the poor in New York.
- Lincoln Steffens—he worked to expose political corruption.
- Upton Sinclair—his book *The Jungle* led to reforms in the meat packing industry.

Through the work of these journalists, many new policies came into being, including workmen's compensation, child labor laws, and trust-busting.

<u>Sixteenth, Seventeenth, Eighteenth and Nineteenth Amendments</u>

The early twentieth century saw several amendments made to the U.S. Constitution. These included:

- Sixteenth Amendment, 1913 established a graduated income tax.
- Seventeenth Amendment, 1913 allowed direct election of Senators.
- Eighteenth Amendment, 1919 prohibited the sale, production and importation of alcohol. This amendment was later repealed by the Twenty-first Amendment.
- Nineteenth Amendment, 1920 gave women the right to vote.

These amendments largely grew out of the Progressive Era, as many citizens worked to improve American society.

Federal Trade Commission and elimination of trusts

Muckrakers such as Ida Tarbell and Lincoln Steffens brought to light the damaging trend of trusts—huge corporations working to monopolize areas of commerce and so control prices and distribution. The Sherman Act and the Clayton Antitrust Act set out guidelines for competition among corporations and set out to eliminate these trusts. The Federal Trade Commission was formed in order to enforce antitrust measures and ensure companies were operated fairly and did not create controlling monopolies.

Government dealings with Native Americans

America's westward expansion led to conflict and violent confrontations with Native Americans such as the Battle of Little Bighorn. In 1876, the American government ordered all Indians to relocate to reservations. Lack of compliance led to the Dawes Act in 1887, which ordered assimilation rather than separation. This act remained in effect until 1934. Reformers also forced Indian children to attend Indian Boarding Schools, where they were not allowed to speak their native language and were forced to accept Christianity. Children were often abused in these schools, and were indoctrinated to abandon their identity as Native Americans.

In 1890, the massacre at Wounded Knee, accompanied by Geronimo's surrender, led the Native Americans to work to preserve their culture rather than fight for their lands.

Native Americans in wartime

The Spanish-American war, 1898-1902, saw a number of Native Americans serving with Teddy Roosevelt in the Rough Riders. Apache scouts accompanied General John J. Pershing to Mexico, hoping to find Pancho Villa. More than 17,000 Native Americans were drafted into service for World War I, though at the time they were not considered as legal citizens. In 1924, Indians were finally granted official citizenship by the Indian Citizenship Act.

After decades of relocation, forced assimilation and outright genocide the number of Native Americans in the U.S. has greatly declined. Though many Native Americans have chosen—or have been forced—to assimilate, about 300 reservations exist today, with most of their inhabitants living in abject poverty.

Spanish-American War

Spain had controlled Cuba since the fifteenth century. Over the centuries, the Spanish had quashed a variety of revolts. In 1886, slavery ended in Cuba, and another revolt was rising.

In the meantime, the US had expressed interest in Cuba, offering Spain $130 million for the island in 1853, during Franklin Pierce's presidency. In 1898, the Cuban revolt was underway. In spite of various factions supporting the Cubans, the US President, William McKinley, refused to recognize the rebellion, preferring negotiation over involvement in war. Then The Maine, a US battleship in Havana Harbor, was blown up, costing nearly 300 lives. The US declared war two months later, and the war ended four months later with a Spanish surrender.

Panama Canal

Initial work began on the Panama Canal in 1880, though the idea had been discussed since the 1500s. The Canal greatly reduces the length and time needed to sail from one ocean to the other by connecting the Atlantic to the Pacific through the Isthmus of Panama, which joins South America to North America. Before the Canal was built, travelers had to sail all the way around South America to reach the West Coast of the US. The French began the work in 1880, after successfully completing the Suez Canal, connecting the Mediterranean Sea to the Red Sea. However, their efforts quickly fell apart. The US moved in to take over, completing the complex canal in 1914. The Panama Canal was constructed as a lock-and-lake canal, with ships actually lifted on locks to travel from one lake to another over the rugged, mountainous terrain. In order to maintain control of the Canal Zone, the US assisted Panama in its battle for independence from Columbia.

Roosevelt's "Big Stick Diplomacy" and foreign policy in Latin America

Theodore Roosevelt's famous quote, "Speak softly and carry a big stick," is supposedly of African origins, at least according to Roosevelt. He used this proverb to justify expanded involvement in foreign affairs during his tenure as President. The US military was deployed to protect American interests in Latin America. Roosevelt also worked to maintain an equal or greater influence in Latin America than those held by European interests. As a result, the US Navy grew larger, and the US generally became more involved in foreign affairs. Roosevelt felt that if any country was left vulnerable to control by Europe, due to economic issues or political instability, the US had not only a right to intervene, but was obligated to do so. This led to US involvement in Cuba, Nicaragua, Haiti and the Dominican Republic over several decades leading into the First and Second World Wars.

William Howard Taft's "Dollar Diplomacy" approach

During William Howard Taft's presidency, Taft instituted "Dollar Diplomacy." This approach was used as a description of American efforts to influence Latin America and East Asia through economic rather than military means. Taft saw past efforts in these areas to be political and warlike, while his efforts focused on peaceful economic goals. His justification of the policy was to protect the Panama Canal, which was vital to US trade interests.

In spite of Taft's assurance that Dollar Diplomacy was a peaceful approach, many interventions proved violent. During Latin American revolts, such as those in Nicaragua, the US sent troops to settle the revolutions. Afterwards, bankers moved in to help support the new leaders through loans. Dollar Diplomacy continued until 1913, when Woodrow Wilson was elected President.

Woodrow Wilson's approach to international diplomacy

Turning away from Taft's "Dollar Diplomacy", Wilson instituted a foreign policy he referred to as "moral diplomacy." This approach still influences American foreign policy today. Wilson felt that representative government and democracy in all countries would lead to worldwide stability. Democratic governments, he felt, would be less likely to threaten American interests. He also saw the US and Great Britain as the great role models in this area, as well as champions of world peace and self-government. Free trade and international commerce would allow the US to speak out regarding world events.
Main elements of Wilson's policies included:

- Maintaining a strong military
- Promoting democracy throughout the world
- Expanding international trade to boost the American economy
-

First World War

The First World War occurred from 1914 to 1918 and was fought largely in Europe. Triggered by the assassination of Austrian Archduke Francis Ferdinand, the war rapidly escalated. At the beginning of the conflict, Woodrow Wilson declared the US neutral. Major events influencing US involvement included:

- Sinking of the Lusitania - The British passenger liner RMS Lusitania was sunk by a German U-boat in 1915. Among the 1,000 civilian victims were 100 Americans. Outraged by this act, many Americans began to push for US involvement in the war, using the Lusitania as a rallying cry.
- German U-boat aggression - Wilson continued to keep the US out of the war, with his 1916 reelection slogan, "He kept us out of war." While he continued to work toward an end of the war, German

U-boats began to indiscriminately attack American and Canadian merchant ships carrying supplies to Germany's enemies in Europe.

- Zimmerman Note - The final event that brought the US into World War I was the interception of the Zimmerman Note. In this telegram, Germany communicated with the Mexican government its intentions to invade the US with Mexico's assistance.

US efforts during World War I

American railroads came under government control in December 1917. The widespread system was consolidated into a single system, with each region assigned a director. This greatly increased the efficiency of the railroad system, allowing the railroads to supply both domestic and military needs. Control returned to private ownership in 1920. In 1918, telegraph, telephone and cable services also came under Federal control, to be returned to private management the next year. The American Red Cross supported the war effort by knitting clothes for Army and Navy troops. They also helped supply hospital and refugee clothing and surgical dressings. Over eight million people participated in this effort. To generate wartime funds, the US government sold Liberty Bonds. In four issues, they sold nearly $25 billion—more than one fifth of Americans purchased them. After the war, Liberty Bonds were replaced with Victory Bonds.

Wilson's Fourteen Points

President Woodrow Wilson proposed Fourteen Points as the basis for a peace settlement to end the war. Presented to the US Congress in January 1918, the Fourteen Points included:

- Five points outlining general ideals
- Eight points to resolve immediate problems of political and territorial nature
- One point proposing an organization of nations with the intent of maintaining world peace

In November of that same year, Germany agreed to an armistice, assuming the final treaty would be based on the Fourteen Points. However, during the peace conference in Paris 1919, there was much disagreement, leading to a final agreement that punished Germany and the other Central Powers much more than originally intended. Henry Cabot Lodge, who had become the Foreign Relations Committee chairman in 1918, wanted an unconditional surrender from Germany. A League of Nations was included in the Treaty of Versailles at Wilson's insistence. The Senate rejected the Treaty of Versailles, and in the end Wilson refused to concede to Lodge's demands. As a result, the US did not join the League of Nations.

America during the 1920s

The post-war '20s saw many Americans moving from the farm to the city, with growing prosperity in the US. The Roaring Twenties, or the Jazz Age, was driven largely by growth in the automobile and entertainment industries. Individuals like Charles Lindbergh, the first aviator to make a solo flight cross the Atlantic Ocean, added to the American admiration of individual accomplishment. Telephone lines, distribution of electricity, highways, the radio, and other inventions brought great changes to everyday life.

<u>Cultural movements influenced or driven by African Americans</u>

The Harlem Renaissance saw a number of African American artists settling in Harlem, New York City. This community produced a number of well-known artists and writers, including Langston Hughes, Nella Larson, Zora Neale Hurston, Claude McKay, Countee Cullen and Jean Toomer. The growth of jazz, also largely driven by African Americans, defined the Jazz Age. Its unconventional, improvisational style matched the growing sense of optimism and exploration of the decade. Originating as an offshoot of the blues, jazz began in New Orleans. Some significant jazz musicians were Duke Ellington, Louis Armstrong and Jelly Roll Morton. Big Band and Swing Jazz also developed in the 1920s.

Well-known musicians of this movement included Bing Crosby, Frank Sinatra, Count Basie, Benny Goodman, Billie Holiday, Ella Fitzgerald and The Dorsey Brothers.

National Origins Act of 1924

The National Origins Act (Johnson-Reed Act) placed limitations on immigration. The number of immigrants allowed into the US was based on the population of each nationality of immigrants who were living in the country in 1890. Only two percent of each nationality's 1890 population numbers were allowed to immigrate. This led to great disparities between immigrants from various nations, and Asian immigration was not allowed at all. Some of the impetus behind the Johnson-Reed Act came as a result of paranoia following the Russian Revolution. Fear of communist influences in the US led to a general fear of immigrants.

Red Scare

World War I created many jobs, but after the war ended these jobs disappeared, leaving many unemployed. In the wake of these employment changes the International Workers of the World and the Socialist Party, headed by Eugene Debs, became more and more visible. Workers initiated strikes in an attempt to regain the favorable working conditions that had been put into place before the war. Unfortunately, many of these strikes became violent, and the actions were blamed on "Reds," or Communists, for trying to spread their views into America. With the Bolshevik Revolution being recent news in Russia, many Americans feared a similar revolution might occur here. The Red Scare ensued, with many individuals jailed for supposedly holding communist, anarchist or socialist beliefs.

Growth of civil rights for African Americans

Marcus Garvey founded the Universal Negro Improvement Association, which became a large and active organization focused on building black nationalism. In 1911, the National Association for the Advancement of Colored People (NAACP) came into being, working to defeat Jim Crow laws. The NAACP also helped prevent racial segregation from becoming federal law, fought against lynchings, helped black soldiers in WWI become officers, and helped defend the Scottsboro Boys, who were unjustly accused of rape.

Ku Klux Klan

In 1866, Confederate Army veterans came together to fight against Reconstruction in the South, forming a group called the Ku Klux Klan (KKK). With white supremacist beliefs, including anti-Semitism, nativism, anti-Catholicism, and overt racism, this organization relied heavily on violence to get its message across. In 1915, they grew again in power, using a film called *The Birth of a Nation*, by D.W. Griffith, to spread their ideas. In the 1920s, the reach of the KKK spread far into the North and Midwest, and members controlled a number of state governments. Its membership and power began to decline during the Great Depression, but experienced a major resurgence later.

American Civil Liberties Union

The American Civil Liberties Union (ACLU), founded in 1920, grew from the American Union Against Militarism. This former organization helped conscientious objectors avoid going to war during WWI, and also helped those being prosecuted under the Espionage Act (1917) and the Sedition Act (1918), many of whom were immigrants. Their major goals were to protect immigrants and other citizens who were threatened with prosecution for their political beliefs, and to support labor unions, which were also under threat by the government during the Red Scare.

Anti-Defamation League

In 1913, the Anti-Defamation League was formed to prevent anti-Semitic behavior and practices. Its actions also worked to prevent all forms of racism, and to prevent individuals from being discriminated against for any reason involving their race. They spoke against the Ku Klux Klan, as well as other racist or anti-Semitic organizations. This organization still exists, and still works to fight discrimination against minorities of all kinds.

Great Depression

The Great Depression, which began in 1929 with the Stock Market Crash, grew out of several factors that had developed over the previous years including:

- Growing economic disparity between the rich and middle-class, with the rich amassing wealth much more quickly than the lower classes
- Disparity in economic distribution in industries
- Growing use of credit, leading to an inflated demand for some goods
- Government support of new industries rather than providing additional support for agriculture
- Risky stock market investments, leading to the stock market crash

Additional factors contributing to the Depression also included the Labor Day Hurricane in the Florida Keys (1935) and the Great Hurricane of 1938, in Long Island, along with the Dust Bowl in the Great Plains, which destroyed crops and resulted in the displacement of as many as 2.5 million people.

Roosevelt administration

Roosevelt's "New Deal"

Franklin D. Roosevelt was elected president in 1932 with his promise of a "New Deal" for Americans. His goals were to provide government work programs to provide jobs, wages and relief to numerous workers throughout the beleaguered US. Congress gave Roosevelt almost free rein to produce relief legislation. The goals of this legislation were:

- Relief: Accomplished largely by creating jobs
- Recovery: Stimulate the economy through the National Recovery Administration
- Reform: Pass legislation to prevent future similar economic crashes

The Roosevelt Administration also passed legislation regarding ecological issues, including the Soil Conservation Service, aimed at preventing another Dust Bowl.

Roosevelt's "alphabet organizations"

So-called alphabet organizations set up during Roosevelt's administration included:

- Civilian Conservation Corps (CCC)—provided jobs in the forestry service
- Agricultural Adjustment Administration (AAA)—increased agricultural income by adjusting both production and prices.
- Tennessee Valley Authority (TVA)—organized projects to build dams in the Tennessee River for flood control and production of electricity, resulting in increased productivity for industries in the area, and easier navigation of the Tennessee River
- Public Works Administration (PWA) and Civil Works Administration (CWA)—initiated over 34,000 projects, providing employment
- Works Progress Administration (WPA)—helped unemployed persons to secure employment on government work projects or elsewhere

Actions taken to prevent future crashes and stabilize the economy

The Roosevelt administration passed several laws and established several institutions to initiate the "reform" portion of the New Deal, including:

- Glass-Steagall Act—separated investment from the business of banking
- Securities Exchange Commission (SEC)—helped regulate Wall Street investment practices, making them less dangerous to the overall economy

- Wagner Act—provided worker and union rights to improve relations between employees and employers.
- Social Security Act of 1935—provided pensions as well as unemployment insurance

Other actions focused on insuring bank deposits and adjusting the value of American currency. Most of these regulatory agencies and government policies and programs still exist today.

Labor regulations

Three major regulations regarding labor that were passed after the Great Depression are:

- The Wagner Act—established that unions were legal, protected members of unions, and required collective bargaining. This act was later amended by the Taft-Hartley Act of 1947 and the Landrum Griffin Act of 1959, which further clarified certain elements.
- Davis-Bacon Act (1931)—provided fair compensation for contractors and subcontractors.
- Walsh-Healey Act (1936)—established a minimum wage, child labor laws, safety standards, and overtime pay.

World War II

Interventionist and Isolationist approaches to involvement

When war broke out in Europe in 1939, President Roosevelt stated that the US would remain neutral. However, his overall approach was considered "interventionist," as he was willing to provide any necessary aid to the Allies short of actually entering the conflict. Thus the US supplied a wide variety of war materials to the Allied nations.

Isolationists believed the US should not provide any aid to the Allies, including supplies. They felt Roosevelt, by assisting the Allies, was leading the US into a war for which it was not prepared. Led by Charles A. Lindbergh, the Isolationists believed any involvement in the European conflict endangered the US by weakening its national defense.

U.S. entry into the war

In 1937, Japan invaded China, prompting the US to halt all exports to Japan. Roosevelt also did not allow Japanese interests to withdraw money held in US banks. In 1941, General Tojo rose to power as the Japanese Premier. Recognizing America's ability to bring a halt to Japan's expansion, he authorized the bombing of Pearl Harbor on December 7, of that year. The US responded by declaring war on Japan. Because of the Tipartite Pact among the Axis Powers, Germany and Italy then declared war on the US, followed by Bulgaria and Hungary.

Surrender of Germany

In 1941, Hitler violated the non-aggression pact he had signed with Stalin in 1939 by invading the USSR. Stalin then joined the Allies. Stalin, Roosevelt and Winston Churchill planned to defeat Germany first, then Japan, bringing the war to an end.

Starting in 1942 through 1943, the Allies drove Axis forces out of Africa. In addition, the Germans were soundly defeated at Stalingrad.

Between July 1943 and May 1945, Allied troops liberated Italy. June 6, 1944, known as D-Day, the Allies invaded France at Normandy. Soviet troops moved on the eastern front at the same time, driving German forces back. April 25, 1945, Berlin was surrounded by Soviet troops. On May 7, Germany surrendered.

Surrender of Japan

War continued with Japan after Germany's surrender. Japanese forces had taken a large portion of Southeast Asia and the Western Pacific, all the way to the Aleutian Islands in Alaska. General Doolittle bombed several Japanese cities while American troops scored a victory at Midway. Additional fighting in the Battle of the Coral Sea further weakened Japan's position. As a final blow, the US dropped two atomic bombs, one on Hiroshima and the other on Nagasaki, Japan. This was the first time atomic bombs had ever been used in warfare, and the devastation was horrific and demoralizing. Japan surrendered on September 2, 1945.

442nd Regimental Combat Team, the Tuskegee Airmen, and the Navajo Code Talkers

The 442nd Regimental Combat Team consisted of Japanese Americans fighting in Europe for the US. The most highly decorated unit per member in US history, they suffered a 93 percent casualty rate during the war. The Tuskegee Airmen were African American aviators, the first black Americans allowed to fly for the military. In spite of not being eligible to become official navy pilots, they flew over 15,000 missions and were highly decorated. The Navajo Code Talkers were native Navajo who used their traditional language to transmit information among Allied forces. Because Navajo is a language and not simply a code, the Axis powers were never able to translate it. Use of Navajo Code Talkers to transmit information was instrumental in the taking of Iwo Jima and other major victories of the war.

Women during World War II

Women served widely in the military during WWII, working in numerous positions, including the Flight Nurses Corps. Women also moved into the workforce while men were overseas, leading to over 19 million women in the US workforce by 1944. Rosie the Riveter stood as a symbol of these women and a means of recruiting others to take needed positions. Women, as well as their families left behind during wartime, also grew Victory Gardens to help provide food.

Atomic bomb

The atomic bomb, developed during WWII, was the most powerful bomb ever invented. A single bomb, carried by a single plane, held enough power to destroy an entire city. This devastating effect was demonstrated with the bombing of Hiroshima and Nagasaki in 1945 in what later became a controversial move, but ended the war. The bombings resulted in as many as 200,000 immediate deaths and many more as time passed after the bombings, mostly due to radiation poisoning.

Whatever the arguments against the use of "The Bomb", the post WWII era saw many countries develop similar weapons to match the newly expanded military power of the US. The impact of those developments and use of nuclear weapons continues to haunt international relations today.

Yalta Conference and the Potsdam Conference

In February 1945, Joseph Stalin, Franklin D. Roosevelt and Winston Churchill met in Yalta to discuss the post-war treatment of Europe, particularly Germany. Though Germany had not yet surrendered, its defeat was imminent. After Germany's official surrender, Clement Attlee, Harry Truman and Joseph Stalin met to formalize those plans. This meeting was called the Potsdam Conference.

Basic provisions of these agreements included:

- Dividing Germany and Berlin into four zones of occupation
- Demilitarization of Germany
- Poland remaining under Soviet control
- Outlawing the Nazi Party
- Trials for Nazi leaders
- Relocation of numerous German citizens
- The USSR joined the United Nations, established in 1945
- Establishment of the United Nations Security Council, consisting of the US, the UK, the USSR, China and France

Agreements made with post-war Japan

General Douglas MacArthur directed the American military occupation of Japan after the country surrendered. The goals the US occupation included removing Japan's military and making the country a democracy. A 1947 constitution removed power from the emperor and gave it to the people, as well as granting voting rights to women. Japan was no longer allowed to declare war, and a group of 25 government officials were tried for war crimes. In 1951, the US finally signed a peace treaty with Japan. This treaty allowed Japan to rearm itself for purposes of self-defense, but stripped the country of the empire it had built overseas.

Alien Registration Act and treatment of Japanese immigrants

In 1940, the US passed the Alien Registration Act, which required all aliens older than fourteen to be fingerprinted and registered. They were also required to report changes of address within five days.

Tension between whites and Japanese immigrants in California, which had been building since the beginning of the century, came to a head with the bombing of Pearl Harbor in 1941. Believing that even those Japanese living in the US were likely to be loyal to their native country, the president ordered numerous Japanese to be arrested on suspicion of subversive action isolated in exclusion zones known as War Relocation Camps. Over 120,000 Japanese Americans, two thirds of them citizens of the US, were sent to these camps during the war.

General state of the US after World War II

Following WWII, the US became the strongest political power in the world, becoming a major player in world affairs and foreign policies. The US determined to stop the spread of Communism, naming itself the "arsenal of democracy." In addition, America had emerged with a greater sense of itself as a single, integrated nation, with many regional and economic differences diminished. The government worked for greater equality and the growth of communications increased contact among different areas of the country. Both the aftermath of the Great Depression and the necessities of WWII had given the government greater control over various institutions as well as the economy. This also meant the American government took on greater responsibility for the well being of its citizens, both in the domestic arena, such as providing basic needs, and in protecting them from foreign threats. This increased role of providing basic necessities for all Americans has been criticized by some as "the welfare state."

Harry S. Truman

Harry S. Truman took over the presidency from Franklin D. Roosevelt near the end of WW II. He made the final decision to drop atomic bombs on Japan, and he played a major role in the final decisions regarding treatment of post-war Germany. On the domestic front, Truman initiated a 21-point plan known as the Fair Deal. This plan expanded Social Security, provided public housing, and made the Fair Employment Practices Act permanent. Truman helped support Greece and Turkey, under threat from the USSR, supported South Korea against communist North Korea, and helped with recovery in Western Europe. He also participated in the formation of NATO, the North Atlantic Treaty Organization.

Korean War

The Korean War began in 1950 and ended in 1953. For the first time in history, a world organization—the United Nations—played a military role in a war. North Korea sent Communist troops into South Korea, seeking to bring the entire country under Communist control. The UN sent out a call to member nations, asking them to support South Korea. Truman sent troops, as did many other UN member nations. The war ended three years later with a truce rather than a peace treaty, and Korea remains divided at 38 degrees North Latitude, with Communist rule remaining in the North and a democratic government ruling the South.

Dwight D. Eisenhower

Eisenhower carried out a middle-of-the-road foreign policy and brought about several steps forward in equal rights. He worked to minimize tensions during the Cold War, and negotiated a peace treaty with Russia after the death of Stalin.

He enforced desegregation by sending troops to Little Rock, Arkansas when the schools there were desegregated, and also ordered the desegregation of the military. Organizations formed during his administration included the Department of Health, Education and Welfare, and the National Aeronautics and Space Administration (NASA).

John F. Kennedy

Although cut short by his assassination, during his term JFK instituted economic programs that led to a period of continuous expansion in the US unmatched since before WW II. He formed the Alliance for Progress and the Peace Corps, organizations intended to help developing nations. He also oversaw the passage of new civil rights legislation, and drafted plans to attack poverty and its causes, along with support of the arts. Kennedy's presidency ended when he was assassinated by Lee Harvey Oswald in 1963.

Cuban Missile Crisis

The Cuban Missile Crisis occurred in 1962, during John F. Kennedy's presidency. Russian Premier Nikita Khrushchev decided to place nuclear missiles in Cuba to protect the island from invasion by the US. American U-2 planes flying over the island photographed the missile bases as they were being built. Tensions rose, with the US concerned about nuclear missiles so close to its shores, and the USSR concerned about American missiles that had been placed in Turkey. Eventually, the missile sites were removed, and a US naval blockade turned back Soviet ships carrying missiles to Cuba. During negotiations, the US agreed to remove their missiles from Turkey and agreed to sell surplus wheat to the USSR. A telephone hot line between Moscow and Washington was set up to allow instant communication between the two heads of state to prevent similar incidents in the future.

Lyndon B. Johnson

Kennedy's Vice President, Lyndon Johnson, assumed the presidency after Kennedy's assassination. He supported civil rights bills, tax cuts, and other wide-reaching legislation that Kennedy had also supported. Johnson saw America as a "Great Society," and enacted legislation to fight disease and poverty, renew urban areas, support education and environmental conservation. Medicare was instituted under his administration. He continued Kennedy's supported of space exploration, and he is also known, although less positively, for his handling of the Vietnam War.

Civil Rights Movement

In the 1950s, post-war America was experiencing a rapid growth in prosperity. However, African Americans found themselves left behind. Following the lead of Mahatma Gandhi, who lead similar class struggles in India; African Americans began to demand equal rights. Major figures in this struggle included:

- Rosa Parks—often called the "mother of the Civil Rights Movement," her refusal to give up her seat on the bus to a white man served as a seed from which the movement grew.
- Martin Luther King, Jr.—the best-known leader of the movement, King drew on Gandhi's beliefs and encouraged non-violent opposition. He led a march on Washington in 1963, received the Nobel Peace Prize in 1968, and was assassinated in 1968.
- Malcolm X—espousing less peaceful means of change, Malcolm X became a Black Muslim, and supported black nationalism.
- Stokely Carmichael—Carmichael invented the term "Black Power" and served as head of the Student Nonviolent Coordinating Committee. He believed in black pride and black culture, and felt separate political and social institutions should be developed for blacks.
- Adam Clayton Powell—chairman of the Coordinating Committee for Employment, he led rent strikes and other actions, as well as a bus boycott, to increase the hiring of blacks.

- Jesse Jackson—Jackson was selected to head the Chicago Operation Breadbasket in 1966 by Martin Luther King, Jr., and went on to organize boycotts and other actions. He also had an unsuccessful run for President.

Three major events of the Civil Rights Movement are:

- Montgomery Bus Boycott—in 1955, Rosa Parks refused to give her seat on the bus to a white man. As a result, she was tried and convicted of disorderly conduct and of violating local ordinances. A 381-day boycott ensued, protesting segregation on public buses.
- Desegregation of Little Rock—In 1957, after the Supreme Court decision on Brown vs. Board of Education, which declared "separate but equal" unconstitutional, the Arkansas school board voted to desegregate their schools. Even though Arkansas was considered progressive, its governor brought in the National Guard to prevent nine black students from entering Central High School in Little Rock. President Eisenhower responded by federalizing the National Guard and ordering them to stand down.
- Birmingham Campaign—Protestors organized a variety of actions such as sit-ins and an organized march to launch a voting campaign. When the City of Birmingham declared the protests illegal, the protestors, including Martin Luther King, Jr., persisted and were arrested and jailed.

Three major pieces of legislation passed as a result of the Civil Rights movement are:

- Brown vs. Board of Education (1954)—the Supreme Court declared that "separate but equal" accommodations and services were unconstitutional.
- Civil Rights Act of 1964—declared discrimination illegal in employment, education, or public accommodation.
- Voting Rights Act of 1965—ended various activities practiced, mostly in the South, to bar blacks from exercising their voting rights. These included poll taxes and literacy tests.

Vietnam War

After World War II, the US pledged, as part of its foreign policy, to come to the assistance of any country threatened by Communism. When Vietnam was divided into a Communist North and democratic South, much like Korea before it, the eventual attempts by the North to unify the country under Communist rule led to intervention by the US.
On the home front, the Vietnam War became more and more unpopular politically, with Americans growing increasingly discontent with the inability of the US to achieve the goals it had set for the Asian country. When President Richard Nixon took office in 1969, his escalation of the war led to protests at Kent State in Ohio, during which several students were killed by National Guard troops.
Protests continued, eventually resulting in the end of the compulsory draft in 1973. In that same year, the US departed Vietnam. In 1975, the south surrendered, and Vietnam became a unified country under Communist rule.

US Cold War foreign policy acts

The following are US Cold War foreign policy acts and how they affected international relationships, especially between the US and the Soviet Union:

- Marshall Plan—sent aid to war-torn Europe after WW II, largely focusing on preventing the spread of communism.
- Containment—proposed by George F. Kennan, Containment focused on containing the spread of Soviet communism.
- Truman Doctrine—Harry S. Truman stated that the US would provide both economic and military support to any country threatened by Soviet takeover.

- National Security Act—passed in 1947, this act created the Department of Defense, the Central Intelligence Agency, and the National Security Council.

The combination of these acts led to the cold war, with Soviet communists attempting to spread their influence and the US and other countries trying to contain or stop this spread.

NATO, the Warsaw Pact, and the Berlin Wall

NATO, the North Atlantic Treaty Organization, came into being in 1949. It essentially amounted to an agreement among the US and Western European countries that an attack on any one of these countries was to be considered an attack against the entire group.

Under the influence of the Soviet Union, the Eastern European countries of USSR, Bulgaria, East Germany, Poland, Romania, Albania, Poland and Czechoslovakia responded with the Warsaw Pact, which created a similar agreement among those nations.
In 1961, a wall was built to separate Communist East Berlin from democratic West Berlin. A similar, though metaphorical, wall lay between east and west, as well, and was referred to as the Iron Curtain.

Arms race

After the World War II, major nations, particularly the US and USSR, rushed to develop the atomic bomb, and later the hydrogen bomb, as well as many other highly advanced weapons systems. These countries seemed determined to outpace each other with the development of numerous, deadly weapons. These weapons were expensive and extremely dangerous, and it is possible that the war between US and Soviet interests remained "cold" due to the fear that one side or the other would use these terrifyingly powerful weapons.

End of the cold war

In the late 1980s, Mikhail Gorbachev ruled the Soviet Union. He introduced a series of reform programs. Also during this period, the Berlin Wall came down, ending the separation of East and West Germany. The Soviet Union relinquished its power over the various republics in Eastern Europe, and they became independent nations with their own individual governments. With the end of the USSR, the cold war also came to an end.

Technological advances after WWII

Numerous technological advances after the Second World War led to more effective treatment of diseases, more efficient communication and transportation, and new means of generating power. Advances in medicine increased the lifespan of people in developed countries, and near-instantaneous communication began to make the world a much smaller place.

- Discovery of penicillin (1945)
- Supersonic air travel (1947)
- First commercial airline flight (1948)
- Nuclear power (1951)
- Orbital leading to manned space flight (Sputnik—1957)
- First man on the moon (1969)

US policy toward immigrants after World War II

Prior to WW II, the US had been limiting immigration for several decades. After WW II, policy shifted slightly to accommodate political refugees from Europe and elsewhere. So many people were displaced by the war that in 1946, The UN formed the International Refugee Organization to deal with the problem. In 1948, the US Congress passed the Displaced Persons Act, which allowed over 400,000 European refugees to enter the US, most of them concentration camp survivors and refugees from Eastern Europe.

In 1952, the President's Escapee Program allowed refugees from Communist Europe to enter the US, as did the Refugee Relief Act, passed in 1953. At the same time, however, the Internal Security Act of 1950 allowed deportation of declared Communists, and Asians were subjected to a quota based on race, rather than country of origin. Later changes included:

- 1962—Migration and Refugee Assistance Act—helped assist refugees in need.
- 1965—Immigration Act—ended quotas based on nation of origin.
- 1986—Immigration Reform and Control Act—prohibited the hiring of illegal immigrants, but also granted amnesty to about three million illegals already in the country.

Richard Nixon

Richard Nixon is best known for illegal activities during his presidency, but other important events marked his tenure as president, including:

- Vietnam War comes to an end
- Improved diplomatic relations between the US and China, and the US and the USSR
- National Environmental Policy Act passed, providing for environmental protection
- Compulsory draft ended
- Supreme Court legalizes abortion in Roe v Wade
- Watergate

The Watergate scandal of 1972 ended Nixon's presidency, when he resigned rather than face impeachment and removal from office.

Gerald Ford

Gerald Ford was appointed to the vice presidency after Nixon's vice president Spiro Agnew resigned under charges of tax evasion. With Nixon's resignation, Ford became president.

Ford's presidency saw negotiations with Russia to limit nuclear arms, as well as struggles to deal with inflation, economic downturn, and energy shortages. Ford's policies sought to reduce governmental control of various businesses and reduce the role of government overall. He also worked to prevent escalation of conflicts in the Middle East.

Carter administration

Jimmy Carter was elected president in 1976. Faced with a budget deficit, high unemployment, and continued inflation, Carter also dealt with numerous matters of international diplomacy including:

- Panama Canal Treaties
- Camp David Accords—negotiations between Anwar el-Sadat, the president of Egypt, and Menachem Begin, the Israeli Prime Minister, leading to a peace treaty between the two nations.
- Strategic Arms Limitation Talks (SALT) and resulting agreements and treaties
- Iran Hostage Crisis—when the Shah of Iran was deposed, an Islamic cleric, the Ayatollah Ruholla Khomeini, came into power. Fifty-three American hostages were taken and held for 444 days in the US Embassy.

Jimmy Carter was awarded the Nobel Peace Prize in 2002.

Ronald Reagan

Ronald Reagan, at 69, became the oldest American president. The two terms of his administration included notable events such as:

- Reaganomics, also known as supply-side or trickle-down economics, involving major tax cuts in the upper income brackets
- Economic Recovery Tax Act of 1981
- First female justice appointed to the Supreme Court, Sandra Day O'Connor
- Massive increase in the national debt—increased from $600 billion to $3 trillion

- Reduction of nuclear weapons via negotiations with Mikhail Gorbachev
- Iran-Contra scandal—cover-up of US involvement in revolutions in El Salvador and Nicaragua
- Deregulation of savings and loan industry
- Loss of the space shuttle Challenger

George Herbert Walker Bush

Reagan's presidency was followed by a term under his former Vice President, George H. W. Bush. His run for president included the famous "thousand points of light" speech, which was instrumental in increasing his standing in the election polls.
During Bush's presidency, numerous major international events took place, including:

- Fall of the Berlin wall and Germany's unification
- Panamanian dictator Manuel Noriega captured and tried on drug and racketeering charges
- Dissolution of the Soviet Union
- Gulf War, or Operation Desert Storm, triggered by Iraq's invasion of Kuwait
- Tiananmen Square Massacre in Beijing, China
- Ruby Ridge
- The arrival of the World Wide Web

William Clinton

William Jefferson Clinton was the second president in US history to be impeached, but he was not convicted, and maintained high approval ratings in spite of the impeachment. Major events during his presidency included:

- Family and Medical Leave Act
- Don't Ask Don't Tell, a compromise position regarding homosexuals serving in the military
- North American Free Trade Agreement, or NAFTA
- Defense of Marriage Act
- Oslo Accords
- Siege at Waco, Texas, involving the Branch Davidians led by David Koresh
- Bombing of the Murrah Federal Building in Oklahoma City, Oklahoma
- Troops sent to Haiti, Bosnia and Somalia to assist with domestic problems in those areas

Expansion of minority rights

Several major acts have been passed, particularly since WW II, to protect the rights of minorities in America. These include:

- Civil Rights Act—1964
- Voting Rights Act—1965
- Age Discrimination Act—1978
- Americans with Disabilities Act—1990

Other important movements for civil rights included a prisoner's rights movement, movements for immigrant rights, and the women's rights movement. The National Organization for Women (NOW) was established in 1966 and worked to pass the Equal Rights Amendment. The amendment was passed, but not enough states ratified it for it to become part of the Constitution.

George W. Bush

Amidst controversy, George W. Bush, son of George Herbert Walker Bush, became president after William Clinton. The election was tightly contested, and though he did not win the popular vote, he won the electoral vote. In the end a Supreme Court ruling was necessary to resolve the issue. His second term was also tightly contested. However, in the election for his second term, Bush won both the popular and the electoral vote. On 9/11/2001, during his first year in office, Bush's presidency was challenged by the first terrorist attack on American soil when al-Qaeda terrorists flew planes into the World Trade Center, destroying it, and into the Pentagon, causing major damage. This event led to major changes in security in the US, especially regarding airline travel. It also led to US troops being deployed in Afghanistan.

Later, Bush initiated war in Iraq with the claim that the country held weapons of mass destruction. On March 20, 2003, the US, along with troops from more than 20 other countries, invaded Iraq. Though no weapons were found, the war continues.

The last months of Bush's administration saw a serious economic meltdown in the US and worldwide. Dramatic increases in oil prices resulted in extreme increases of gasoline prices. This, along with the meltdown of the mortgage industry, created serious and overwhelming economic issues for the Bush administration.

Obama Presidency to date

In 2008, Barack Obama, a Senator from Illinois, became the first African-American US president. His administration has focused on improving the lot of a country suffering from a major recession. His major initiatives have included:

- Economic bailout packages
- Improvements in women's rights
- Moves to broaden gay rights
- Health care reform legislation
- Reinforcement of the war in Afghanistan

World History

Prehistory

Prehistory is the period of human history before writing was developed. The three major periods of prehistory are:

- Lower Paleolithic—Humans used crude tools.
- Upper Paleolithic—Humans began to develop a wider variety of tools. These tools were better made and more specialized. They also began to wear clothes, organize in groups with definite social structures, and to practice art. Most lived in caves during this time period.
- Neolithic—Social structures became even more complex, including growth of a sense of family and the ideas of religion and government. Humans learned to domesticate animals and produce crops, build houses, start fires with friction tools, and to knit, spin and weave.

Anthropology

Anthropology is the study of human culture. Anthropologists study groups of humans, how they relate to each other, and the similarities and differences between these different groups and cultures. Anthropological research takes two approaches: cross-cultural research and comparative research. Most anthropologists work by living among different cultures and participating in those cultures in order to learn about them.
There are three major divisions within anthropology:

- Biological and cultural anthropology
- Archaeology
- Linguistics

Archeology

Archeology studies past human cultures by evaluating what they leave behind. This can include bones, buildings, art, tools, pottery, graves, and even trash. Archeologists maintain detailed notes and records of their findings and use special tools to evaluate what they find. Photographs, notes, maps, artifacts, and surveys of the area can all contribute to evaluation of an archeological site. By studying all these elements of numerous archeological sites, scientists have been able to theorize that humans or near-humans have existed for about 600,000 years. Before that, more primitive humans are believed to have appeared about one million years ago. These humans eventually developed into Cro-Magnon man, and then Homo sapiens, or modern man.

Human development from the Lower Paleolithic to the Iron Age

Human development has been divided into several phases:

- Lower Paleolithic or Old Stone Age, about one million years ago—early humans used tools like needles, hatchets, awls, and cutting tools.
- Upper Paleolithic or New Stone Age, 6,000-8,000 BCE—also known as the Neolithic, textiles and pottery are developed. Humans of this era discovered the wheel, began to practice agriculture, made polished tools, and had some domesticated animals.
- Bronze Age, 3,000 BCE—metals are discovered and the first civilizations emerge as humans become more technologically advanced.

- Iron Age, 1,200-1,000 BCE—metal tools replace stone tools as humans develop knowledge of smelting.

Civilizations

Civilizations are defined as having the following characteristics:

- Use of metal to make weapons and tools
- Written language
- A defined territorial state
- A calendar

The earliest civilizations developed in river valleys where reliable, fertile land was easily found, including:

- Nile River valley in Egypt
- Mesopotamia
- Indus River
- Hwang Ho in China

The very earliest civilizations developed in the Tigris-Euphrates valley in Mesopotamia, which is now part of Iraq, and in Egypt's Nile valley. These civilizations arose between 4,000 and 3,000 BCE. The area where these civilizations grew is known as the Fertile Crescent. There, geography and the availability of water made large-scale human habitation possible.

Importance of rivers and water

The earliest civilizations are also referred to as fluvial civilizations because they were founded near rivers. Rivers and the water they provide were vital to these early groupings, offering:

- Water for drinking and cultivating crops
- A gathering place for wild animals that could be hunted
- Easily available water for domesticated animals
- Rich soil deposits as a result of regular flooding

Irrigation techniques helped direct water where it was most needed, to sustain herds of domestic animals and to nourish crops of increasing size and quality.

Fertile Crescent

James Breasted, an archeologist from the University of Chicago, coined the term Fertile Crescent to describe the area in the Near East where the earliest civilizations arose. The region includes modern day Iraq, Syria, Lebanon, Israel/Palestine and Jordan. It is bordered on the south by the Arabian Desert, the west by the Mediterranean Sea, and to the north and east by the Taurus and Zagros Mountains respectively. This area not only provided the raw materials for the development of increasingly advanced civilizations, but also saw waves of migration and invasion, leading to the earliest wars and genocides as groups conquered and absorbed each other's cultures and inhabitants.

Egyptian, Sumerian, Babylonian and Assyrian cultures

The Egyptians were one of the most advanced ancient cultures, having developed construction methods to build the great pyramids, as well as a form of writing known as hieroglyphics. Their religion was highly developed and complex, and included advanced techniques for the preservation of bodies after death. They also made paper by processing papyrus, a plant commonly found along the Nile, invented the decimal system, devised a solar calendar, and advanced overall knowledge of arithmetic and geometry.

The Sumerians were the first to invent the wheel, and also brought irrigation systems into use. Their cuneiform writing was simpler than Egyptian hieroglyphs, and they developed the timekeeping system we still use today.

The Babylonians are best known for the Code of Hammurabi, an advanced law code.

The Assyrians developed horse-drawn chariots and an organized military.

Hebrew, Persian, Minoan, and Mycenaean cultures

The Hebrew or ancient Israelite culture developed the monotheistic religion that eventually developed into modern Judaism, Christianity, and Islam.

The Persians were conquerors, but those they conquered were allowed to keep their own laws, customs, and religious traditions rather than being forced to accept those of their conquerors. They also developed an alphabet and practicing Zoroastrianism, Mithraism and Gnosticism, religions that have influenced modern religious practice.

The Minoans used a syllabic writing system and built large, colorful palaces. These ornate buildings included sewage systems, running water, bathtubs, and even flush toilets. Their script, known as Linear Script A, has yet to be deciphered.

The Mycenaeans practiced a religion that grew into the Greek pantheon, worshipping Zeus and other Olympian gods. They developed Linear Script B, a writing system used to write an ancient form of classical Greek.

Phoenicians and early culture in India and ancient China

Skilled seafarers and navigators, the Phoenicians used the stars to navigate their ships at night. They developed a purple dye that was in great demand in the ancient world, and worked with glass and metals. They also devised their own phonetic alphabet, using symbols to represent individual sounds rather than whole words or syllables.

In the Indus Valley, an urban civilization arose in what is now India. These ancient humans developed the concept of zero in mathematics, practiced an early form of the Hindu religion, and developed a caste system which is still prevalent in India today. Archeologists are still uncovering information about this highly developed ancient civilization.

In ancient China, human civilization developed along the Yangtze River, starting as long as 500,000 years ago. These people produced silk, grew millet, and made pottery, including Longshan black pottery.

Civilizations of Mesopotamia

The major civilizations of Mesopotamia, in what is now called the Middle East, were:

- Sumerians
- Amorites
- Hittites
- Assyrians
- Chaldeans
- Persians

These cultures controlled different areas of Mesopotamia during various time periods, but were similar in that they were autocratic. This meant a single ruler served as the head of the government and often, the main religious ruler, as well. These, often tyrannical, militaristic leaders, controlled all aspects of life, including law, trade, and religious activity. Portions of the legacies of these civilizations remain in cultures today. These include mythologies, religious systems, mathematical innovations and even elements of various languages.

Sumer

Sumer, located in the southern part of Mesopotamia, consisted of a dozen city-states. Each city-state had its own gods, and the leader of each city-state also served as the high priest. Cultural legacies of Sumer include:

- The invention of writing
- Invention of the wheel
- The first library—established in Assyria by Ashurbanipal
- The Hanging Gardens of Babylon—one of the Seven Wonders of the Ancient World
- First written laws—Ur-Nammu's Codes and the Codes of Hammurabi
- The *Epic of Gilgamesh*—the first epic story in history

Kushite culture

Kush, or Cush, was located south of ancient Egypt, and the earliest existing records of this civilization were found in Egyptian texts. At one time, Kush was the largest empire on the Nile River, surpassing even Egypt.

In Neolithic times, Kushites lived in villages, with buildings made of mud bricks. They were settled rather than nomadic, and practiced hunting and fishing, cultivated grain, and also herded cattle. Kerma, the capitol, was a major center of trade.

Kush determined leadership through matrilineal descent of their kings, as did Egypt. Their heads of state, the Kandake or Kentake, were female. Their polytheistic religion included the primary Egyptian gods as well as regional gods, including a lion god, which is commonly found in African cultures.

Archeological evidence indicates the Kushites were a mix of Mediterranean and Negroid peoples. Kush was conquered by Nubia in 800 BCE.

Minoan civilization

The Minoans lived on the island of Crete, just off the coast of Greece. This civilization reigned from 2700 to 1450 BCE. The Minoans developed writing systems known to linguists as Linear A and Linear B. Linear A has not yet been translated; Linear B evolved into classical Greek script. "Minoans" is not the name they used for themselves, but is instead a variation on the name of King Minos, a king in Greek mythology believed by some to have been a denizen of Crete. The Minoan civilization subsisted on trade, and their way of life was often disrupted by earthquakes and volcanoes. Much is still unknown about the Minoans, and archeologists continue to study their architecture and archeological remains. The Minoan culture eventually fell to Greek invaders and was supplanted by the Mycenaean civilization.

Influences of ancient Indian civilization

The civilizations of ancient India gave rise to both Hinduism and Buddhism, major world religions that have found their way to countries far away from their place of origin. Practices such as yoga, increasingly popular in the West, can trace their roots to these earliest Indian civilizations. Literature from ancient India includes the *Mahabharata* containing the *Bhagavad Gita,* the *Ramayana*, *Arthashastra*, and the *Vedas*, a collection of sacred texts. Indo-European languages, including English, find their beginnings in these ancient cultures. Ancient Indo-Aryan languages such as Sanskrit are still used in some formal Hindu practices. Yoga poses are still formally referred to by Sanskrit names.

Earliest civilizations in China

Many historians believe Chinese civilization is the oldest uninterrupted civilization in the world. The Neolithic age in China goes back 10,000 years, with agriculture in China beginning as early as 7,000 years ago. Their system of writing dates to 1,500 BCE. The Yellow River served as the center for the earliest Chinese settlements. In Ningxia, in northwest China, there are carvings on cliffs that date back to the Paleolithic Period, at least 6,000 years ago, indicating the extreme antiquity of Chinese culture. Literature from ancient China includes works by Confucius, *Analects*, the *Tao Te Ching*, and a variety of poetry.

Ancient American cultures

Less is known of ancient American civilizations since less was left behind. Those we know something of include:

- The Norte Chico civilization in Peru, an agricultural society of 20 individual communities, that existed over 5,000 years ago. This culture is also known as Caral-Supe, and is the oldest known civilization in the Americas.
- The Anasazi, or Ancient Pueblo People, in what is now the southwestern United States. Emerging about 1200 BCE, the Anasazi built complex adobe dwellings, and were the forerunners of later Pueblo Indian cultures.
- The Maya emerged in southern Mexico and northern Central America as early as 2,600 BCE. They developed a written language and a complex calendar.

Mycenaean civilization

The Mycenaean civilization was the first major civilization in Europe. In contrast to the Minoans, whom they displaced, the Mycenaeans relied more on conquest than on trade. Mycenaean states included Sparta, Metropolis and Corinth. The history of this civilization, including the Trojan War, was recorded by the Greek poet, Homer. His work was largely considered mythical until archeologists discovered evidence of the city of Troy in Hisarlik, Turkey. Archeologists continue to add to the body of information about this ancient culture, translating documents written in Linear B, a script derived from the Minoan Linear A. It is theorized that the Mycenaean civilization was eventually destroyed in either a Dorian invasion or an attack by Greek invaders from the north. This theory has not been proven, nor is it certain who the invaders might have been

Dorian invasion

A Dorian invasion does not refer to an invasion by a particular group of people, but rather is a hypothetical theory to explain the end of the Mycenaean civilization and the growth of classical Greece. Ancient tradition refers to these events as "the return of the Heracleidae," or the sons (descendents) of Hercules. Archeologists and historians still do not know exactly who conquered the Mycenaean, but it is believed to have occurred around 1200 BCE, contemporaneous with the destruction of the Hittite civilization in what is now modern Turkey. The Hittites speak of an attack by people of the Aegean Sea, or the "Sea People." Only Athens was left intact.

Spartans and Athenians

Both powerful city-states, the Spartans and the Athenians nurtured contrasting cultures.

- The Spartans, located in Peloponnesus, were ruled by an oligarchic military state. They practiced farming, disallowed trade for Spartan citizens, and valued military arts and strict discipline. They emerged as the strongest military force in the area, and maintained this status for many years. In one memorable encounter, a small group of Spartans held off a huge army of Persians at Thermopylae.
- The Athenians were centered in Attica, where there was little land available for farming. Like the Spartans, they descended from invaders who spoke Greek. Their government was very different from Sparta's; it was in Athens that democracy was created by Cleisthenes of Athens in 510 BCE. Athenians excelled in art, theater, architecture, and philosophy.

Athens and Sparta fought each other in the Peloponnesian War, 431-404 BCE.

Contributions of ancient Greece

Ancient Greece made numerous major contributions to cultural development, including:

- Theater—Aristophanes and other Greek playwrights laid the groundwork for modern theatrical performance.
- Alphabet—the Greek alphabet, derived from the Phoenician alphabet, developed into the Roman alphabet, and then into our modern-day alphabet.
- Geometry—Pythagoras and Euclid pioneered much of the system of geometry still taught today. Archimedes made various mathematical discoveries, including the value of pi.
- Historical writing—much of ancient history doubles as mythology or religious texts. Herodotus and Thucydides made use of research and interpretation to record historical events.
- Philosophy—Socrates, Plato, and Aristotle served as the fathers of Western philosophy. Their work is still required reading for philosophy students.

Alexander the Great

Born to Philip II of Macedon and tutored by Aristotle, Alexander the Great is considered one of the greatest conquerors in history. He conquered Egypt, the Achaemenid/Persian Empire, a powerful empire founded by Cyrus the Great that spanned three continents, and he traveled as far as India and the Iberian Peninsula. Though Alexander died at the early age of 32, his conquering efforts spread Greek culture into the east. This cultural diffusion left a greater mark on history than did his empire, which fell apart due to internal conflict not long after his death. Trade between the East and West increased, as did an exchange of ideas and beliefs that influenced both regions greatly. The Hellenistic traditions his conquest spread were prevalent in Byzantine culture until as late as the 15th century.

Hittite Empire

The Hittites were centered in what is now Turkey, but their empire extended into Palestine and Syria. They conquered the Babylonian civilization, but adopted their religion and their system of laws. Overall, the Hittites tended to tolerate other religions, unlike many other contemporary cultures, and absorbed foreign gods into their own belief systems rather than forcing their religion onto peoples they conquered. The Hittite Empire reached its peak in 1600-1200 BCE. After a war with Egypt, which weakened them severely, they were eventually conquered by the Assyrians in 700 BCE.

Persian Wars

The Persian Empire, ruled by Cyrus the Great, encompassed an area from the Black Sea to Afghanistan, and beyond into Central Asia. After the death of Cyrus, Darius became king in 522 BCE. The empire reached its zenith during his reign.
From 499-448 BCE, the Greeks and Persians fought in the Persian Wars. Battles of the Persian Wars included:

- The Battle of Marathon, in which heavily outnumbered Greek forces managed to achieve victory.
- The Battle of Thermopylae, in which a small band of Spartans held off a throng of Persian troops for several days.
- The Battle of Salamis, a naval battle that again saw outnumbered Greeks achieving victory.
- The Battle of Plataea, another Greek victory, but one in which they outnumbered the Persians.

The Persian Wars did not see the end of the Persian Empire, but discouraged additional attempts to invade Greece.

Maurya Empire

The Maurya Empire was a large, powerful empire established in India. It was one of the largest ever to rule in the Indian subcontinent, and existed from 322 to 185 BCE, ruled by Chandragupta after the withdrawal from India of Alexander the Great. The Maurya Empire was highly developed, including a standardized economic system, waterworks, and private corporations. Trade to the Greeks and others became common, with goods including silk, exotic foods, and spices. Religious development included the rise of Buddhism and Jainism. The laws of the Maurya Empire protected not only civil and social rights of the citizens, but also protected animals, establishing protected zones for economically important creatures such as elephants, lions and tigers. This period of time in Indian history was largely peaceful due to the strong Buddhist beliefs of many of its leaders. The empire finally fell after a succession of weak leaders, and was taken over by Demetrius, a Greco-Bactrian king who took advantage of this lapse in leadership to conquer southern Afghanistan and Pakistan around 180 BCE.

Chinese empires

In China, history was divided into a series of dynasties. The most famous of these, the Han Dynasty, existed from 206 BCE to 220 CE. Accomplishments of the Chinese Empires included:

- Building the Great Wall of China
- Numerous inventions, including paper, paper money, printing, and gunpowder
- High level of artistic development
- Silk production

The Chinese Empires were comparable to Rome as far as their artistic and intellectual accomplishments, as well as the size and scope of their influence.

Roman Empire and Republic

Rome began humbly, in a single town that grew out of Etruscan settlements and traditions, founded, according to legend, by twin brothers Romulus and Remus, who were raised by wolves. Romulus killed Remus, and from his legacy grew Rome. A thousand years later, the Roman Empire covered a significant portion of the known world, from what is now Scotland, across Europe, and into the Middle East. Hellenization, or the spread of Greek culture throughout the world, served as an inspiration and a model for the spread of Roman culture. Rome brought in belief systems of conquered peoples as well as their technological and scientific accomplishments, melding the disparate parts into a Roman core. Rome's overall government was autocratic, but local officials came from the provinces where they lived. This limited administrative system was probably a major factor in the long life of the empire.

Byzantine Empire

In the early fourth century, the Roman Empire split, with the eastern portion becoming the Eastern Empire, or the Byzantine Empire. In 330 CE, Constantine founded the city of Constantinople, which became the center of the Byzantine Empire. Its major influences came from Mesopotamia and Persia, in contrast to the Western Empire, which maintained traditions more closely linked to Greece and Carthage. Byzantium's position gave it an advantage over invaders from the west and the east, as well as control over trade from both regions. It protected the Western empire from invasion from the Persians and the Ottomans, and practiced a more centralized rule than in the West. The Byzantines were famous for lavish art and architecture, as well as the Code of Justinian, which collected Roman law into a clear system.

Nicene Creed

The Byzantine Empire was Christian-based but incorporated Greek language, philosophy and literature and drew its law and government policies from Rome. However, there was as yet no unified doctrine of Christianity, as it was a relatively new religion that had spread rapidly and without a great deal of organization. In 325, the First Council of Nicaea addressed this issue. From this conference came the Nicene Creed, addressing the Trinity and other basic Christian beliefs. The Council of Chalcedon in 451 stated that any rejection of the Trinity was blasphemy.

Fall of the Western Roman Empire

Germanic tribes, including the Visigoths, Ostrogoths, Vandals, Saxons and Franks, controlled most of Europe. The Roman Empire faced major opposition on that front. The increasing size of the empire also made it harder to manage, leading to dissatisfaction throughout the empire as Roman government became less efficient. Germanic tribes refused to adhere to the Nicene Creed, instead following Arianism, which led the Roman Catholic Church to declare them heretics. The Franks proved a powerful military force in their defeat of the Muslims in 732. In 768, Charlemagne became king of the Franks. These tribes waged several wars against Rome, including the invasion of Britannia by the Angles and Saxons. Far-flung Rome lost control over this area of its Empire, and eventually Rome itself was invaded.

Iconoclasm and conflict between Roman Catholic and Eastern Orthodox churches

Emperor Leo III ordered the destruction of all icons throughout the Byzantine Empire. Images of Jesus were replaced with a cross, and images of Jesus, Mary or other religious figures were considered blasphemy on grounds of idolatry. The current Pope, Gregory II, called a synod to discuss the issue. The synod declared that destroying these images was heretical, and that strong disciplinary measures would result for anyone who took this step. Leo's response was an attempt to kidnap Pope Gregory, but this plan ended in failure when his ships were destroyed by a storm.

Viking invasions

Vikings invaded Northern France in the tenth century, eventually becoming the Normans. Originating in Scandinavia, the Vikings were accomplished seafarers with advanced knowledge of trade routes. With overpopulation plaguing their native lands, they began to travel. From the eighth to the eleventh centuries, they spread throughout Europe, conquering and colonizing. Vikings invaded and colonized England through several waves, including the Anglo-Saxon invasions that displaced Roman control. Their influence remained significant in England, affecting everything from the language of the country to place names and even the government and social structure. By 900, Vikings had settled in Iceland. They proceeded then to Greenland and eventually to North America, arriving in the New World even before the Spanish and British who claimed the lands several centuries later. They also traded with the Byzantine Empire until the eleventh century when their significant level of activity came to an end.

Tenth century events in the West and the East

In Europe, the tenth century is largely known as the Dark Ages, as numerous Viking invasions disrupted societies that had been more settled under Roman rule. Vikings settled in Northern France, eventually becoming the Normans. By the eleventh century, Europe would rise again into the High Middle Ages with the beginning of the Crusades.
In China, wars also raged. This led the Chinese to make use of gunpowder for the first time in warfare.

In the Americas, the Mayan Empire was winding down while the Toltec became more prominent. Pueblo Indian culture was also at its zenith.

In the East, the Muslims and the Byzantine Empire were experiencing a significant period of growth and development.

European feudalism in the Middle Ages

A major element of the social and economic life of Europe, feudalism developed as a way to ensure European rulers would have the wherewithal to quickly raise an army when necessary. Vassals swore loyalty and promised to provide military service for lords, who in return offered a fief, or a parcel of land, for them to use to generate their livelihood. Vassals could work the land themselves, have it worked by peasants or serfs—workers who had few rights and were little more than slaves—or grant the fief to someone else. The king legally owned all the land, but in return promised to protect the vassals from invasion and war. Vassals returned a certain percentage of their income to the lords, who in turn passed a portion of their income on to the king. A similar practice was manorialism, in which the feudal system was applied to a self-contained manor. These manors were often owned by the lords who ran them, but were usually included in the same system of loyalty and promises of military service that drove feudalism.

Influence of the Roman Catholic Church over medieval society

The Roman Catholic Church extended significant influence both politically and economically throughout medieval society. The church supplied education, as there were no established schools or universities. To a large extent, the church had filled a power void left by various invasions throughout the former Roman Empire, leading it to exercise a role that was far more political than religious. Kings were heavily influenced by the Pope and other church officials, and churches controlled large amounts of land throughout Europe.

Black Death

The Black Death, believed to be bubonic plague, came to Europe probably brought by fleas carried on rats that were regular passengers on sailing vessels. It killed in excess of a third of the entire population of Europe and effectively ended feudalism as a political system. Many who had formerly served as peasants or serfs found different work, as a demand for skilled labor grew. Nation-states grew in power, and in the face of the pandemic, many began to turn away from faith in God and toward the ideals of ancient Greece and Rome for government and other beliefs.

Crusades

The Crusades began in the eleventh century and progressed well into the twelfth. The major goal of these various military ventures was to slow the progression of Muslim forces into Europe and to expel them from the Holy Land, where they had taken control of Jerusalem and Palestine. Alexius I, the Eastern emperor, called for helped from Pope Urban II when Palestine was taken. In 1095, the Pope, hoping to reunite Eastern and Western Christian influences, encouraged all Christians to help the cause. Amidst great bloodshed, this Crusade recaptured Jerusalem, but over the next centuries, Jerusalem and other areas of the Holy Land changed hands numerous times. The Second Crusade, in 1145, consisted of an unsuccessful attempt to retake Damascus. The Third Crusade, under Pope Gregory VIII, attempted to recapture Jerusalem, but failed. The Fourth Crusade, under Pope Innocent III, attempted to come into the Holy Land via Egypt. The Crusades led to greater power for the Pope and the Catholic Church in general and also opened numerous trading and cultural routes between Europe and the East.

Developments through the eleventh century

<u>Politics in India</u>
After the Mauryan dynasty, the Guptas ruled India, maintaining a long period of peace and prosperity in the area. During this time, the Indian people invented the decimal system as well as the concept of zero. They produced cotton and calico, as well as other products in high demand in Europe and Asia, and developed a complex system of medicine.

The Gupta Dynasty ended in the eleventh century with a Muslim invasion of the region. These sultans ruled for several centuries. Tamerlane, one of the most famous, expanded India's borders and founded the Mogul Dynasty. His grandson Akbar promoted freedom of religion and built a wide-spread number of mosques, forts, and other buildings throughout the country.

<u>Chinese and Japanese governments</u>
After the Mongols, led by Genghis Khan and his grandson Kublai Khan, unified the Mongol Empire, China was led by the Ming and Manchu Dynasties. Both these Dynasties were isolationist, ending China's interaction with other countries until the eighteenth century. The Ming Dynasty was known for its porcelain, while the Manchus focused on farming and road construction as the population grew.

Japan developed independent of China, but borrowed the Buddhist religion, the Chinese writing system, and other elements of Chinese society. Ruled by the divine emperor, Japan basically functioned on a feudal system led by Daimyos, or lords, and soldiers known as samurai. Japan remained isolationist, not interacting significantly with the rest of the world until the 1800s.

<u>Africa</u>
Only a few areas of Africa were amenable to habitation, due to the large amount of desert and other inhospitable terrain. Egypt remained important, though most of the northern coast became Muslim as their armies spread through the area. Ghana rose as a trade center in the ninth century, lasting into the twelfth century, primarily trading in gold, which it exchange for Saharan salt. Mali rose somewhat later, with the trade center Timbuktu becoming an important exporter of goods such as iron, leather and tin.

Mali also dealt in agricultural trade, becoming one of the most significant trading centers in West Africa. The Muslim religion dominated, and technological advancement was sparse.

African culture was largely defined through migration, as Arab merchants and others settled on the continent, particularly along the east coast. Scholars from the Muslim nations gravitated to Timbuktu, which in addition to its importance in trade, had also become a magnet for those seeking knowledge and education.

Islam

Born in 570 CE, Mohammed became prominent in 610, leading his followers in a new religion called Islam, which means submission to God's will. Before this time, the Arabian Peninsula was inhabited largely by Bedouins, nomads who battled amongst each other and lived in tribal organizations. But by the time Mohammed died in 632, most of Arabia had become Muslim to some extent.

Mohammed conquered Mecca, where a temple called the Kaaba had long served as a center of the nomadic religions. He declared this temple the most sacred of Islam, and Mecca as the holy city. His writings became the Koran, or Qur'an, divine revelations he said had been delivered to him by the angel Gabriel.

Mohammed's teachings gave the formerly tribal Arabian people a sense of unity that had not existed in the area before. After his death, the converted Muslims of Arabia conquered a vast territory, creating an empire and bringing advances in literature, technology, science and art just as Europe was declining under the scourge of the Black Death. Literature from this period includes the *Arabian Nights* and the *Rubaiyat* of Omar Khayyam.

Later in its development, Islam split into two factions, the Shiite and the Sunni Muslims. Conflict continues today between these groups.

Ottoman Empire

By 1400, the Ottomans had grown in power in Anatolia and had begun attempts to take Constantinople. In 1453 they finally conquered the Byzantine capital and renamed it Istanbul. The Ottoman Empire's major strength, much like Rome before it, lay in its ability to unite widely disparate people through religious tolerance. This tolerance grew from the Islamic belief that Muslims, Christians and Jews were fundamentally related as "People of the Book," and enabled the Ottomans to develop a widely varied culture. They also believed in just laws and just government, with government centered in a monarch, known as the sultan.

Renaissance

Renaissance literally means "rebirth." After the darkness of the Dark Ages and the Black Plague, interest rose again in the beliefs and politics of ancient Greece and Rome. Art, literature, music, science, and philosophy all burgeoned during the Renaissance.

Many of the ideas of the Renaissance began in Florence, Italy, spurred by the Medici family. Education for the upper classes expanded to include law, math, reading, writing, and classical Greek and Roman works. As the Renaissance progressed, the world was presented through art and literature in a realistic way that had never been explored before. This realism drove culture to new heights.

Artists, authors and scientists

Artists of the Renaissance included Leonardo da Vinci, also an inventor, Michelangelo, also an architect, and others who focused on realism in their work. In literature, major contributions came from the humanist, authors like Petrarch, Erasmus, Sir Thomas More, and Boccaccio, who believed man should focus on reality rather than on the ethereal. Shakespeare, Cervantes and Dante followed in their footsteps, and their works found a wide audience thanks to Gutenberg's development of the printing press.

Scientific developments of the Renaissance included the work of Copernicus, Galileo and Kepler, who challenged the geocentric philosophies of the church by proving the earth was not the center of the solar system.

Reformation

The Reformation consisted of the Protestant Revolution and the Catholic Reformation. The Protestant Revolution rose in Germany when Martin Luther protested abuses of the Catholic Church. John Calvin led the movement in Switzerland, while in England King Henry VIII made use of the Revolution's ideas to further his own political goals. The Catholic Reformation occurred in response to the Protestant Revolution, leading to various changes in the Catholic Church. Some provided wider tolerance of different religious viewpoints, but others actually increased the persecution of those deemed to be heretics.

From a religious standpoint, the Reformation occurred due to abuses by the Catholic Church such as indulgences and dispensations, religious offices being offered up for sale, and an increasingly dissolute clergy. Politically, the Reformation was driven by increased power of various ruling monarchs, who wished to take all power to themselves rather than allowing power to remain with the church. They also had begun to chafe at papal taxes and the church's increasing wealth. The ideas of the Protestant Revolution removed power from the Catholic Church and the Pope himself, playing nicely into the hands of those monarchs, such as Henry VIII, who wanted out from under the church's control.

Scientific Revolution

In addition to holding power in the political realm, church doctrine also governed scientific belief. During the Scientific Revolution, astronomers and other scientists began to amass evidence that challenged the church's scientific doctrines. Major figures of the Scientific Revolution included:

- Nicolaus Copernicus—wrote *Revolutions of the Celestial Spheres*, arguing that the Earth revolved around the sun.
- Tycho Brahe—catalogued astronomical observations.
- Johannes Kepler—developed Laws of Planetary Motions.
- Galileo Galilei—defended the heliocentric theories of Copernicus and Kepler, discovered four moons of Jupiter, and died under house arrest by the Church, charged with heresy.
- Isaac Newton—discovered gravity, studied optics, calculus and physics, and believed the workings of nature could be observed, studied, and proven through observation.

Enlightenment

During the Enlightenment, philosophers and scientists began to rely more and more on observation to support their ideas, rather than building on past beliefs, particularly those held by the church. A focus on ethics and logic drove their work. Major philosophers of the Enlightenment included:

- Rene Descartes—"I think, therefore I am." He believed strongly in logic and rules of observation.
- David Hume—pioneered empiricism and skepticism, believing that truth could only be found through direct experience, and that what others said to be true was always suspect.
- Immanuel Kant—believed in self-examination and observation, and that the root of morality lay within human beings.
- Jean-Jacques Rousseau—developed the idea of the social contract, that government existed by the agreement of the people, and that the government was obligated to protect the people and their basic rights. His ideas influenced John Locke and Thomas Jefferson.

American Revolution and French Revolution

Both the American and French Revolution came about as a protest against the excesses and overly controlling nature of their respective monarchs. In America, the British colonies had been left mostly self-governing until the British monarchs began to increase control, leading the colonies to revolt. In France, the nobility's excesses had led to increasingly difficult economic conditions, with inflation, heavy taxation and food shortages creating horrible burdens on the people. Both revolutions led to the development of republics to replace the monarchies that were displaced. However, the French Revolution eventually led to the rise of the dictator Napoleon Bonaparte, while the American Revolution produced a working republic from the beginning.

In 1789, King Louis XVI, faced with a huge national debt, convened parliament. The Third Estate, or Commons, a division of the French parliament, then claimed power, and the king's resistance led to the storming of the Bastille, the royal prison. The people established a constitutional monarchy. When King Louis XVI and Marie Antoinette attempted to leave the country, they were executed on the guillotine. From 1793 to 1794, Robespierre and extreme radicals, the Jacobins, instituted a Reign of Terror, executing thousands of nobles as well as anyone considered an enemy of the Revolution. Robespierre was then executed, as well, and the Directory came into power. This governing body proved incompetent and corrupt, allowing Napoleon Bonaparte to come to power in 1799, first as a dictator, then as emperor. While the French Revolution threw off the power of a corrupt monarchy, its immediate results were likely not what the original perpetrators of the revolt had intended.

Russian Revolution of 1905

In Russia, rule lay in the hands of the Czars, and the overall structure was feudalistic. Beneath the Czars was a group of rich nobles, landowners whose lands were worked by peasants and serfs. The Russo-Japanese War (1904-1905) made conditions much worse for the lower classes. When peasants demonstrated outside the Czar's Winter Palace, the palace guard fired upon the crowd. The demonstration had been organized by a trade union leader, and after the violent response, many unions as well as political parties blossomed and began to lead numerous strikes. When the economy ground to a halt, Czar Nicholas II signed a document known as the October Manifesto, which established a constitutional monarchy and gave legislative power to parliament. However, he violated the Manifesto shortly thereafter, disbanding parliament and ignoring the civil liberties granted by the Manifesto. This eventually led to the Bolshevik Revolution of 1917.

Bolshevik Revolution of 1917

Throughout its modern history, Russia had lagged behind other countries in development. The continued existence of a feudal system, combined with harsh conditions and the overall size of the country, led to massive food shortages and increasingly harsh conditions for the majority of the population. The tyrannical rule favored by the Czars only made this worse, as did repeated losses in various military conflicts. Increasing poverty, decreasing supplies, and the Czar's violation of the October Manifesto which had given some political power and civil rights to the people finally came to a head with the Bolshevik Revolution.

<u>Major events</u>

A workers' strike in Petrograd in 1917 set the revolutionary wheels in motion when the army sided with the workers. While parliament set up a provisional government made up of nobles, the workers and military joined to form their own governmental system known as soviets, which consisted of local councils elected by the people. The ensuing chaos opened the doors for formerly exiled leaders Vladimir Lenin, Joseph Stalin and Leon Trotsky to move in and gain popular support as well as the support of the Red Guard. Overthrowing parliament, they took power, creating a communist state in Russia.

This development led to the spread of Communism throughout Eastern Europe and elsewhere, greatly affecting diplomatic policies throughout the world for several decades.

Industrial Revolution

The Industrial Revolution began in Great Britain, bringing coal- and steam-powered machinery into widespread use. Industry began a period of rapid growth with these developments. Goods that had previously been produced in small workshops or even in homes were produced more efficiently and in much larger quantities in factories. Where society had been largely agrarian based, the focus swiftly shifted to an industrial outlook. As electricity and internal combustion engines replaced coal and steam as energy sources, even more drastic and rapid changes occurred. Western European countries in particular turned to colonialism, taking control of portions of Africa and Asia to assure access to the raw materials needed to produce factory goods. Specialized labor became very much in demand, and businesses grew rapidly, creating monopolies, increasing world trade, and creating large urban centers. Even agriculture changed fundamentally as the Industrial Revolution led to a second Agricultural Revolution as the addition of the new technologies advanced agricultural production.

First and second phases

The first phase of the Industrial Revolution took place from roughly 1750 to 1830. The textile industry experienced major changes as more and more elements of the process became mechanized. Mining benefited from the steam engine. Transportation became easier and more widely available as waterways were improved and the railroad came into prominence. In the second phase, from 1830 to 1910, industries further improved in efficiency and new industries were introduced as photography, various chemical processes, and electricity became more widely available to produce new goods or new, improved versions of old goods. Petroleum and hydroelectric became major sources of power. During this time, the industrial revolution spread out of Western Europe and into the US and Japan.

Political, social and economic side effects

The Industrial Revolution led to widespread education, a wider franchise, and the development of mass communication in the political arena. Economically, conflicts arose between companies and their employees, as struggles for fair treatment and fair wages increased. Unions gained power and became more active. Government regulation over industries increased, but at the same time, growing businesses fought for the right to free enterprise. In the social sphere, populations increased and began to concentrate around centers of industry. Cities became larger and more densely populated. Scientific advancements led to more efficient agriculture, greater supply of goods, and increased knowledge of medicine and sanitation, leading to better overall health.

Nationalism in the eighteenth and nineteenth centuries

Nationalism, put simply, is a strong belief in, identification with, and allegiance to a particular nation and people. Nationalistic belief unified various areas that had previously seen themselves as fragmented which led to patriotism and, in some cases, imperialism. As nationalism grew, individual nations sought to grow, bringing in other, smaller states that shared similar characteristics such as language and cultural beliefs. Unfortunately, a major side effect of these growing nationalistic beliefs was often conflict and outright war.

In Europe, imperialism led countries to spread their influence into Africa and Asia. Africa was eventually divided among several European countries that needed the raw materials to be found there. Asia also came under European control, with the exception of China, Japan and Siam (now Thailand). In the US, Manifest Destiny became the rallying cry as the country expanded west. Italy and Germany formed larger nations from a variety of smaller states.

WWI

Europe

WW I began in 1914 with the assassination of Archduke Franz Ferdinand, heir to the throne of Austria-Hungary, by a Serbian national. This led to a conflict between Austria-Hungary and Serbia that quickly escalated into the First World War. Europe split into the Allies—Britain, France and Russia, and later Italy, Japan and the US, against the Central Powers—Austria-Hungary, Germany and Turkey. As the war spread, countries beyond Europe became involved. The war left Europe deeply in debt, and particularly devastated the German economy. The ensuing Great Depression made matters worse, and economic devastation opened the door for Communist, Fascist and Socialist governments to gain power.

Trench warfare

Fighting during WW I took place largely in a series of trenches built along the Eastern and Western Fronts. These trenches added up to about 24,000 miles, each side having dug at least 12,000 miles' worth during the course of the war. This produced fronts that stretched nearly 400 miles, from the coast of Belgium to the border of Switzerland. The Allies made use of straightforward open-air trenches with a front line, supporting lines, and communications lines. By contrast, the German trenches sometimes included well-equipped underground living quarters.

Communism and Socialism

At their roots, socialism and communism both focus on public ownership and distribution of goods and services. However, communism works toward revolution by drawing on what it sees to be inevitable class antagonism, eventually overthrowing the upper classes and the systems of capitalism. Socialism makes use of democratic procedures, building on the existing order. This was particularly true of the Utopian-Socialists, who saw industrial capitalism as oppressive, not allowing workers to prosper. While socialism struggled between the World Wars, communism took hold, especially in Eastern Europe. After WW II, democratic socialism became more common. Later, capitalism took a stronger hold again, and today most industrialized countries in the world function under an economy that mixes elements of capitalism and socialism.

Rise of the Nazi party

The Great Depression had a particularly devastating effect on Germany's economy, especially after the US was no longer able to supply reconstruction loans to help the country regain its footing. With unemployment rising rapidly, dissatisfaction with the government grew. Fascist and Communist parties rose, promising change and improvement.

Led by Adolf Hitler, the Fascist, Nazi Party eventually gained power in Parliament based on these promises and the votes of desperate German workers. When Hitler became Chancellor, he launched numerous expansionist policies, violating the peace treaties that had ended WW I. His military buildup and conquering of neighboring countries sparked the aggression that soon led to WW II.

Blitzkrieg

The blitzkrieg, or "lightning war," consisted of fast, powerful surprise attacks that disrupted communications, made it difficult if not impossible for the victims to retaliate, and demoralized Germany's foes. The "blitz," or the aerial bombing of England in 1940, was one example, with bombings occurring in London and other cities 57 nights in a row. The Battle of Britain, from 1940 to 1941, also brought intense raids by Germany's air force, the Luftwaffe, mostly targeting ports and British air force bases. Eventually, Britain's Royal Air Force blocked the Luftwaffe, ending Germany's hopes for conquering Britain.

Battle of the Bulge

Following the D-Day Invasion, Allied forces gained considerable ground, and began a major campaign to push through Europe. In December of 1944, Hitler launched a counteroffensive, attempting to retake Antwerp, an important port. The ensuing battle became the largest land battle on the war's Western Front, and was known as the Battle of the Ardennes, or the Battle of the Bulge. The battle lasted from December 16, 1944 to January 28, 1945. The Germans pushed forward, making inroads into Allied lines, but in the end the Allies brought the advance to a halt. The Germans were pushed back, with massive losses on both sides. However, those losses proved crippling to the German army.

Holocaust

As Germany sank deeper and deeper into dire economic straits, the tendency was to look for a person or group of people to blame for the problems of the country. With distrust of the Jewish people already ingrained, it was easy for German authorities to set up the Jews as scapegoats for Germany's problems. Under the rule of Hitler and the Nazi party, the "Final Solution" for the supposed Jewish problem was devised. Millions of Jews, as well as Gypsies, homosexuals, Communists, Catholics, the mentally ill and others, simply named as criminals, were transported to concentration camps during the course of the war. At least six million were slaughtered in death camps such as Auschwitz, where horrible conditions and torture of prisoners were commonplace. The Allies were aware of rumors of mass slaughter throughout the war, but many discounted the reports. Only when troops went in to liberate the prisoners was the true horror of the concentration camps brought to light.

The Holocaust resulted in massive loss of human life, but also in the loss and destruction of cultures. Because the genocide focused on specific ethnic groups, many traditions, histories, knowledge, and other cultural elements were lost, particularly among the Jewish and Gypsy populations. After World War II, the United Nations recognized genocide as a "crime against humanity." The UN passed the Universal Declaration of Human Rights in order to further specify what rights the organization protected. Nazi war criminals faced justice during the Nuremberg Trials. There individuals, rather than their governments, were held accountable for war crimes.

Cold War

With millions of military and civilian deaths and over 12 million persons displaced, WW II left large regions of Europe and Asia in disarray. Communist governments moved in with promises of renewed prosperity and economic stability. The Soviet Union backed Communist regimes in much of Eastern Europe. In China, Mao Zedong led communist forces in the overthrow of the Chinese Nationalist Party and instituted a Communist government in 1949. While the new Communist governments restored a measure of stability to much of Eastern Europe, it brought its own problems, with dictatorial governments and an oppressive police force. The spread of Communism also led to several years of tension between Communist countries and the democratic west, as the west fought to slow the spread of oppressive regimes throughout the world. With both sides in possession of nuclear weapons, tensions rose. Each side feared the other would resort to nuclear attack. This standoff lasted until 1989, when the Berlin Wall fell. The Soviet Union was dissolved two years later.

United Nations

The United Nations (UN) came into being toward the end of World War II. A successor to the less-than-successful League of Nations, formed after World War I, the UN built and improved on those ideas. Since its inception, the UN has worked to bring the countries of the world together for diplomatic solutions to international problems, including sanctions and other restrictions. It has also initiated military action, calling for peacekeeping troops from member countries to move against countries violating UN policies.

One example of UN involvement in an international conflict is the Korean War, the first war in which an international alliance of this kind was actively involved.

Decolonization

A rise of nationalism among European colonies led to many of them declaring independence. India and Pakistan became independent of Britain at this time, and numerous African and Asian colonies declared independence, as well. This period of decolonization lasted into the 1960s. Some colonies moved successfully into independence but many, especially in Africa and Asia, struggled to create stable governments and economies, and suffered from ethnic and religious conflicts. Some of those countries still struggle today.

Korean War

In 1910, Japan annexed Korea and maintained this control until 1945, when Soviet and US troops occupied the country. The Soviet Union controlled North Korea, while the US controlled South Korea. In 1947, the UN ordered elections in Korea to unify the country but the Soviet Union refused to allow them to take place, instead setting up a communist government in North Korea. In 1950, the US withdrew troops, and the North Korean troops moved to invade South Korea. The Korean War was the first war in which the UN—or any international organization—played a major role. The US, Australia, Canada, France, Netherlands, Great Britain, Turkey, China, USSR and other countries sent troops at various times, for both sides, throughout the war. In 1953, the war ended in a truce, but no peace agreement was ever achieved, and Korea remains divided.

Vietnam War and involvement of France

Vietnam had previously been part of a French colony called French Indochina.

The Vietnam War began with the French Indochina War from 1946-1954, in which France battled with the Democratic Republic of Vietnam, ruled by Ho Chi Minh.

In 1954, a siege at Dien Bien Phu ended in a Vietnamese victory. Vietnam was then divided into North and South, much like Korea. Communist forces controlled the North and the South was controlled by South Vietnamese forces, supported by the US. Conflict ensued, leading to a war. US troops eventually lead the fight, in support of South Vietnam. The war became a major political issue in the US, with many citizens protesting American involvement. In 1976, South Vietnam surrendered, and Vietnam became the Socialist Republic of Vietnam.

Globalism

In the modern era, globalism has emerged as a popular political ideology. Globalism is based in the idea that all people and all nations are interdependent. Each nation is dependent on one or more other nations for production of and markets for goods, and for income generation. Today's ease of international travel and communication, including technological advances such as the airplane, has heightened this sense of interdependence. The global economy, and the general idea of globalism, has shaped many economic and political choices since the beginning of the twentieth century. Many of today's issues, including environmental awareness, economic struggles, and continued warfare, often require the cooperation of many countries if they are to be dealt with effectively.

Effects of globalization

With countries worldwide often seeking the same resources, some, particularly nonrenewable resources, have experienced high demand. At times this has resulted in wild price fluctuations. One major example is the demand for petroleum products such as oil and natural gas. Increased travel and communication make it possible to deal with diseases in remote locations; however, it also allows diseases to be spread via travelers, as well.

A major factor contributing to increased globalization over the past few decades has been the Internet. By allowing instantaneous communication with anyone nearly anywhere on the globe, the Internet has led to interaction between far-flung individuals and countries, and an ever increasing awareness of happenings all over the world.

Middle East in international relations and economics

Its location on the globe, with ease of access to Europe and Asia, and its preponderance of oil deposits, makes the middle eastern countries a crucial factor in many international issues both diplomatic and economic. Because of its central location, the Middle East has been a hotbed for violence since before the beginning of recorded history. Conflicts over land, resources, religious and political power continue in the area today, spurred by conflict over control of the area's vast oil fields as well as over territories that have been disputed for literally hundreds—and even thousands—of years.

Genocide

The three major occurrences of genocide in modern history other than the Holocaust are as follows:

- Armenian genocide—occurred in the 1900s when the Young Turks, heirs to the Ottoman Empire, slaughtered over a million Armenians between 1915 and 1917. This constituted nearly half the Armenian population at the time.
- Russian purges under Stalin—Scholars have attributed deaths between 3 and 60 million, both directly and indirectly, to the policies and edicts of Joseph Stalin's regime. The deaths took place from 1921 to 1953, when Stalin died. In recent years, many scholars have settled on a number of deaths near 20 million but this is still disputed today.
- Rwandan Genocide—in 1994, hundreds of thousands of Tutsi and Hutu sympathizers were slaughtered during the Rwandan Civil War. The UN did not act or authorize intervention during these atrocities.

Government/Civics/ Political Science

Political science

Political science focuses on studying different governments and how they compare to each other, general political theory, ways political theory is put into action, how nations and governments interact with each other, and a general study of governmental structure and function. Other elements of political science include the study of elections, governmental administration at various levels, development and action of political parties, and how values such as freedom, power, justice and equality are expressed in different political cultures.

Political science also encompasses elements of other disciplines, including:

- History—how historical events have shaped political thought and process
- Sociology—the effects of various stages of social development on the growth and development of government and politics
- Anthropology—the effects of governmental process on the culture of an individual group and its relationships with other groups
- Economics—how government policies regulate distribution of products and how they can control and/or influence the economy in general

Government

Based on general political theory, the four major purposes of any given government are:

- Ensuring national security—the government protects against international, domestic and terrorist attack and also ensures ongoing security through negotiating and establishing relationships with other governments.
- Providing public services—government should "promote the general welfare," as stated in the Preamble to the US Constitution, by providing whatever is needed to its citizens.
- Ensure social order—the government supplies means of settling conflicts among citizens as well as making laws to govern the nation, state, or city.
- Make decisions regarding the economy—laws help form the economic policy of the country, regarding both domestic and international trade and related issues. The government also has the ability to distribute goods and wealth among its citizens.

Origin of the state

The four main theories regarding the origin of the state are as follows:

- Evolutionary—the state evolved from the family, with the head of state the equivalent of the family's patriarch or matriarch.
- Force—one person or group of people brought everyone in an area under their control, forming the first government.
- Divine Right—certain people were chosen by the prevailing deity to be the rulers of the nation, which is itself created by the deity or deities.
- Social Contract—there is no natural order. The people allow themselves to be governed to maintain social order, while the state in turn promises to protect the people they govern. If the government fails to protect its people, the people have the right to seek new leaders.

Influences of philosophers on political study

Ancient Greek philosophers Aristotle and Plato believed political science would lead to order in political matters, and that this scientifically organized order would create stable, just societies.

Thomas Aquinas adapted the ideas of Aristotle to a Christian perspective. His ideas stated that individuals should have certain rights, but also certain duties, and that these rights and duties should determine the type and extent of government rule. In stating that laws should limit the role of government, he laid the groundwork for ideas that would eventually become modern constitutionalism.

Niccolò Machiavelli, author of *The Prince*, was a proponent of politics based solely on power.

Thomas Hobbes, author of *Leviathan* (1651), believed that individual's lives were focused solely on a quest for power, and that the state must work to control this urge. Hobbes felt that people were completely unable to live harmoniously without the intervention of government.

John Locke wrote *Two Treatises of Civil Government* in 1690. This work argued against the ideas of Thomas Hobbes. He put forth the theory of *tabula rasa*—that people are born with minds that are a blank slate. Experience molds individual minds, not innate knowledge or intuition. He also believed that all men are essentially good, as well as independent and equal. Many of Locke's ideas found their way into the Constitution of the United States.
The two French philosophers, Montesquieu and Rousseau, heavily influenced the French Revolution (1789-1815). They believed government policies and ideas should change to alleviate existing problems, an idea referred to as "liberalism." Rousseau in particular directly influenced the Revolution with writings such as *The Social Contract* (1762), *Declaration of the Rights of Man,* and *The Citizen* (1789). Other ideas Rousseau and Montesquieu espoused included:

- Individual freedom and community welfare are of equal importance
- Man's innate goodness leads to natural harmony
- Reason develops with the rise of civilized society
- Individual citizens carry certain obligations to the existing government

Hume and Bentham believed politics should have as its main goal maintaining "the greatest happiness of the greatest number." Hume also believed in empiricism, or that ideas should not be believed until the proof has been observed. He was a natural skeptic, as well, and always sought out the truth of matters himself rather than believing what he was told.

John Stuart Mill, a British philosopher as well as an economist, believed in progressive policies such as women's suffrage, emancipation, and the development of labor organizations and farming cooperatives.

Fichte and Hegel were eighteenth century German philosophers who supported a form of liberalism grounded largely in socialism and a sense of nationalism.

Political orientations

The four main political orientations are:

- Liberal—believes in working to increase equality, sometimes at the expense of some freedoms, but overall the government should not interfere with individual freedom. Focus on health, justice, and education for citizens should be a major focus.
- Conservative—government should be limited in all cases except those of supporting longstanding moral values, often tied to religious beliefs. The government should allow its citizens to solve social issues rather. Businesses should not be regulated, allowing a free market.
- Moderate—incorporates some liberal and some conservative values, generally falling somewhere in between in overall belief.
- Libertarian—believes in limiting the role of government to the defense of the country and supporting social as well as economic freedom.

Principles of government

The six major principles of government as outlined in the United States Constitution are:

- Federalism—the power of the government does not belong entirely to the national government, but is divided between national and state governments.
- Popular sovereignty—the government is determined by the people, and gains its authority and power from the people.
- Separation of powers—the government is divided into three branches, executive, legislative and judicial, with each branch having its own set of powers.
- Judicial review—courts at all levels of government can declare laws invalid if they contradict the constitutions of individual states, or the US Constitution, with the Supreme Court serving as the final judicial authority on decisions of this kind.
- Checks and balances—no single branch can act without input from another, and each branch has the power to "check" any other, as well as balance other branches' powers.
- Limited government—governmental powers are limited and certain individual rights are defined as inviolable by the government.

Powers delegated to the national government

The structure of the US government divides powers between national and state governments. Powers delegated to the national government by the Constitution are:

- Expressed powers—powers directly defined in the Constitution, including power to declare war, regulate commerce, make money, and collect taxes.
- Implied powers—powers the national government must have in order to carry out the expressed powers.
- Inherent powers—powers inherent to any government. These powers are not expressly defined in the constitution.

Some of these powers, such as collection and levying of taxes, are also granted to the individual state governments.

Federalism

Debate on how federalism should function in practice has gone on since the period when the Constitution was being written. There were—and still are—two main factions regarding this issue:

- States' rights—those favoring the states' rights position feel that the state governments should take the lead in performing local actions to manage various problems.
- Nationalist—those favoring a nationalist position feel the national government should take the lead to deal with those same matters.

The flexibility of the Constitution has allowed US government to shift and adapt as the needs of the country have changed. Power has often shifted from the state governments to the national government and back again, and both levels of government have developed various ways to influence each other.

Federalism has three major effects on public policy in the US.

- Determining whether the local, state or national government originates policy
- Affecting how policies are made
- Ensuring policy-making functions under a set of limitations

Federalism also influences the political balance of power in the US by:

- making it difficult if not impossible for a single political party to seize total power.
- ensuring that individuals can participate in the political system at various levels.
- making it possible for individuals working within the system to be able to affect policy at some level, whether local or more widespread.

Branches of the US government

The following are the three branches of the US Federal government and the individuals that belong to each branch:

- Legislative Branch—consists of the two Houses of Congress: the House of Representatives and the Senate. All members of the Legislative Branch are elected officials.
- Executive Branch—consists of the President, Vice President, presidential advisors, and other various cabinet members. These advisors are appointed by the President, but must be approved by Congress.
- Judicial Branch—is made up of the federal court system, headed by the Supreme Court.

The major responsibilities of the three branches of the Federal government are as follows:

- The Legislative Branch is largely concerned with law-making. All laws must be approved by Congress before they go into effect. They are also responsible for regulating money and trade, approving presidential appointments, and establishing organizations like the postal service and federal courts. Congress can also propose amendments to the Constitution, and can impeach, or bring charges against, the president. Only Congress can declare war.
- The Executive Branch carries out laws, treaties, and war declarations enacted by Congress. The President can also veto bills approved by Congress, and serves as commander-in-chief of the US military. The president appoints cabinet members, ambassadors to foreign countries, and federal judges.
- The Judicial Branch makes decisions on challenges as to whether laws passed by Congress meet the requirements of the US Constitution. The Supreme Court may also choose to review decisions made by lower courts to determine their constitutionality.

US citizenship

Anyone born in the US, born abroad to a US citizen, or who has gone through a process of naturalization to become a citizen, is considered a citizen of the United States. It is possible to lose US citizenship as a result of conviction of certain crimes such as treason. Citizenship may also be lost if a citizen pledges an oath to another country or serves in the military of a country engaged in hostilities with the US. A US citizen can also choose to hold dual citizenship, work as an expatriate in another country without losing US citizenship, or even to renounce citizenship if he or she so chooses.

Citizens are granted certain rights under the US government. The most important of these are defined in the Bill of Rights, and include freedom of speech, religion, assembly, and a variety of other rights the government is not allowed to remove.
Duties of a US citizen include:

- Paying taxes
- Loyalty to the government, though the US does not prosecute those who criticize or seek to change the government
- Support and defend the Constitution
- Serve in the Armed Forces as required by law
- Obeying laws as set forth by the various levels of government.

Responsibilities of a US citizen include:

- Voting in elections
- Respecting one another's rights and not infringing upon them
- Staying informed about various political and national issues
- Respecting one another's beliefs

Bill of Rights

The first ten amendments of the US Constitution are known as the Bill of Rights. These amendments prevent the government from infringing upon certain freedoms that the founding fathers felt were natural rights that already belonged to all people. These rights included freedom of speech, freedom of religion, right to bear arms, and freedom of assembly. Many of the rights were formulated in direct response to the way the colonists felt they had been mistreated by the British government.

The first ten amendments were passed by Congress in 1789. Three-fourths of the existing thirteen states had ratified them by December of 1791, making them official additions to the Constitution.

The rights granted in the Bill of Rights are:

- First Amendment—grants freedom of religion, speech, freedom of the press, and the right to assemble.
- Second Amendment—right to bear arms.
- Third Amendment—Congress cannot force individuals to house troops.
- Fourth Amendment—protection from unreasonable search and seizure.
- Fifth Amendment—no individual is required to testify against himself, and no individual may be tried twice for the same crime.
- Sixth Amendment—right to criminal trial by jury, right to legal counsel.
- Seventh Amendment—right to civil trial by jury.
- Eighth Amendment—no excessive bail, no cruel and unusual punishment.
- Ninth Amendment—prevents the absence of rights not explicitly named in the Constitution from being interpreted as a reason to have them taken away.
- Tenth Amendment—any rights not directly delegated to the national government, or not directly prohibited, belong to the states or to the people

In some cases, the government restricts certain elements of First Amendment rights. Some examples include:

- Freedom of religion—when a religion espouses activities that are otherwise illegal, the government often restricts these forms of religious expression. Examples include polygamy, animal sacrifice, and use of illicit drugs or illegal substances.
- Freedom of speech—can be restricted if exercise of free speech endangers other people.
- Freedom of the press—laws prevent the press from publishing falsehoods.

In emergency situations such as wartime, stricter restrictions are sometimes placed on these rights, especially rights to free speech and assembly, and freedom of the press, in order to protect national security.

Constitutional rights of criminals

The US Constitution makes allowances for the rights of criminals, or anyone who has transgressed established laws. There must be laws to protect citizens from criminals, but those accused of crimes must also be protected and their basic rights as individuals preserved. In addition, the Constitution protects individuals from the power of authorities who act in case of transgressions to prevent police forces and other enforcement organizations from becoming oppressive.

The Fourth, Fifth, Sixth and Eighth amendments specifically address these issues:

- No unreasonable search and seizure (Fourth Amendment)
- No self-incrimination or double jeopardy—being tried for the same crime more than once (Fifth Amendment)
- Right to trial by jury and right to legal counsel (Sixth Amendment)
- No cruel or unusual punishment (Eighth Amendment)

Equal protection under the law for all individuals

When the Founding Fathers wrote in the Declaration of Independence that "all men are created equal," they meant "men," and, in fact, defined citizens as white men who owned land. However, as the country has developed and changed, the definition has expanded to more wholly include all people.

"Equality" does not mean all people are inherently the same, but it does mean they all should be granted the same rights and should be treated the same by the government. Amendments to the Constitution have granted citizenship and voting rights to all Americans. The Supreme Court evaluates various laws and court decisions to determine if they properly represent the idea of equal protection. One sample case was Brown v. Board of Education, in 1954, which declared separate-but-equal to be unconstitutional.

Civil liberty challenges addressed in current political discussions

The civil rights movements of the 1960s and ongoing struggle for women's rights and rights of other minorities have led to challenges to existing law. In addition, debate has raged over how much information the government should be required to divulge to the public. Major issues in today's political climate include:

- Continued debate over women's rights, especially as regards equal pay for equal work
- Debate over affirmative action to encourage hiring of minorities
- Debate over civil rights of homosexuals, including marriage and military service
- Decisions as to whether any minorities should be compensated for past discriminatory practices
- Balance between the public's right to know and the government's need to maintain national security
- Balance between the public's right to privacy and national security

Civil liberties and civil rights

While the terms civil liberties and civil rights are often used synonymously, in actuality their definitions are slightly different. The two concepts work together, however, to define the basics of a free state.

- "Civil liberties" defines the role of the state in providing equal rights and opportunities to individuals within that state. An example is non-discrimination policies with regards to granting citizenship.
- "Civil rights" defines the limitations of state rights, describing those rights that belong to individuals and which cannot be infringed upon by the government. Examples of these rights include freedom of religion, political freedom, and overall freedom to live how we choose.

Suffrage and franchise

Suffrage and franchise are both terms referring to the right to vote. Which individuals actually have the right to vote has changed as the US has developed as a nation.

In the early years, only white male landowners were granted suffrage. By the nineteenth century, most states had franchised, or granted the right to vote to, all adult white males. The Fifteenth Amendment of 1870 granted suffrage to former slaves. The Nineteenth Amendment gave women the right to vote, and in 1971 the Twenty-sixth Amendment expanded voting rights to include any US citizen over the age of eighteen. However, those who have not been granted full citizenship and citizens who have committed certain crimes do not have voting rights.

Changes in voting process

The first elections in the US were held by public ballot. However, election abuses soon became common, since public ballot made it easy to intimidate, threaten, or otherwise influence the votes of individuals or groups of individuals.

New practices were put into play, including registering voters before elections took place, and using a secret or Australian ballot. In 1892, the introduction of the voting machine further privatized the voting process, since it allowed voters to vote in complete privacy. Even today debate continues about the accuracy of various voting methods, including high-tech voting machines and even low tech punch cards.

Political parties

Affects on government

Different types and numbers of political parties can have a significant effect on how a government is run. If there is a single party, or a one-party system, the government is defined by that one party, and all policy is based on that party's beliefs. In a two-party system, two parties with different viewpoints compete for power and influence. The US is basically a two-party system, with checks and balances to make it difficult for one party to gain complete power over the other. There are also multi-party systems, with three or more parties. In multiparty systems, various parties will often come to agreements in order to form a majority and shift the balance of power.

Development in the US

George Washington was adamantly against the establishment of political parties, based on the abuses perpetrated by such parties in Britain. However, political parties developed in US politics almost from the beginning. Major parties throughout US History have included:

- Federalists and Democratic-Republicans—formed in the late 1700s and disagreed on the balance of power between national and state government
- Democrats and Whigs—developed before the Civil War, based on disagreements about various issues such as slavery
- Democrats and Republicans—developed after the Civil War, with issues centering on the treatment of the post-war South.

While third parties sometimes enter the picture in US politics, the government is basically a two-party system, dominated by the Democrats and Republicans.

Functions and determination of nominations for elections

Political parties form organizations at all levels of government. Activities of individual parties include:

- Recruiting and backing candidates for offices
- Discussing various issues with the public, increasing public awareness
- Working toward compromise on difficult issues
- Staffing government offices and providing administrative support

At the administrative level, parties work to ensure that viable candidates are available for elections and that offices and staff are in place to support candidates as they run for office and afterwards, when they are elected.

Process for choosing political candidate

Historically, in the quest for political office, a potential candidate has followed one of the following four processes:

- Nominating conventions—an official meeting of the members of a party for the express purpose of nominating candidates for upcoming elections. The Democratic National Convention and the Republican National Convention, convened to announce candidates for presidency, are examples of this kind of gathering.
- Caucuses—a meeting, usually attended by a party's leaders. Some states still use caucuses, but not all.
- Primary elections—the most common method of choosing candidates today, the primary is a publicly held election to choose candidates.
- Petitions—signatures are gathered to place a candidate on the ballot. Petitions can also be used to place legislation on a ballot.

Participation of average citizens in political process

In addition to voting for elected officials, American citizens are able to participate in the political process through several other avenues. These include:

- Participating in local government
- Participating in caucuses for large elections
- Volunteering to help political parties
- Running for election to local, state, or national offices

Individuals can also donate money to political causes, or support political groups that focus on specific causes such as abortion, wildlife conservation or women's rights. These groups often make use of representatives who lobby legislators to act in support of their efforts.

Campaign funding

Political campaigns are very expensive ventures. In addition to the basic necessities of a campaign office, including office supplies, office space, etc., a large quantity of the money that funds a political campaign goes toward advertising. Television advertising in particular is quite costly.
Money to fund a political campaign can come from several sources including:

- The candidate's personal funds
- Donations by individuals
- Special interest groups

The most significant source of campaign funding is special interest groups. Groups in favor of certain policies will donate money to candidates they believe will support those policies. Special interest groups also do their own advertising in support of candidates they endorse.

Free press and the media

The right to free speech guaranteed in the first amendment to the Constitution allows the media to report on government and political activities without fear of retribution. Because the media has access to information about the government, its policies and actions, as well as debates and discussions that occur in Congress, it can ensure that the people are informed about the inner workings of the government. The media can also draw attention to injustices, imbalances of power, and other transgressions the government or government officials might commit. However, media outlets may, like special interest groups, align themselves with certain political viewpoints and skew their reports to fit that viewpoint. The rise of the Internet has made media reporting even more complex, as news can be found from an infinite variety of sources, both reliable and unreliable.

Anarchism, communism and dictatorship

Anarchists believe that all government should be eliminated and that individuals should rule themselves. Historically, anarchists have used violence and assassination to further their beliefs. Communism is based on class conflict, revolution and a one-party state. Ideally, a communist government would involve a single government for the entire world. Communist government controls the production and flow of goods and services rather than leaving this to companies or individuals. Dictatorship involves rule by a single individual. If rule is enforced by a small group, this is referred to as an oligarchy. Few malevolent dictatorships have existed. Dictators tend to rule with a violent hand, using a highly repressive police force to ensure control over the populace.

Fascism and monarchy

Fascism centers on a single leader and is, ideologically, an oppositional belief to Communism. Fascism includes a single party state and centralized control. The power of the fascist leader lies in the "cult of personality," and the fascist state often focuses on expansion and conquering of other nations. Monarchy was the major form of government for Europe through most of its history. A monarchy is led by a king or a queen. This position is hereditary, and the rulers are not elected. In modern times, constitutional monarchy has developed, where the king and queen still exist but most of the governmental decisions are made by democratic institutions such as a parliament.

Presidential System and Socialism

A Presidential System, like a parliamentary system, has a legislature and political parties, but there is no difference between the head of state and the head of government. Instead of separating these functions, an elected president performs both. Election of the president can be direct or indirect, and the president may not necessarily belong to the largest political party. In Socialism, the state controls production of goods, though it does not necessarily own all means of production. The state also provides a variety of social services to citizens and helps guide the economy. A democratic form of government often exists in socialist countries.

Totalitarian and authoritarian systems of government

A totalitarian system believes everything should be under the control of the government, from resource production to the press to religion and other social institutions. All aspects of life under a totalitarian system must conform to the ideals of the government. Authoritarian governments practices widespread state authority, but do not necessarily dismantle all public institutions. If a church, for example, exists as an organization but poses no threat to the authority of the state, an authoritarian government might leave it as it is. While all totalitarian governments are by definition authoritarian, a government can be authoritarian without becoming totalitarian.

Parliamentary and democratic systems of government

In a parliamentary system, government involves a legislature and a variety of political parties. The head of government, usually a Prime Minister, is typically the head of the dominant party. A head of state can be elected, or this position can be taken by a monarch, such as in Great Britain's constitutional monarchy system.

In a democratic system of government, the people elect their government representatives. The term democracy is a Greek term that means "for the rule of the people." There are two forms of democracy—direct and indirect. In a direct democracy, each issue or election is decided by a vote where each individual is counted separately. An indirect democracy employs a legislature that votes on issues that affect large number of people whom the legislative members represent. Democracy can exist as a Parliamentary system or a Presidential system. The US is a presidential, indirect democracy.

Realism, liberalism, institutionalism, and constructivism

The theory of realism states that nations are by nature aggressive, and work in their own self-interest. Relations between nations are determined by military and economic strength. The nation is seen as the highest authority. Liberalism believes states can cooperate, and that they act based on capabilities rather than power. This term was originally coined to describe Woodrow Wilson's theories on international cooperation. In institutionalism, institutions provide structure and incentive for cooperation among nations. Institutions are defined as a set of rules used to make international decisions. These institutions also help distribute power and determine how nations will interact. Constructivism, like liberalism, is based on international cooperation, but recognizes that perceptions countries have of each other can affect their relations.

Foreign policy

Foreign policy is a set of goals, policies and strategies that determine how an individual nation will interact with other countries. These strategies shift, sometimes quickly and drastically, according to actions or changes occurring in the other countries. However, a

nation's foreign policy is often based on a certain set of ideals and national needs.
Examples of US foreign policy include isolationism versus internationalism. In the 1800s, the US leaned more toward isolationism, exhibiting a reluctance to become involved in foreign affairs. The World Wars led to a period of internationalism, as the US entered these wars in support of other countries and joined the United Nations. Today's foreign policy tends more toward interdependence, or globalism, recognizing the widespread affects of issues like economic health.

US foreign policy is largely determined by Congress and the president, influenced by the secretary of state, secretary of defense, and the national security adviser. Executive officials actually carry out policies. The main departments in charge of these day-to-day issues are the US Department of State, also referred to as the State Department. The Department of State carries out policy, negotiates treaties, maintains diplomatic relations, assists citizens traveling in foreign countries, and ensures that the president is properly informed of any international issues. The Department of Defense, the largest executive department in the US, supervises the armed forces and provides assistance to the president in his role as commander in chief.

International organizations

Two types of international organizations are:

- Intergovernmental organizations (IGOs). These organizations are made up of members from various national governments. The UN is an example of an intergovernmental organization. Treaties among the member nations determine the functions and powers of these groups.
- Nongovernmental organizations (NGOs). An NGO lies outside the scope of any government and are usually supported through private donations. An example of an NGO is the International Red Cross, which works with governments all over the world when their countries are in crisis, but is formally affiliated with no particular country or government.

Diplomats

Diplomats are individuals who reside in foreign countries in order to maintain communications between that country and their home country. They help negotiate trade agreements, environmental policies, and convey official information to foreign governments. They also help resolve conflicts between the countries, often working to sort out issues without making the conflicts official in any way. Diplomats, or ambassadors, are appointed in America by the president. Appointments must be approved by Congress.

UN

The United Nations (UN) helps form international policies by hosting representatives of various countries who then provide input into policy decisions. Countries who are members of the UN must agree to abide by all final UN resolutions, but this is not always the case in practice, as dissent is not uncommon. If countries do not follow UN resolutions, the UN can decide on sanctions against those countries, often economic sanctions, such as trade restriction. The UN can also send military forces to problem areas, with "peace keeping" troops brought in from member nations. An example of this function is the Korean War, the first war in which an international organization played a major role.

Geography

Geography

Geography literally means the study of the earth. Geographers study physical characteristics of the earth as well as man-made borders and boundaries. They also study the distribution of life on the planet, such as where certain species of animals can be found, as well as how different forms of life interact.
Major elements of the study of geography include:

- Locations
- Regional characteristics
- Spatial relations
- Natural and manmade forces that change elements of the earth

These elements are studied from regional, topical, physical and human perspectives. Geography also focuses on the origins of the earth as well as the history and backgrounds of different human populations.

<u>Physical and cultural geography</u>
Physical geography is the study of the physical characteristics of the earth, how they relate to each other, how they were formed, and how they develop. These characteristics include climate, land, and water, and also how they affect human populations in various areas. Different landforms in combination with various climates and other conditions determine characteristics of various cultures.

Cultural geography is the study of how the various aspects of physical geography affect individual cultures. Cultural geography also compares various cultures, how their lifestyles and customs are affected by their geographical location, climate, and other factors, and how they interact with their environment.

Divisions of geographical study

The four divisions of geographical study and tools used are:

- Topical—the study of a single feature of the earth or one specific human activity that occurs world-wide.
- Physical—the various physical features of the earth, how they are created, the forces that change them, and how they are related to each other and to various human activities.
- Regional—specific characteristics of individual places and regions.
- Human—how human activity affects the environment. This includes study of political, historical, social, and cultural activities.

Tools used in geographical study include special research methods like mapping, field studies, statistics, interviews, mathematics, and use of various scientific instruments.

Ancient geographers

The following are three important ancient geographers and their contributions to the study of geography:

- Eratosthenes lived in ancient Greek times, and mathematically calculated the circumference of the earth.
- Strabo wrote a description of the ancient world called Geographica. The work consisted of seventeen volumes.
- Ptolemy, primarily an astronomer, was also an experienced mapmaker. His skills also contributed to overall knowledge of the earth's geography.

Analysis of areas of human population

In cities, towns, or other areas where many people have settled, geographers focus on distribution of populations, neighborhoods, industrial areas, transportation, and other elements important to the society in question. For example, they would map out the locations of hospitals, airports, factories, police stations, schools, and housing groups. They would also make note of how these facilities are distributed in relation to the areas of habitation, such as the number of schools a certain neighborhood, or how many grocery stores are located in a specific suburban area. Another area of study and discussion is the distribution of towns themselves, from widely spaced rural towns to large cities that merge into each other to form a megalopolis.

Cartographers and maps

A cartographer is a mapmaker. Mapmakers produce detailed illustrations of geographic areas to record where various features are located within that area. These illustrations can be compiled into maps, charts, graphs, and even globes. When constructing maps, cartographers must take into account the phenomenon of distortion. Because the earth is round, a flat map does not accurately represent the correct proportions, especially if a very large geographical area is being depicted. Maps must be designed in such a way as to minimize this distortion and maximize accuracy. Accurately representing the earth's features on a flat surface is achieved through projection.

Map projections

The three major types of projection used in creating world maps are:

- Cylindrical projection—created by wrapping the globe of the Earth in a cylindrical piece of paper, then using a light to project the globe onto the paper. The largest distortion occurs at the outermost edges.
- Conical projection—the paper is shaped like a cone and contacts the globe only at the cone's base. This type of projection is most useful for middle latitudes.
- Flat-Plane projections—also known as a Gnomonic projection, this type of map is projected onto a flat piece of paper that only touches the globe at a single point. Flat-plane projections make it possible to map out Great-Circle Routes, or the shortest route between one point and another on the globe, as a straight line.

Four specific types of map projections that are commonly used today are:

- Winkel tripel projection—the most common projection used for world maps, since it was accepted in 1998 by the National Geographic Society as a standard. The Winkel tripel projection balances size and shape, greatly reducing distortion.
- Robinson projection—east and west sections of the map are less distorted, but continental shapes are somewhat inaccurate.
- Goode's interrupted equal-area projection—Sizes and shapes are accurate, but distances are not. This projection basically represents a globe that has been cut in a way that allows it to lie flat.
- Mercator projection—though distortion is high, particularly in areas farther from the equator, this cylindrical projection is commonly used by seafarers.

Map elements

The five major elements of any map are:

- Title—tells basic information about the map, such as the area represented.
- Legend—also known as the key, the legend explains what symbols used on a particular map represent, such as symbols for major landmarks.
- Grid—most commonly represents the Geographic Grid System, or latitude and longitude marks used to precisely locate specific locations.
- Directions—a compass rose or other symbol used to indicate the cardinal directions.
- Scale—shows the relation between a certain distance on the map and the actual distance. For example, one inch might represent one mile, or ten miles, or even more depending on the size of the map.

Equal area map and conformal map

An equal area map is designed such that the proportional sizes of various areas are accurate. For example, if one land mass is one-fifth the size of another, the lines on the map will be shifted to accommodate for distortion so that the proportional size is accurate. In many maps, areas farther from the equator are greatly distorted; this type of map compensates for this phenomenon.

A conformal map focuses on representing the correct shape of geographical areas, with less concern for comparative size.

Consistent scale map and thematic map

With a consistent scale map, the same scale, such as one inch=ten miles, is used throughout the entire map. This is most often used for maps of smaller areas, as maps that cover larger areas, such as the full globe, must make allowances for distortion. Maps of very large areas often make use of more than one scale, with scales closer to the center representing a larger area than those at the edges.

A thematic map is constructed to show very specific information about a chosen theme. For example, a thematic map might represent political information, such as how votes were distributed in an election, or show population distribution or climactic features.

Relief map

A relief map is constructed to show details of various elevations across the area of the map. Higher elevations are represented by different colors than lower elevations. Relief maps often also show additional details, such as the overall ruggedness or smoothness of an area. Mountains would be represented as ridged and rugged, while deserts would be shown as smooth.

Elevation in relief maps can also be represented by contour lines, or lines that connect points of the same elevation. Some relief maps even feature textures, reconstructing details in a sort of miniature model.

Mountains, hills, plains and valleys

The following are geographical features of mountains, hills, plains, and valleys:

- Mountains are elevated areas that measure 2,000 feet or more above sea level. Often steep and rugged, they usually occur in groups called chains or ranges. Six of the seven continents on Earth contain at least one range.
- Hills are of lower elevation than mountains, at about 500-2,000 feet. Hills are usually more rounded, and are found everywhere on Earth.
- Plains are large, flat areas and are usually very fertile. The majority of Earth's population is supported by crops grown on the Earth's vast plains.
- Valleys lie between hills and mountains. Depending on where they are located, their specific features can vary greatly, from fertile and habitable to rugged and inhospitable.

Plateaus, deserts, deltas, mesas, basins, foothills, marshes and swamps

Plateaus, deserts, deltas, mesas, basins, foothills, marshes and swamps are described below:

- Plateaus are elevated, but flat on top. Some plateaus are extremely dry, such as the Kenya Plateau, because surrounding mountains prevent them from receiving moisture.
- Deserts receive less than ten inches of rain per year. They are usually large areas, such as the Sahara Desert in Africa or the Australian Outback.
- Deltas occur at river mouths. Because the rivers carry sediment to the deltas, these areas are often very fertile.
- Mesas are flat, steep-sided mountains or hills. The term is sometimes used to refer to plateaus.
- Basins are areas of low elevation where rivers drain.

- Foothills are the transition area between the plains and the mountains, usually consisting of hills that gradually increase in size as they approach the mountain range.
- Marshes and swamps are also lowlands, but they are very wet and largely covered in vegetation such as reeds and rushes.

Bodies of water

Oceans, seas, lakes, rivers and canals are described below:

- Oceans are the largest bodies of water on Earth. They are salt water, and cover about two-thirds of the earth's surface. The four major oceans are the Atlantic, Pacific, Indian and Arctic.
- Seas are generally also salt water, but are smaller than oceans and surrounded by land. Examples include the Mediterranean Sea, the Caribbean Sea, and the Caspian Sea.
- Lakes are bodies of freshwater found inland. Sixty percent of all lakes are located in Canada.
- Rivers are moving bodies of water that flow from higher elevations to lower. They usually start as rivulets or streams, and grow until they finally empty into a sea or an ocean.
- Canals, such as the Panama Canal and the Suez Canal, are manmade waterways connecting two large bodies of water.

Communities

Communities, or groups of people who settle together in a specific area, typically gather where certain conditions exists. These conditions include:

- Easy access to resources such as food, water, and raw materials
- Ability to easily transport raw materials and goods, such as access to a waterway
- Room to house a sufficient work force

People also tend to form groups with others who are similar to them. In a typical community, people can be found who share values, a common language, and common or similar cultural characteristics and religious beliefs. These factors will determine the overall composition of a community as it develops.

Cities

Cities develop and grow as an area develops. Modern statistics show over half of the world's people living in cities. That percentage is even higher in developed areas of the globe. Cities are currently growing more quickly in developing regions, and even established cities continue to experience growth throughout the world. In developing or developed areas, cities often are surrounded by a metropolitan area made up of both urban and suburban sections. In some places, cities have merged into each other and become a megalopolis, or a single, huge city.

Cities develop differently in different areas of the world. The area available for cities to grow, as well as cultural and economic forces, drives how cities develop. For example, North American cities tend to cover wider areas. European cities tend to have better developed transportation systems. In Latin America, the richest inhabitants can be found in the city centers, while in North America wealthier inhabitants tend to live in suburban areas.

In other parts of the world, transportation and communication between cities is less developed. Recent technological innovations such as the cell phone have increased communication even in these areas. Urban areas must also maintain communication with rural areas in order to procure food, resources and raw materials that cannot be produced within the city limits.

Weather and climate

Weather and climate are physical systems that affect geography. Though they deal with similar information, the way this information is measured and compiled is different.

Weather involves daily conditions in the atmosphere that affect temperature, precipitation (rain, snow, hail or sleet), wind speed, air pressure, and other factors. Weather focuses on the short-term—for example what the conditions will be today, tomorrow, or over the next few days. By contrast, climate aggregates information about daily and seasonal weather conditions in a region over a long period of time. The climate takes into account average monthly and yearly temperatures, average precipitation over long periods of time, and the growing season of an area.

Climates are classified according to latitude, or how close they lie to the Earth's equator. The three major divisions are:

- Low Latitudes, lying from 0 to 23.5 degrees latitude
- Middle Latitudes, found from 23.5 to 66.5 degrees
- High Latitudes, found from 66.5 degrees to the poles

Desert, savanna and rainforest climates occur in low latitudes:

- Rainforest climates, near the equator, experience high average temperatures and humidity, as well as relatively high rainfall.
- Savannas are found to either side of the rainforest region. Mostly grasslands, they typically experience dry winters and wet summers.
- Beyond the savannas lie the desert regions, with hot, dry climates, sparse rainfall (less than ten inches per year on average) and temperature fluctuations of up to fifty degrees from day into night.

The climate regions found in the middle latitudes are:

- Mediterranean - The Mediterranean climate occurs between 30 and 40 degrees latitude, both north and south, and on the western coasts. Characteristics include a year-long growing season, hot, dry summers followed by mild winters, and sparse rainfall that occurs mostly during the winter months.
- Humid-subtropical - Humid-subtropical regions are located on southeastern coastal areas. Winds that blow in over warm ocean currents produce long summers, mild winters, and a long growing season. These areas are highly productive, and support a larger part of the Earth's population than any other climate.
- Humid-continental - The humid continental climate produces the familiar four seasons typical of a good portion of the US. Some of the most productive farmlands in the world lie in these climates. Winters are cold, summers are hot and humid.
- Marine - Marine climates are found near water or on islands. Ocean winds help make these areas mild and rainy. Summers are cooler than humid-subtropical summers, but winters also bring milder temperatures due to the warmth of the ocean winds.
- Steppe - Steppe climates, or prairie climates, are found far inland in large continents. Summers are hot and winters are cold, but rainfall is sparser than in continental climates.
- Desert - Desert climates occur where steppe climates receive even less rainfall. Examples include the Gobi desert in Asia as well as desert areas of Australia and the southwestern US.

The high latitudes consist of two major climate areas, the tundra and taiga.

- Tundra means marshy plain. Ground is frozen throughout long, cold winters, but there is little snowfall. During the short summers, it becomes wet and marshy. Tundras are not amenable to crops, but many plants and animals have adapted to the conditions.
- Taigas lie south of tundra regions, and include the largest forest areas in the world, as well as swamps and marshes. Large mineral deposits exist here, as well

as many animals valued for their fur. In the winter, taiga regions are colder than the tundra, and summers are hotter. The growing season is short.

A vertical climate exists in high mountain ranges. Increasing elevation leads to varying temperatures, growing conditions, types of vegetation and animals, and occurrence of human habitation, often encompassing elements of various other climate regions.

Factors that affect climate
Because the earth is tilted, its rotation brings about the changes in seasons. Regions closer to the equator, and those nearest the poles, experience very little change in seasonal temperatures. Mid-range latitudes are most likely to experience distinct seasons. Large bodies of water also affect climate. Ocean currents and wind patterns can change the climate for an area that lies in typically cold latitude, such as England, to a much more temperate climate. Mountains can affect both short-term weather and long-term climates. Some deserts occur because precipitation is stopped by the wall of a mountain range.

Over time, established climate patterns can shift and change. While the issue is hotly debated, it has been theorized that human activity has also led to climate change.

Human systems

Human systems affect geography in the way in which they settle, form groups that grow into large-scale habitations, and even create permanent changes in the landscape. Geographers study movements of people, how they distribute goods among each other and to other settlements or cultures, and how ideas grow and spread. Migrations, wars, forced relocations, and trade all can spread cultural ideas, language, goods and other practices to wide-spread areas. Some major migrations or the conquering of one people by another have significantly changed cultures throughout history. In addition, human systems can lead to various conflicts or alliances to control access to and the use of natural resources.

North America
North America consists of the countries of the United States and Canada. These two countries support similarly diverse cultures, as both were formed from groups of native races as well as large numbers of immigrants. Both functioned for a period under British rule. The United States broke from British rule via violent revolution, while Canada became independent in 1931 through diplomatic means. Agriculture is important to both countries, while service industries and technology also play a large part in the North American economy. North America in general supports a high standard of living and a high level of development, and supports trade with countries throughout the world

Latin America
Including Mexico, Central America and South America, Latin America is largely defined by its prevailing languages. The majority of countries in Latin America speak Spanish or Portuguese. Most of Latin America has experienced a similar history, having been originally dominated by Native cultures, conquered by European nations. The countries of Latin America have since gained independence, but there is a wide disparity between various countries' economic and political factors. Most Latin American countries rely on only one or two exports, usually agricultural, with suitable lands often controlled by rich families. Most societies in Latin America feature major separations between classes, both economically and socially. Challenges faced by developing Latin American countries include geographical limitations, economic issues, and sustainable development, including the need to preserve the existing rainforests.

Europe
Europe contains a wide variety of cultures, ethnic groups, physical geographical features, climates, and resources, all of which have influenced the distribution of its varied population. Europe in general is industrialized and developed, with cultural differences giving

each individual country its own unique characteristics. Greek and Roman influences played a major role in European culture, as did Christian beliefs. European countries spread their beliefs and cultural elements throughout the world by means of migration and colonization. They have had a significant influence on nearly every other continent in the world. While Western Europe has been largely democratic, Eastern Europe functioned under Communist rule for many years. The recent formation of the European Union (EU) has increased stability and positive diplomatic relations among European nations. Like other industrialized regions, Europe is now focusing on various environmental issues.

Russia

After numerous conflicts, Russia became a Communist state, known as the USSR. With the collapse of the USSR in 1991, the country has struggled in its transition to a market driven economy. Attempts to build a workable system have led to the destruction of natural resources as well as problems with nuclear power, including accidents such as Chernobyl. To complete the transition to a market economy, Russia needs to improve its transportation and communication systems, and find a way to more efficiently use its natural resources.

The population of Russia is not distributed evenly, with three quarters of the population living west of the Ural Mountains. The people of Russia encompass over a hundred different ethnic groups. Over eighty percent of the population is ethnically Russian, and Russian is the official language of the country.

North Africa and Southwest and Central Asia

The largely desert climate of these areas has led most population centers to arise around sources of water, such as the Nile River. This area is the home of the earliest known civilizations and the place of origin for Christianity, Judaism and Islam. After serving as the site of huge, independent civilizations in ancient times, North Africa and Southwest and Central Asia were largely parceled out as European Colonies during the eighteenth and nineteenth centuries. The beginning of the twentieth century saw many of these countries gain their independence. Islam has served as a unifying force for large portions of these areas, and many of the inhabitants speak Arabic. In spite of the arid climate, agriculture is a large business, but the most valuable resource is oil. Centuries of conflict throughout this area has led to ongoing political problems. These political problems have also contributed to environmental issues.

Southern Africa

South of the Sahara Desert, Africa is divided into a number of culturally diverse nations. The inhabitants are unevenly distributed due to geographical limitations that prevent settlement in vast areas. AIDS has become a major plague throughout this part of Africa, killing millions, largely due to restrictive beliefs that prevent education about the disease, as well as abject poverty and unsettled political situations that make it impossible to manage the pandemic. The population of this area of Africa is widely diverse due to extensive migration. Many of the people still rely on subsistence farming for their welfare. Starvation and poverty are rampant due to drought and political instability. Some areas are far more stable than others due to greater availability of resources. These have been able to begin the process of industrialization.

South Asia

South Asia is home to one of the first human civilizations, which grew up in the Indus River Valley. With a great deal of disparity between rural and urban life, South Asia has much to do to improve the quality of life for its lower classes. Two major religions, Hinduism and Buddhism, have their origins in this region. Parts of South Asia, most notably India, were subject to British rule for several decades, and are still working to improve independent governments and social systems. Overall, South Asia is very culturally diverse, with a wide mix of religions and languages throughout. Many individuals are farmers, but a growing number have found prosperity in the spread of high-tech industries. Industrialization is growing in South Asia, but continues to face environmental, social, religious and economic challenges.

<u>East Asia</u>
Governments in East Asia are varied, ranging from communist to democratic governments, with some governments that mix both approaches. Isolationism throughout the area limited the countries' contact with other nations until the early twentieth century. The unevenly distributed population of East Asia consists of over one and a half billion people with widely diverse ethnic backgrounds, religions and languages. More residents live in urban areas than in rural areas, creating shortages of farm workers for some. Japan, Taiwan and South Korea are overall more urban, while China and Mongolia are more rural. Japan stands as the most industrial country of East Asia. Some areas of East Asia are suffering from major environmental issues. Japan has dealt with many of these problems and now has some of the strictest environmental laws in the world.

<u>Southeast Asia</u>
Much of Southeast Asia was colonized by European countries during the eighteenth and nineteenth centuries, with the exception of Siam, now known as Thailand. All the countries of the area are now independent, but the twentieth century saw numerous conflicts between communist and democratic forces.

Southeast Asia has been heavily influenced by both Buddhist and Muslim religions. Industrialization is growing, with the population moving in large numbers from rural to urban areas. Some have moved to avoid conflict, oppression, and poverty.

Natural disasters, including volcanoes, typhoons and flash flooding, are fairly common in Southeast Asia, creating extensive economic damage and societal disruption.

<u>Australia, Oceana and Antarctica</u>
South Pacific cultures originally migrated from Southeast Asia, creating hunter-gatherer or sometimes settled agricultural communities. European countries moved in during later centuries, seeking the plentiful natural resources of the area. Today, some South Pacific islands remain under the control of foreign governments, and culture in these areas mix modern, industrialized society and indigenous culture. Population is unevenly distributed, largely due to the inhabitability of many parts of the South Pacific, such as the extremely hot desert areas of Australia. Agriculture still drives much of the economy, with tourism growing. Antarctica remains the only continent not claimed by a single country. There are no permanent human habitations in Antarctica, but scientists and explorers visit the area on a temporary basis.

Human-environment interaction

Geography also studies the way people interact with, use and change their environment. The effects, reasons and consequences of these changes are studied, as are the ways the environment limits or influences human behavior. This kind of study can help determine the best course of action when a nation or group of people are considering making changes to the environment, such as building a dam or removing natural landscape to build or expand roads. Study of the consequences can help determine if these actions are manageable and how long-term detrimental results can be mitigated.

Physical geography and climate

<u>US and Canada</u>
The US and Canada have a similar distribution of geographical features, with shared mountain ranges in both east and west, similar stretches of fertile plains through the center, and some shared lakes and waterways. Both areas were shaped by glaciers, which also deposited highly fertile soil. Because they are so large, Canada and the US experience several varieties of climate, including continental climates with four seasons in median areas, tropical climates in the southern part of the US, and arctic climes in the far north. Human intervention has greatly

influenced the productivity of agricultural regions, and many areas have been reshaped to accommodate easier, more economical transportation.

Latin America

Latin America contains a wide variety of geographical features including high mountains such as the Andes, wide plains, and high altitude plateaus. The region contains numerous natural resources, but many of them have remained unused due to various obstacles, including political issues, geographic barriers, and lack of sufficient economic power.

Climate zones in Latin America are largely tropical, with rainforests and savannahs, but vertical climate zones and grasslands are also included.

Europe

Europe spans a wide area with a variety of climate zones. In the east and south are mountain ranges, while the north is dominated by a plains region. The long coastline and the island nature of some countries, such as Britain, mean the climate is often warmer than other lands at similar latitudes, as the area is warmed by ocean currents. Many areas of western Europe have a moderate climate, while areas of the south are dominated by the classic Mediterranean climate. Europe carries a high level of natural resources. Numerous waterways help connect the inner regions with the coastal areas. Much of Europe is industrialized, and agriculture has existed in the area for thousands of years.

Russia

Russia's area encompasses part of Asia and Europe. From the standpoint of square footage alone, Russia is the largest country in the world. Due to its size Russia encompasses a wide variety of climatic regions, including plains, plateaus, mountains and tundra.

Russia's climate can be quite harsh, with rivers that are frozen through most of the year making transportation of the country's rich natural resources more difficult. Siberia, in the north of Russia, is dominated by permafrost. Native peoples in this area still live hunting and gathering existence, live in portable yurts and subsisting largely on herds of reindeer or caribou. Other areas include taiga with extensive, dense woods in north central Russia and more temperate steppes and grasslands in the southwest.

North Africa and Southwest and Central Asia

This area of the world is complex in its geographical structure and climate, incorporating seas, peninsulas, rivers, mountains, and numerous other features. Earthquakes remain common, with tectonic plates in the area remaining active. Much of the world's oil lies in this area. The tendency of the large rivers of North Africa, especially the Nile, to follow a set pattern of drought and extreme fertility, led people to settle there from prehistoric times. As technology has advanced, people have tamed this river, making its activity more predictable and the land around it more productive. The extremely arid nature of many other parts of this area has also led to human intervention such as irrigation to increase agricultural production.

Southern Africa

South of the Sahara Desert, the high elevations and other geographical characteristics have made it very difficult for human travel or settlement to occur. The geography of the area is dominated by a series of plateaus. There are also mountain ranges and a large rift valley in the eastern part of the country. Contrasting the wide desert areas, Southern Africa contains numerous lakes, rivers, and world-famous waterfalls. The area contains tropical climates, including rain forests, as well as savannahs, steppes, and desert areas. The main natural resources are minerals, including gems, and water.

South Asia

The longest alluvial plain, a plain caused by shifting floodplains of major rivers and river systems over time, exists in South Asia. South Asia boasts three major river systems in the

Ganges, Indus and Brahmaputra. It also has large deposits of minerals, including iron ore that are in great demand internationally. South Asia holds mountains, plains, plateaus, and numerous islands. The climates range from tropical to highlands and desert areas. South Asia also experiences monsoon winds that cause a long rainy season. Variations in climate, elevation and human activity influence agricultural production.

East Asia

East Asia includes North and South Korea, Mongolia, China, Japan and Taiwan. Mineral resources are plentiful but not evenly distributed throughout. The coastlines are long, and while the population is large, farmlands are sparse. As a result, the surrounding oceans have become a major source of sustenance. East Asia is large enough to also encompass several climate regions. Ocean currents provide milder climates to coastal areas, while monsoons provide the majority of the rainfall for the region. Typhoons are somewhat common, as are earthquakes, volcanoes and tsunamis. The latter occur because of the tectonic plates that meet beneath the continent, and remain somewhat active.

Southeast Asia

Southeast Asia lies largely on the equator, and roughly half of the countries of the region are island nations. These countries include Borneo, Thailand, Vietnam, Laos, Myanmar, New Guinea and Malaysia. Malaysia is partially on the mainland and partially an island country. The island nations of Southeast Asia feature mountains that are considered part of the Ring of Fire, an area where tectonic plates remain quite active, leading to extensive volcanic activity as well as earthquakes and tsunamis. Southeast Asia boasts many rivers as well as abundant natural resources, including gems, fossil fuels and minerals. There are basically two seasons—wet and dry. The wet season arrives with the monsoons. In general, Southeast Asia consists of tropical rainforest climates, but there are some mountain areas and tropical savannas.

Australia, Oceania and Antarctica

In the far southern hemisphere of the globe, Australia and Oceania present their own climatic combinations. Australia, the only island on earth that is also a continent, has extensive deserts as well as mountains and lowlands. The economy is driven by agriculture, including ranches and farms, and minerals. While the steppes bordering extremely arid inland areas are suitable for livestock, only the coastal areas receive sufficient rainfall for crops without using irrigation. Oceania refers to literally thousands of Pacific islands, created by volcanic activity. Most of these have tropical climates with wet and dry seasons. New Zealand, Australia's nearest neighbor, boasts rich forests as well as mountain ranges and relatively moderate temperatures, including rainfall throughout the year. Antarctica is covered with ice. Its major resource consists of scientific information. It supports some wildlife, such as penguins, and little vegetation, mostly mosses or lichens.

Plate tectonics

According to the geological theory of plate tectonics, the earth's crust is made up of ten major and several minor tectonic plates. These plates are the solid areas of the crust. They float on top of the earth's mantle, which is made up of molten rock. Because the plates float on this liquid component of the earth's crust, they move, creating major changes in the earth's surface. These changes can happen very slowly, over time, such as in continental drift, or can happen rapidly, such as when earthquakes occur. Interaction between the different continental plates can create mountain ranges, volcanic activity, major earthquakes, and deep rifts.

Plate boundaries

Plate tectonics defines three types of plate boundaries, determined by the way in which the edges of the plates interact. These plate boundaries are:

- Convergent boundaries—the bordering plates move toward one another. When they collide directly, this is known as continental collision, which can create

very large, high mountain ranges such as the Himalayas and the Andes. If one plate slides under the other, this is called subduction. Subduction can lead to intense volcanic activity. One example is the Ring of Fire that lies along the northern Pacific coastlines.
- Divergent boundaries—plates move away from each other. This movement leads to rifts such as the Mid-Atlantic Ridge and east Africa's Great Rift Valley.
- Transform boundaries—plate boundaries slide in opposite directions against each other. Intense pressure builds up along transform boundaries as the plates grind along each other's edges, leading to earthquakes. Many major fault lines, including the San Andreas Fault, lie along transform boundaries.

Erosion, weathering, transportation and deposition

Erosion involves movement of any loose material on the earth's surface. This can include soil, sand, or rock fragments. These loose fragments can be displaced by natural forces such as wind, water, ice, plant cover, and human factors. Mechanical erosion occurs due to natural forces. Chemical erosion occurs as a result of human intervention and activities. Weathering occurs when atmospheric elements affect the earth's surface. Water, heat, ice, and pressure all lead to weathering. Transportation refers to loose material being moved by wind, water or ice. Glacial movement, for example, carries everything from pebbles to boulders, sometimes over long distances. Deposition is the result of transportation. When material is transported, it is eventually deposited, and builds up to form formations like moraines and sand dunes.

Effects of human interaction and conflict on geographical boundaries

Human societies and their interaction have led to divisions of territories into countries and various other subdivisions. While these divisions are at their root artificial, they are important to geographers in the discussion of interactions of various populations.
Geographical divisions often occur through conflict between different human populations. The reasons behind these divisions include:
- Control of resources
- Control of important trade routes
- Control of populations

Conflict often occurs due to religious or political differences, language differences, or race differences. Natural resources are finite and so often lead to conflict over how they are distributed among populations.

State sovereignty

State sovereignty recognizes the division of geographical areas into areas controlled by various governments or groups of people. These groups control not only the territory, but also all its natural resources and the inhabitants of the area. The entire planet Earth is divided into political or administratively sovereign areas recognized to be controlled by a particular government with the exception of the continent of Antarctica.

Alliances

Alliances form between different countries based on similar interests, political goals, cultural values, or military issues. Six existing international alliances include:
- North Atlantic Treaty Organization (NATO)
- Common Market
- European Union (EU)
- United Nations (UN)
- Caribbean Community
- Council of Arab Economic Unity

In addition, very large companies and multi-national corporations can create alliances and various kinds of competition based on the need to control resources, production, and the overall marketplace.

Agricultural revolution

The agricultural revolution began six thousand years ago when the plow was invented in Mesopotamia. Using a plow drawn by animals, people were able to cultivate crops in large quantities rather than gathering available seeds and grains and planting them by hand. Because large-scale agriculture was labor intensive, this led to the development of stable communities where people gathered to make farming possible. As stable farming communities replaced groups of nomadic hunter-gatherers, human society underwent profound changes. Societies became dependent on limited numbers of crops as well as subject to the vagaries of weather. Trading livestock and surplus agricultural output led to the growth of large-scale commerce and trade routes.

Modification of surrounding environments by human populations

The agricultural revolution led human societies to begin changing their surroundings in order to accommodate their needs for shelter and room to cultivate food and to provide for domestic animals. Clearing ground for crops, redirecting waterways for irrigation purposes, and building permanent settlements all create major changes in the environment. Large-scale agriculture can lead to loose topsoil and damaging erosion. Building large cities leads to degraded air quality, water pollution from energy consumption, and many other side effects that can severely damage the environment. Recently, many countries have taken action by passing laws to reduce human impact on the environment and reduce the potentially damaging side effects. This is called environmental policy.

Ecology

Ecology is the study of the way living creatures interact with their environment. Biogeography explores the way physical features of the earth affect living creatures.

Ecology bases its studies on three different levels of the environment. These are:

- Ecosystem—a specific physical environment and all the organisms that live there.
- Biomes—a group of ecosystems, usually consisting of a large area with similar flora and fauna as well as similar climate and soil. Examples of biomes include deserts, tropical rain forests, taigas, and tundra.
- Habitat—an area in which a specific species usually lives. The habitat includes the necessary soil, water, and resources for that particular species, as well as predators and other species that compete for the same resources.

Interactions between species

Different interactions occur among species and members of single species within a habitat. These interactions fall into three categories:

- Competition — Competition occurs when different animals, either of the same species or of different species, compete for the same resources. Robins can compete with other robins for available food, but other insectivores also compete for these same resources.
- Predation— Predation occurs when one species depends on the other species for food, such as a fox who subsists on small mammals.
- Symbiosis — Symbiosis occurs when two different species exist in the same environment without affecting the other. Some symbiotic relationships are beneficial to one or both organisms without harm occurring to either.

Ability to adapt

If a species is relocated from one habitat to another, it must adapt in order to survive. Some species are more capable of adapting than others. Those that cannot adapt will not survive. There are different ways a creature can adapt, including behavior modification as well as structure or physiological changes. Adaptation is also vital if an organism's environment changes around it. Although the creature has not been relocated, it finds itself in a new environment that requires changes in order to survive. The more readily an organism can adapt, the more likely it is to survive. The almost infinite ability of humans to adapt is a major reason why they are able to survive in almost any habitat in any area of the world.

Biodiversity

Biodiversity refers to the variety of habitats that exist on the planet, as well as the variety of organisms that can exist within these habitats. A greater level of biodiversity makes it more likely that an individual habitat will flourish along with the species that depend upon it. Changes in habitat, including climate change, human intervention, or other factors, can reduce biodiversity by causing the extinction of certain species.

Economics

Economics

Economics is the study of the ways specific societies allocate resources to individuals and groups within that society. Also important are the choices society makes regarding what efforts or initiatives are funded and which are not. Since resources in any society are finite, allocation becomes a vivid reflection of that society's values.

In general, the economic system that drives an individual society is based on:

- What goods are produced
- How those goods are produced
- Who acquires the goods or benefits from them

Economics consists of two main categories, macroeconomics, which studies larger systems, and microeconomics, which studies smaller systems.

Market economy

A market economy is based on supply and demand. Demand has to do with what customers want and need, as well as how quantity those consumers are able to purchase based on other economic factors. Supply refers to how much can be produced to meet demand, or how much suppliers are willing and able to sell. Where the needs of consumers meet the needs of suppliers is referred to as a market equilibrium price. This price varies depending on many factors, including the overall health of a society's economy, overall beliefs and considerations of individuals in society, and other factors.

The following is a list of terms defined in the context of a market economy:

- Elasticity—based on how the quantity of a particular product responds to the price demanded for that product. If quantity responds quickly to changes in price, the supply/demand for that product is said to be elastic. If they do not respond quickly, then it is inelastic.
- Market efficiency—when a market is capable of producing output high enough to meet consumer demand, that market is efficient.
- Comparative advantage—in the field of international trade, this refers to a country focusing on a specific product that it can produce more efficiently and more cheaply, or at a lower opportunity cost, than another country, thus giving it a comparative advantage in production of that product.

<u>Comparison to planned economy</u>
In a market economy, supply and demand are determined by consumers. In a planned economy, a public entity or planning authority makes the decisions about what resources will be produced, how they will be produced, and who will be able to benefit from them. The means of production, such as factories, are also owned by a public entity rather than by private interests. In market socialism, the economic structure falls somewhere between the market economy and the planned economy. Planning authorities determine allocation of resources at higher economic levels, while consumer goods are driven by a market economy.

Microeconomics

While economics generally studies how resources are allocated, microeconomics focuses on economic factors such as the way consumers behave, how income is distributed, and output and input markets. Studies are limited to the industry or firm level, rather than an entire country or society. Among the elements studied in microeconomics are factors of production, costs of production, and factor income. These factors determine production decisions of individual firms, based on resources and costs.

Classification of markets

The conditions prevailing in a given market are used to classify markets. Conditions considered include:

- Existence of competition
- Number and size of suppliers
- Influence of suppliers over price
- Variety of available products
- Ease of entering the market

Once these questions are answered, an economist can classify a certain market according to its structure and the nature of competition within the market.

Market failure

When any of the elements for a successfully competitive market are missing, this can lead to a market failure. Certain elements are necessary to create what economists call "perfect competition." If one of these factors is weak or lacking, the market is classified as having "imperfect competition." Worse than imperfect competition, though, is a market failure.

There are five major types of market failure:

- Competition is inadequate
- Information is inadequate
- Resources are not mobile
- Negative externalities, or side effects
- Failure to provide public goods

Externalities are side effects of a market that affect third parties. These effects can be either negative or positive.

Factors of production and costs of production

Every good and service requires certain resources, or inputs. These inputs are referred to as factors of production. Every good and service requires four factors of production:

- Labor
- Land
- Capital
- Entrepreneurship

These factors can be fixed or variable, and can produce fixed or variable costs. Examples of fixed costs include land and equipment. Variable costs include labor. The total of fixed and variable costs makes up the costs of production.

Factor income

Factors of production all have an associated factor income. Factors that earn income include:

- Labor—earns wages
- Capital—earns interest
- Land—earns rent
- Entrepreneurs—earn profit

Each factor's income is determined by its contribution. In a market economy, this income is not guaranteed to be equal. How scarce the factor is and the weight of its contribution to the overall production process determines the final factor income.

Output market

The four kinds of market structures in an output market are:

- Perfect competition—all existing firms sell an identical product. The firms are not able to control the final price. In addition, there is nothing that makes it difficult to become involved in or leave the industry. Anything that would prevent entering or leaving an industry is called a barrier to entry. An example of this market structure is agriculture.
- Monopoly—a single seller controls the product and its price. Barriers to entry, such as prohibitively high fixed cost structures, prevent other sellers from entering the market.
- Monopolistic competition—a number of firms sell similar products, but they are not identical, such as different brands of clothes or food. Barriers to entry are low.
- Oligopoly—only a few firms control the production and distribution of products, such as automobiles. Barriers to entry are high, preventing large numbers of firms from entering the market.

Monopolies

Four types of monopolies are:

- Natural monopoly—occurs when a single supplier has a distinct advantage over the others
- Geographic monopoly—only one business offers the product in a certain area
- Technological monopoly—a single company controls the technology necessary to supply the product
- Government monopoly—a government agency is the only provider of a specific good or service

Control by the US government

The US government has passed several acts to regulate businesses, including:

- Sherman Antitrust Act (1890) — prohibited trusts, monopolies, and any other situations that eliminated competition.
- Clayton Antitrust Act (1914) — prohibited price discrimination.
- Robinson-Patman Act (1936) — strengthened provisions of the Clayton Antitrust Act.

The government has also taken other actions to ensure competition, including requirements for public disclosure. The Securities and Exchange Commission (SEC) requires companies that provide public stock to provide financial reports on a regular basis. Because of the nature of their business, banks are further regulated and required to provide various types of information to the government.

Marketing and utility

Marketing consists of all of the activity necessary to convince consumers to acquire goods. One major way to move products into the hands of consumers is to convince them that any single product will satisfy a need. The ability of a product or service to satisfy the need of a consumer is called utility.

There are four types of utility:

- Form utility—a product's desirability lies in its physical characteristics.
- Place utility—a product's desirability is connected to its location and convenience.
- Time utility—a product's desirability is determined by its availability at a certain time.
- Ownership utility—a product's desirability is increased because ownership of the product passes to the consumer.

Marketing behavior will stress any or all of the types of utility to the consumer to which the product is being marketed.

Determining a product's market

Successful marketing depends not only on convincing customers they need the product, but also on focusing the marketing towards those who have a need or desire for the product. Before releasing a product into the general marketplace, many producers will test markets to determine which will be the most receptive to the product.

There are three steps usually taken to evaluate a product's market:

- Market research—researching a market to determine if the market will be receptive to the product.
- Market surveys—a part of market research, market surveys ask specific questions of consumers to help determine the marketability of a product to a specific group.
- Test marketing—releasing the product into a small geographical area to see how it sells. Often test marketing is followed by wider marketing if the product does well.

Marketing plan

The four major elements of a marketing plan are:

- Product—any elements pertaining directly to the product, including packaging, presentation, or services to include along with it.
- Price—calculates cost of production, distribution, advertising, etc. as well as the desired profit to determine the final price.
- Place—what outlets will be used to sell the product, whether traditional outlets such as brick and mortar stores or through direct mail or Internet marketing.
- Promotion—ways to let consumers know the product is available, through advertising and other means.

Once these elements have all been determined, the producer can proceed with production and distribution of his product.

Distribution channels

Distribution channels determine the route a product takes on its journey from producer to consumer, and can also influenced the final price and availability of the product. There are two major forms of distributions: wholesale and retail. A wholesale distributor buys in large quantities and then resells smaller amounts to other businesses. Retailers sell directly to the consumers rather than to businesses. In the modern marketplace, additional distribution channels have grown up with the rise of markets such as club warehouse stores as well as purchasing through catalogs or over the Internet. Most of these newer distribution channels bring products more directly to the consumer, eliminating the need for middlemen.

Distribution of income and poverty

Distribution of income in any society lies in a range from poorest to richest. In most societies, income is not distributed evenly. To determine income distribution, family incomes are ranked, lowest to highest. These rankings are divided into sections called quintiles, which are compared to each other. The uneven distribution of income is often linked to higher levels of education and ability in the upper classes, but can also be due to other factors such as discrimination and existing monopolies. The income gap in America continues to grow, largely due to growth in the service industry, changes in the American family unit and reduced influence of labor unions. Poverty is defined by comparing incomes to poverty guidelines. Poverty guidelines determine the level of income necessary for a family to function. Those below the poverty line are often eligible for assistance from government agencies.

Consumer behavior

The two major types of consumer behavior as defined in macroeconomics are:

- Marginal propensity to consume defines the tendency of consumers to increase spending in conjunction with increases in income. In general, individuals with greater income will buy more. As individuals increase their income through job changes or growth of experience, they will also increase spending.
- Utility is a term that describes the satisfaction experienced by a consumer in relation to acquiring and using a good or service. Providers of goods and services will stress utility to convince consumers they want the products being presented.

Macroeconomics

Macroeconomics examines economies on a much larger level than microeconomics. While microeconomics studies economics on a firm or industry level, macroeconomics looks at economic trends and structures on a national level. Variables studied in macroeconomics include:

- Output
- Consumption

- Investment
- Government spending
- Net exports

The overall economic condition of a nation is defined as the Gross Domestic Product, or GDP. GDP measures a nation's economic output over a limited time period, such as a year.

GDP

The two major ways to measure the Gross Domestic Product of a country are:

- The expenditures approach calculates the GDP based on how much money is spent in each individual sector.
- The income approach calculates based on how much money is earned in each sector.

Both methods yield the same results and both of these calculation methods are based on four economic sectors that make up a country's macro economy:

- Consumers
- Business
- Government
- Foreign sector

Several factors must be considered in order to accurately calculate the GDP using the incomes approach. Income factors are:

- Wages paid to laborers, or Compensation of Employees
- Rental income derived from land
- Interest income derived from invested capital
- Entrepreneurial income

Entrepreneurial income consists of two forms. Proprietor's Income is income that comes back to the entrepreneur himself. Corporate Profit is income that goes back into the corporation as a whole. Corporate profit is divided by the corporation into corporate profits taxes, dividends, and retained earnings. Two other figures must be subtracted in the incomes approach. These are indirect business taxes, including property and sales taxes, and depreciation.

<u>Effects of the population</u>
Changes in population can affect the calculation of a nation's GDP, particularly since GDP and GNP are generally measure per capita. If a country's economic production is low, but the population is high, the income per individual will be lower than if the income is high and the population is lower. Also, if the population grows quickly and the income grows slowly, individual income will remain low or even drop drastically.

Population growth can also affect overall economic growth. Economic growth requires both consumers to purchase goods and workers to produce them. A population that does not grow quickly enough will not supply enough workers to support rapid economic growth.

Ideal balance in an economy and phases in national economies

Ideally, an economy functions efficiently, with the aggregate supply, or the amount of national output, equal to the aggregate demand, or the amount of the output that is purchased. In these cases, the economy is stable and prosperous.

However, economies more typically go through phases. These phases are:

- Boom—GDP is high and the economy prospers
- Recession—GDP falls, unemployment rises
- Trough—the recession reaches its lowest point
- Recovery—Unemployment lessens, prices rise, and the economy begins to stabilize again

These phases happen often, in cycles that are not necessarily predictable or regular.

Unemployment and inflation

When demand outstrips supply, prices are driven artificially high, or inflated. This occurs when too much spending causes an imbalance in the economy. In general, inflation occurs because an economy is growing too quickly. When there is too little spending and supply has moved far beyond demand, a surplus of product results. Companies cut back on production, reduce the number of workers they employ, and unemployment rises as people lose their jobs. This imbalance occurs when an economy becomes sluggish. In general, both these economic instability situations are caused by an imbalance between supply and demand. Government intervention is often necessary to stabilize an economy when either inflation or unemployment becomes too serious.

<u>Five different forms of unemployment are:</u>

- Frictional—when workers change jobs and are unemployed while waiting for a new job.
- Structural—when economical shifts reduce the need for workers.
- Cyclical—when natural business cycles bring about loss of jobs.
- Seasonal—when seasonal cycles reduce the need for certain jobs.
- Technological—when advances in technology result in elimination of certain jobs.

Any of these factors can increase unemployment in certain sectors.

Inflation is classified by the overall rate at which it occurs:

- Creeping inflation—an inflation rate of about one to three percent annually.
- Galloping inflation—a high inflation rate of 100 to 300 percent annually.
- Hyperinflation—an inflation rate over 500 percent annually. Hyperinflation usually leads to complete monetary collapse in a society, as individuals become unable to generate sufficient income to purchase necessary goods.

<u>Government intervention policies</u>

When an economy becomes too imbalanced, either due to excessive spending or not enough spending, government intervention often becomes necessary to put the economy back on track. Government Fiscal Policy can take several forms, including:

- Monetary policy
- Contractionary policies
- Expansionary policies

Contractionary policies help counteract inflation. These include increasing taxes and decreasing government spending to slow spending in the overall economy. Expansionary policies increase government spending and lower taxes in order to reduce unemployment and increase the level of spending in the economy overall. Monetary policy can take several forms, and affects the amount of funds available to banks for making loans.

Populations and population growth

Populations are studied by size, rates of growth due to immigration, the overall fertility rate, and life expectancy. For example, though the population of the United States is considerably larger than it was two hundred years ago, the rate of population growth has decreased greatly, from about three percent per year to less than one percent per year.

In the US, the fertility rate is fairly low, with most women choosing not to have large families, and life expectancy is high, creating a projected imbalance between older and younger people in the near future. In addition, immigration and the mixing of racially diverse cultures are projected to increase the percentages of Asian, Hispanic and African Americans.

Money

Money is used in three major ways:

- As an accounting unit
- As a store of value
- As an exchange medium

In general, money must be acceptable throughout a society in exchange for debts or to purchase goods and services. Money should be relatively scarce, its value should remain stable, and it should be easily carried, durable, and easy to divide up. There are three basic types of money: commodity, representative and fiat. Commodity money includes gems or precious metals. Representative money can be exchanged for items such as gold or silver which have inherent value. Fiat money, or legal tender, has no inherent value but has been declared to function as money by the government. It is often backed by gold or silver, but not necessarily on a one-to-one ratio.

US money
Money in the US is not just currency. When economists calculate the amount of money available, they must take into account other factors such as deposits that have been placed in checking accounts, debit cards and "near moneys" such as savings accounts, that can be quickly converted into cash. Currency, checkable deposits and traveler's checks, referred to as M1, are added up, and then M2 is calculated by adding savings deposits, CDs and various other monetary deposits. The final result is the total quantity of available money.

Monetary policy and the Federal Reserve System

The Federal Reserve System, also known as the Fed, implements all monetary policy in the US. Monetary policy regulates the amount of money available in the American banking system. The Fed can decrease or increase the amount of available money for loans, thus helping regulate the national economy. Monetary policies implemented by the Fed are part of expansionary or contractionary monetary policies that help counteract inflation or unemployment. The Discount Rate is an interest rate charged by the Fed when banks borrow money from them. A lower discount rate leads banks to borrow more money, leading to increased spending. A higher discount rate has the opposite effect.

Banks

Banks earn their income by loaning out money and charging interest on those loans. If less money is available, fewer loans can be made, which affects the amount of spending in the overall economy. While banks function by making loans, they are not allowed to loan out all the money they hold in deposit. The amount of money they must maintain in reserve is known as the reserve ratio. If the reserve ratio is raised, less money is available for loans and spending decreases. A lower reserve ratio increases available funds and increases spending. This ratio is determined by the Federal Reserve System.

Open Market Operations

The Federal Reserve System can also expand or contract the overall money supply through Open Market Operations. In this case, the Fed can buy or sell bonds it has purchased from banks, or from individuals. When they buy bonds, more money is put into circulation, creating an expansionary situation to stimulate the economy. When the Fed sells bonds, money is withdrawn from the system, creating a contractionary situation to slow an economy suffering from inflation. Because of international financial markets, however, American banks often borrow and lend money in markets outside the US. By shifting their attention to international markets, domestic banks and other businesses can circumvent whatever contractionary policies the Fed may have put into place in order to help a struggling economy.

International trade

International trade can take advantage of broader markets, bringing a wider variety of products within easy reach. By contrast, it can also allow individual countries to specialize in particular products that they can produce easily, such as those for which they have easy access to raw materials. Other products, more difficult to make domestically, can be acquired through trade with other nations. International trade requires efficient use of native resources as well as sufficient disposable income to purchase native products and imported products. Many countries in the world engage extensively in international trade, but others still face major economic challenges.

Developing nations

The five major characteristics of a developing nation are:

- Low GDP
- Rapid growth of population
- Economy that depends on subsistence agriculture
- Poor conditions, including high infant mortality rates, high disease rates, poor sanitation, and insufficient housing
- Low literacy rate

Developing nations often function under oppressive governments that do not provide private property rights and withhold education and other rights from women. They also often feature an extreme disparity between upper and lower classes, with little opportunity for lower classes to improve their position.

Stages of economic development
Economic development occurs in three stages that are defined by the activities that drive the economy:

- Agricultural stage
- Manufacturing stage
- Service sector stage

In developing countries, it is often difficult to acquire the necessary funding to provide equipment and training to move into the advanced stages of economic development. Some can receive help from developed countries via foreign aid and investment or international organizations such as the International Monetary Fund or the World Bank. Having developed countries provide monetary, technical, or military assistance can help developing countries move forward to the next stage in their development.

Obstacles to economic growth
Developing nations typically struggle to overcome obstacles that prevent or slow economic development. Major obstacles can include:

- Rapid, uncontrolled population growth
- Trade restrictions
- Misused resources, often perpetrated by the nation's government
- Traditional beliefs that can slow or reject change.

Corrupt, oppressive governments often hamper the economic growth of developing nations, creating huge economic disparities and making it impossible for individuals to advance, in turn preventing overall growth. Governments sometimes export currency, called capital flight, which is detrimental to a country's economic development. In general, countries are more likely to experience economic growth if their governments encourage entrepreneurship and provide private property rights.

Problems with rapid industrialization

Rapid growth throughout the world leaves some nations behind, and sometimes spurs their governments to move forward too quickly into industrialization and artificially rapid economic growth. While slow or nonexistent economic growth causes problems in a country, overly rapid industrialization carries its own issues. Four major problems encountered due to rapid industrialization are:

- Use of technology not suited to the products or services being supplied
- Poor investment of capital
- Lack of time for the population to adapt to new paradigms
- Lack of time to experience all stages of development and adjust to each stage

Economic failures in Indonesia were largely due to rapid growth that was poorly handled.

E-commerce

The growth of the Internet has brought many changes to our society, not the least of which is the ways we do business. Where supply channels used to have to move in certain ways, many of these channels are now bypassed as e-commerce makes it possible for nearly any individual to set up a direct market to consumers, as well as direct interaction with suppliers. Competition is fierce. In many instances e-commerce can provide nearly instantaneous gratification, with a wide variety of products. Whoever provides the best product most quickly often rises to the top of a marketplace. How this added element to the marketplace will affect the economy in the near and not-so-near future remains to be seen. Many industries are still struggling with the best ways to adapt to the rapid, continuous changes.

Knowledge economy

The knowledge economy is a growing sector in the economy of developed countries, and includes the trade and development of:

- Data
- Intellectual property
- Technology, especially in the area of communications

Knowledge as a resource is steadily becoming more and more important. What is now being called the Information Age may prove to bring about changes in life and culture as significant as those brought on by the Agricultural and Industrial Revolutions.

Cybernomics

Related to the knowledge economy is what has been dubbed "cybernomics," or economics driven by e-commerce and other computer-based markets and products. Marketing has changed drastically with the growth of cyber communication, allowing suppliers to connect one-on-one with their customers. Other issues coming to the fore regarding cybernomics include:

- Secure online trade
- Intellectual property rights
- Rights to privacy
- Bringing developing nations into the fold

As these issues are debated and new laws and policies developed, the face of many industries continues to undergo drastic change. Many of the old ways of doing business no longer work, leaving industries scrambling to function profitably within the new system.

Behavioral Sciences

Sociology

Sociology is a scientific discipline that focuses on the study of societies. Human societies are made up of institutions, groups, and finally individuals. How all these levels of organization interact is the major interest of sociologists. The way individuals organize themselves, how they interact with each other, and the attitudes and beliefs different groups develop, all define those groups' cultural backgrounds. Groups of people in the same geographical area often develop similar organizational structures, beliefs and attitudes.

The five major study areas covered by sociology are:

- Population studies: These studies involve observing social patterns of groups of people who live in the same area.
- Social behaviors: Sociology studies how general behaviors change over time, as well as attitudes such as morale, need for conformity, and other elements of social interaction.
- Cultural influences: Influences of culture on social groups include art, religion, language, and overall knowledge and learning.
- Social change: Ways societies change over time. This includes major events such as wars and revolutions, or the way technology changes how people interact.
- Social institutions: Large groups of people organized to fit specific niches in society, such as churches, hospitals, government, businesses and schools. These organizations change over time and according to the overall needs and beliefs of an individual society.

Gathering and testing data

The three major methods of gathering data for sociological studies are:

- Surveys—gathering information via direct questioning of members of the social group being studied.
- Controlled experiments—performing experiments that change an element of society.
- Field observations—living among members of a particular group or culture and observing how they interact and how they live their everyday lives.

Socialization within cultures

Individuals learn how to function within a specific culture, group or society via a process called socialization. Social contact with other human beings is vitally important to early development so that children can grow up to function in society as expected.

During the early years, children receive socialization from their families, siblings, peers, schoolmates, and from exposure to mass media, when applicable. Observing the behavior of others and adapting it to their own use helps children learn to interact with others. This process continues throughout life as individuals learn to adapt to various situations and interact with new groups.

Social groups and social interaction

Social groups are defined based on how they come into being, how they develop, and how they interact with wider society. The five major classifications are:

- Primary groups—focused on members' need for support, such as a family or friend grouping.
- Secondary groups—form around the need to complete a task.
- Reference groups—help form an individual's identity.
- In-groups and out-groups—oppose each other or exclude members of other groups.
- Social networks—provide multiple links to an often large number of other individuals.

Five main forms of social interaction help define social groups:

- Cooperation
- Coercion
- Conflict
- Conformity
- Social exchange

All of these elements can bring a group into existence, break it apart, or transform it.

Social institutions

Six major social institutions that characterize and meet the needs of any society are:

- Family—the basic unit of any society and the most important social institution in all sociological study.
- Education—in many societies, the values and norms of culture are communicated through institutionalized education as well as via the family.
- Political institutions—political institutions in a society determine the distribution of power.
- Economic institutions—these institutions determine distribution of wealth.
- Religion—provides mores and beliefs that help unify a culture. Unfortunately many religions also function in an in-group/out-group capacity.
- Sport—reflects values of society, promotes unity, and provides an outlet for aggression

Cultural change and cultural traits

Three major processes bring about the majority of changes in a culture:

- Discovery—finding things that already exist, such as fire, a major cultural transformer.
- Invention—Creating new equipment, machinery, etc. that changes the way tasks are accomplished.
- Diffusion—borrowing elements from other cultures.

Over 70 traits have been identified that are found in nearly every culture to some level. These traits can be divided into five categories that determine the basic structure, mores, norms, and other characteristics of a culture.

- Arts
- Language
- Environment
- Recreation
- Economy
- Institution
- Beliefs

Race and ethnicity relationships

In general, relationships within cultures involving race and ethnicity are defined by either assimilation or conflict. Assimilation can involve:

- Anglo-conformity—immigrants and racial minorities conform to the expectations of Anglo-American society, whether by choice, necessity or force.
- Cultural pluralism—acceptance of varieties of racial and ethnic groups.
- Accommodation—mutual adaptation between majority and minority groups.
- Melting pot—the mixing together of various ethnic groups will bring about a new cultural group.

Patterns of conflict include:

- Population transfer—one group is required or forced to leave by another group.
- Subjugation—one group exercises control over the other.
- Genocide—one group slaughters another.

Gender and age discrimination

In spite of legislation, education, and other attempts to bring about a higher level of equality, discrimination still exists against women and the elderly, particularly as involves law, politics and economic standing. Discrimination against women is particularly profound in most developing countries. It is believed that increasing the standing of women in a society is a major element in increasing the overall livelihood of that society.

While some societies value the elderly for their knowledge and experience, others discriminate against older people because of their decreased physical ability and ability to contribute economically. In the US, the poverty level for the elderly still stands at about ten percent. As lifespan increases, all societies must find a way to accommodate the needs of the elderly population.

Auguste Comte

Auguste Comte, a French philosopher, first used the term sociology to describe the study of human organizations and culture. His major theory was positivism. Positivism relies entirely on physical and sensory data to describe and evaluate human experience, completely discounting anything metaphysical. Social behavior, according to Comte, could be measured scientifically, as could major events that occurred in different populations. Comte is considered to be the first sociologist in the Western world.

Emile Durkheim's

Through Durkheim's efforts, sociology eventually came to be considered a discipline in major universities. Heavily influenced by Comte's views of positivism, Durkheim felt the larger world was influenced by group beliefs, attitudes and cultural aspects rather than by individuals. He performed in-depth studies on the cause of higher suicide rates among certain social groups. In the course of this study, he discussed anomie, or people affected by larger changes in society, such as unemployment or alienation of social groups.

Karl Marx and Friedrich Engels

According to Marx and Engels, society world-wide could be boiled down to a constant struggle between classes. This socio-economic battle, as explained in *The Communist Manifesto*, would eventually lead to a revolution by the working class, since work itself is a social organization that involves large groups of people.

Herbert Spencer

Herbert Spencer is credited with the idea known as Social Darwinism. Though he and Darwin were technically rivals, Spencer applied Darwin's idea of "survival of the fittest" (though Spencer actually coined that term) to the way society develops. According to Spencer, competition is the major driving force behind the development and changes inherent in human society.

Max Weber

Weber's major thesis stated that the differing religions of East and West led to differences in societal development. Weber believed Protestantism as a religion influenced the development of Capitalism in the West. He also stated that the organization of the state felt violence was a legitimate means of protecting citizenry or enforcing rule. Police action, military action, and violence of individuals against each other in order to protect themselves or property demonstrate the state's propensity to solve problems through violence.

Anthropology

While archeology studies the physical remains of populations, anthropology by contrast studies human culture, its development, and how different cultural groups are similar or different. Anthropologists often engage in direct study of cultures by living among them, observing and participating in everyday activities. This is referred to as "participant observation." Anthropologists also perform cross-cultural and comparative research.

Anthropology can be divided into four major areas of study. Each one addresses a slightly different approach to culture and how it affects human beings, as well as how culture develops over time.

- Archeology—studies materials and physical items left behind by human settlements
- Social-cultural—social-cultural anthropology focuses on cultural standards, beliefs, values and norms
- Biological—biological anthropology studies specific genetic characteristics of different populations
- Linguistics—studies the development of languages over time

Culture

"Culture" refers to all learned human behaviors and behavioral patterns. Culture is made up of:

- Cultural universals—traits shared by all human beings such as language.
- Culture—all traditions that define a society.
- Subculture—groups within a culture that share specific traits.

While culture serves as a survival mechanism by bringing people together in groups and helping individuals identify with each other, it also undergoes frequent and sometimes profound change as groups respond to new technologies, knowledge, or contact with other cultures.

Subsistence patterns

The term subsistence patterns are a reference to ways in which societies obtain the necessities of life such as food and shelter. The subsistence pattern of a society often is directly correlated to its economy, population size, political systems, and overall technological development. Certain subsistence patterns can only support lower levels of societal development, while others can support a much more developed culture.

The four major subsistence patterns are:

- Foraging, or hunter-gatherer
- Pastoralism—herding
- Horticulture—small-scale farming
- Intensive agriculture—large-scale farming

Hunter-gatherer societies by nature are nomadic and do not tend to support highly developed cultures. Intensive agriculture, by contrast, can support a large population to a high subsistence level, allowing for the development of a sophisticated, modern culture.

Religion

Strictly defined, religion consists of a belief system and usually a set of rituals involving worship of a supernatural force or forces that have some effect upon both everyday life and the overall structure and functioning of the world around us. Religion provides meaning and explanation for various life events and profoundly affects a cultures worldviews. Religion provides emotional support for individuals and a sense of community within a group that has shared religious views. Religious organization also provides structured sets of moral norms and motivation to abide by these norms and rules.

Increased secularization, particularly in developed countries, has reduced the role of religion in everyday life, leading individuals to find other systems to fill these basic human needs.

Margaret Mead

Margaret Mead studied sexual beliefs and norms among South Pacific and Southeast Asian cultures. She acquired a Ph.D. from Columbia University, and her work popularized sociology, bringing it to the attention of a wide number of people. She also studied how children were treated and brought up in different cultures, and how breastfeeding was viewed in different population groups. Among other works, she wrote a book called *Coming of Age in Samoa*, about the culture of these Pacific Islanders.

Mary and Louis Leakey and Olduvai Gorge

The Leakeys made major discoveries regarding the origin of the human species during their excavations in Olduvai Gorge in Africa, excavating wide varieties of stone tools and other artifacts dating back as far as two million years. Mary Leakey discovered footprints of Laetoli and developed a system by which to classify early humans. The Leakeys also discovered prehistoric remains of humans, including early humans dating nearly four million years old and fifteen new species and one new genus of early human ancestors. They also discovered the first fossil ape skull, and only three similar specimens exist to this day. Their findings fundamentally changed theories regarding development and evolution of ancient humans.

Psychology

Psychology studies human behavior and how the mind works. Some psychologists pursue scientific psychology, while others focus on applied psychology. Psychology correlates human behavior and can make use of this data to predict behavior or determine why a particular behavior has occurred. Psychologists also help work with people who have specific problems with relationships or with how they perceive the world. By observing patterns and recording them in detail, psychologists can apply these patterns to predictions about human behavior in individuals, groups, cultures, and even countries.

<u>Methods of psychological study</u>
Psychological researchers study their discipline in various ways. Based on what they are studying, they generally use one of the following methods.

- Naturalistic observation—much as with sociological study, psychologists observe people and their natural behavior without interfering.
- Survey method—surveys are distributed among a wide range of people and the answers are correlated.
- Case studies—specific individuals or groups are studied in depth over a period of time, sometimes for many years.
- Experimental method—involves experimental and control groups and use of specific experiments to prove or disprove a theory.
- Correlational design—is concerned with relationships between variables, such as whether one factor causes or influences another.

Aristotle

Aristotle is often cited as founding the science of psychology through his overall interest in the working of the human mind. His beliefs stated that the mind was part of the body, while the psyche functioned as a receiver of knowledge. He felt psychology's major focus was to uncover the soul. Later philosophers and scientists built on these ideas to eventually develop the modern science of psychology.

Nativism

Nativism is a theory that states that there is a certain body of knowledge all people are born with. This knowledge requires no learning or experience on the part of the individual. Rene Descartes, a French philosopher, developed this concept. He believed the body and mind affected each other profoundly, largely because they are separate from each other. The physical site of this interaction took place in the pineal gland according to his theory. The pineal gland is a small gland in the brain. Descartes developed several theories in the field of philosophy and psychology that are still studied in modern universities.

Empiricism

Empiricism was in direct opposition to Descartes' theory of nativism. Nativism states that people are born with a certain body of knowledge that they do not have to learn. Empiricism theorizes that all knowledge is acquired through life experience, impressing itself on a mind and brain that are blank at the time of birth. Major proponents of empiricism were Thomas Hobbes, John Locke, David Hume and George Berkeley.

Johannes P. Muller, Hermann L.F. von Hemholtz, William James and William Wundt

Johannes P. Muller and Hermann L.F. von Hemholtz, both German, conducted scientific, organized studies of sensation and perception. As the first psychologists to attempt this kind of study, they showed that it was possible to study actual physical processes that work to produce mental activity.

William James was the founder of the world's first psychology laboratory. William Wundt, also German, published the first experimental psychology journal. Together, James and Wundt helped bring psychology into its own, separating it from philosophy. The method of psychological study called introspection grew out of their work.

Sigmund Freud

An Austrian doctor, Freud developed a number of theories regarding human mental processes and behavior. He believed the subconscious to hold numerous repressed experiences and feelings that drove behavior without the individual being aware of it, and that these subconscious motivators could lead to severe personality problems and disorders. He particularly stressed sexual desire as a motivating force. He developed the method of psychoanalysis to help discover the hidden impulses driving individual behavior.

Freud's psychoanalytic theory proposed three major components to an individual's psychological makeup:

- Id—driven by instinct and basic drives.
- Ego—most conscious and producing self-awareness.
- Superego—strives for perfection and appropriate behavior.

The ego acts as mediator between the id and superego, which function in opposition to each other.

Carl Jung

A student of Freud, Jung eventually developed different theories regarding the workings of the human mind. With an intense interest in both Eastern and Western philosophy, he incorporated ideas from both into his psychological explorations. He developed the theories of extroversion and introversion, as well as proposing the existence of the collective unconscious and the occurrence of synchronicity.

Behaviorism

John B. Watson, an American, developed the idea of behaviorism. In his theory, growth, learning and training would always win out over any possible inborn tendencies. He believed that any person, regardless of origin, could learn to perform any type of art, craft or enterprise with sufficient training and experience.

Ivan Pavlov and B.F. Skinner

Ivan Pavlov and B.F. Skinner both built on the theories of John B. Watson, who developed the idea of behaviorism. This work came about largely as a counter to the growing importance of introspective techniques to psychological study. Believing environment strongly influenced individual behavior, Pavlov and Skinner searched for connections between outside stimuli and behavioral patterns. Pavlov's experiments proved the existence of conditioned response. His most famous experiment conditioned dogs to salivate at the sound of a ringing bell. Skinner went on to build further on these ideas, developing the "Skinner Box," a device used to develop and study conditioned response in rats.

Gestalt psychology, social psychology, and modern psychology

Gestalt psychology is a theory developed by Max Wertheimer. In Gestalt theory, events are not considered individually, but as part of a larger pattern. Social psychology is the study of how social conditions affect individuals. Modern psychology, as it has developed, combines earlier schools of psychology, including Freudian, Jungian, behaviorism, cognitive, humanistic and stimulus-response theories.

Divisions of the human lifespan

Development psychologists divide the human lifespan into stages, and list certain developmental milestones that generally take place during these stages:

- Infancy and childhood—the most rapid period of human development during which, the child learns to experience its world, relate to other people, and perform tasks necessary to function in its native culture. Debate exists as to what characteristics are inborn and what are learned.
- Adolescence—this period represents the shift from child to adult. Changes are rapid and can involve major physical and emotional shifts.
- Adulthood—individuals take on new responsibilities, become self-sufficient, and often form their own families and other social networks.
- Old age—priorities shift again as children become adults and no longer require support and supervision.

Learning

Psychologists define learning as a permanent change in behavior. They divide types of learning into three basic categories, depending upon on how the behavioral change is acquired.

- Classical conditioning—a learning process in which a specific stimulus is associated with a specific response over time.
- Operant conditioning—a learning process in which behavior is punished or rewarded, leading to a desired long-term behavior.
- Social learning—learning based on observation of others and modeling others' behavior.

These three learning processes work together to produce the wide variety of human behavior.

Social psychology

Social psychology studies the ways in which people interact as well as why and how they decide who to interact with. The ways people react with each other are defined in several ways, including:

- Social perception—how we perceive others and their behavior as we make judgments based on our own experiences and prejudices.
- Personal relationships—close relationships developed among people for various reasons, including the desire to reproduce and form a family unit.
- Group behavior—people gather into groups with similar beliefs, needs, or other characteristics. Sometimes group behavior differs greatly from behavior that would be practiced by individuals alone.
- Attitudes—individual attitudes toward others develop over time based on individual history, experience, knowledge, and other factors. Attitudes can change over time, but some are deeply ingrained and can lead to prejudice.

Practice Test

Multiple Choice Questions

1. How did Plato's Theory of Forms most influence Christianity?
   A. It held that what is most real and most good is outside the physical realm.
   B. The theory described a cosmic conflict between ideal forms of good and evil.
   C. It held that the form of the good formed a trinity with ideal forms of knowledge and reason.
   D. The theory described Socratic reasoning as a means of redemption from sin.

2. How did Egypt's geographical features most contribute to the stability of ancient Egyptian culture?
   A. The Nile River regularly and predictably flooded, irrigating crops.
   B. The expanse of the Nile River prevented Egyptians from settling elsewhere.
   C. The Valley of the Kings divided Upper Egypt from Lower Egypt.
   D. The Mediterranean Sea enabled contact between Egyptians and other ancient peoples.

3. How does the prevalence of ziggurats in ancient Mesopotamia illustrate a central factor of Mesopotamian culture?
   A. Intended as lookouts, the number of ziggurats illustrates a Mesopotamian concern for security from invaders.
   B. Used for stargazing, the number of ziggurats shows how Mesopotamian culture depended on astrology.
   C. Dedicated to Mesopotamian rulers, the ziggurats illustrate the complete control Mesopotamian kings held over their subjects.
   D. Structures dedicated to gods, the ziggurats illustrate the importance of religion in Mesopotamian culture.

4. Which of the following played the most influential role in the Spanish defeat of the Incas in the 16th century?
   A. The scarcity of roads in the Incan Empire prevented the Incas from easily defending their cities.
   B. Francisco Pizarro's forces outnumbered the Incan warriors.
   C. The centralized power structure of the Incan Empire left the Incas vulnerable after Atahualpa was captured.
   D. New diseases introduced by the Spanish decimated the Incan army.

5. How did Charlemagne's coronation as Holy Roman Emperor influence European politics?
   A. It united much of Western Europe under a single ruler.
   B. It strengthened papal authority regarding the right of political leaders to rule.
   C. It made Catholicism the official religion throughout Charlemagne's empire.
   D. It led to Charlemagne's renunciation of conquest by force.

6. In about 1428, the Mesoamerican city-states Tenochtitlan, Texcoco, and Tlacopan formed a Triple Alliance. How did this influence Aztec history?
   A. Texcoco and Tlacopan secretly conspired against Tenochtitlan, using the Alliance as a front.
   B. Disagreements about strategy between the city-states weakened Aztec resistance to Spanish invaders.
   C. The alliance agreed that each city-state would offer a specific number of human sacrifices each year.
   D. The allied city-states joined forces to conquer other city-states, incorporating them into an Aztec Empire.

7. Which statement best describes the feudal society of Western Europe in the Middle Ages?
   A. Religious institutions owned most of the land and leased portions to vassals.
   B. Rulers granted land strictly on the basis of blood relationships.
   C. Rulers granted vassals land in exchange for military and political service.
   D. Feudalism shifted a spice-based economy to a land-based economy.

8. Which statement best describes the role of the Catholic Church in medieval Western Europe?
   A. Powerful and wealthy, the Church was important to both poor and rich people.
   B. The Church concerned itself mainly with the poorer members of medieval society.
   C. Weakened by infighting about Church doctrine, the Church struggled to wield power.
   D. The Catholic Church served as a neutral force between competing political leaders.

9. What effect did the Crusades have on Europe's Jewish population?
   A. Entire European Jewish communities were killed during the First Crusade.
   B. Persecution of Jewish people declined as the Crusaders focused on Muslims.
   C. Most Jewish traders and merchants profited through Crusades-related business.
   D. To avoid persecution, some Jewish-only battalions fought in each Crusade.

10. During the 15th century, Johann Gutenberg invented a printing press with moveable type. How did his invention influence science?
   A. It did not influence science; the printing of Gutenberg Bibles directed public attention away from science and toward reforming the Catholic Church.
   B. It led to scientific advances throughout Europe by spreading scientific knowledge.
   C. It influenced scientific advancement in Germany only, where Gutenberg's press was based.
   D. It did not influence science; though texts with scientific knowledge were printed, distribution of these texts was limited.

11. In the 16th century, Akbar ruled the Mughal Empire, which covered much of present-day India. Which statement best describes one means by which Akbar maintained control of the Empire?

A. He paid administrative officials with land instead of money.
B. He accommodated the religious practices of Hindus as well as Muslims.
C. He refused to allow certain defeated rulers to keep their land.
D. He refused to allow the construction of Hindu temples.

12. Which statement best describes how Martin Luther's religious Reformation influenced Western civilization?

A. It contributed to the decline of women's and girls' education.
B. It weakened civil authorities in European towns.
C. It contributed to the rise of individualism.
D. It delayed reform within the Catholic Church itself.

13. Which statement best describes the role played by the French economy in causing the 1789 French Revolution?

A. France's very large national debt led to heavy tax burdens on the French peasantry.
B. Nearly sixty percent of annual national expenditures financed luxuries for the French nobility.
C. Reforms in the guild system allowed many peasants to rise to the middle class.
D. The king's attempt to curtail free trade led skilled journeymen to rebel against the monarchy.

14. Which statement best describes the role of natural selection in Charles Darwin's theory of evolution?

A. Natural selection describes the diversity of environmental pressures.
B. Natural selection is the process by which individual organisms adapt.
C. Natural selection explains how organisms inherit acquired characteristics.
D. Natural selection is the mechanism by which species are said to evolve.

15. How did Russia's participation in World War I influence the Russian Revolution?

A. Civilian suffering and military setbacks served as a catalyst for revolutionary forces.
B. Nicholas III capitalized on battlefield successes to temporarily silence critics.
C. The government eased laws banning collective action by factory workers to appease social discontent about the war.
D. Anti-government protesters temporarily ceased protesting to show patriotism in a difficult war.

16. How did World War II influence American society?

A. Consumption decreased in postwar American society.
B. Thousands of people moved to find work in war-related factories.
C. Racially integrated army units helped desegregate American society.
D. Japanese-Americans were banned from serving in the U.S. military.

17. How did the Truman Doctrine shape U.S. foreign policy after World War II?
   A. It influenced President Truman's decision to create commissions on civil rights.
   B. It shaped the U.S. role in rebuilding the economies of postwar Europe.
   C. It led the U.S. government to refrain from interfering with the U.S. economy.
   D. It led to U.S. military involvement in countries such as Korea.

18. The United States fought North Vietnam in the 1960s and 1970s primarily to:
   A. spread democracy modeled on the U.S. system.
   B. demonstrate U.S. power to the Soviet Union.
   C. protect U.S. trade interests in Southeast Asia.
   D. prevent the spread of communism.

19. Which statement best describes the significance of the Mayflower Compact on colonial America?
   A. It declared that the colonists were independent from King James.
   B. It served as a blueprint for the later Bill of Rights.
   C. It provided the Pilgrims the first written basis for laws in the New World.
   D. It established Puritanism as the official religion for Puritan colonies.

20. European colonization of present-day Pennsylvania in the late 17th century is most closely associated with:
   A. the desire for freedom of the press.
   B. escape from high taxes.
   C. the desire for religious freedom.
   D. escape from trade restrictions.

21. Which statement best describes the significance of the Peter Zenger trial in colonial America?
   A. It was the earliest American case on the right to bear arms.
   B. It established a precedent for freedom of the press.
   C. It was the earliest American case on right of peaceable assembly.
   D. It established a precedent for freedom of religion.

22. Which of the following is a significant structural similarity between the government of the Iroquois Confederacy and the government of the United States?
   A. Many decisions require compromise between two separate entities. In the Iroquois Confederacy, those entities were two different sets of Lords; in the U.S. government, those entities are the House of Representatives and the Senate.
   B. A single leader has significant executive powers: in the Iroquois Confederacy, a chief, and in the U.S. government, the president.
   C. The level of representation in at least one legislative body depended on population. In the Iroquois Confederacy, the population of tribes partially determined representation, and in the United States, the population of states partially determines representation.
   D. A third judicial branch served as a check on the executive power in both the Iroquois Confederacy and the U.S. government.

23. Some American colonists reacted angrily to Great Britain's Navigation Acts in the seventeenth and eighteenth centuries primarily because
A. the Acts restricted manufacturing in the colonies.
B. the Acts forced the colonists to buy sugar from the French West Indies.
C. the Acts gave the British a monopoly on tobacco.
D. the Acts placed high taxes on the cost of shipping goods to Britain.

24. One of the earliest political parties in the United States was the Federalist Party. Its decline is best explained by:
A. a failure to organize state political parties.
B. the enmity of wealthy Americans.
C. its opposition to the War of 1812.
D. its advocacy of a strong central government.

25. In 1777, the United States Congress adopted the Articles of Confederation. The Articles of Confederation limited the power of the federal government by denying it:
A. the power to borrow money.
B. the power to declare war.
C. the power to make international treaties.
D. the power to raise taxes.

26. The French and Indian War ended in 1763. Which subsequent British policy regarding the American colonies was most important to the American Revolution?
A. Increasingly limited oversight of the colonies in order to focus on Canadian territories
B. A determination that the colonies should help pay for the War
C. The Proclamation of 1763 limiting the location of new American colonies
D. Increasing the colonies' dependence on the British military

27. Which of the following is the most significant justification for United States expansion as advocated by the Manifest Destiny?
A. It was the duty of the United States to spread democracy.
B. The United States would spread material wealth.
C. It was the duty of the United States to prevent the spread of slavery.
D. The United States would spread religious freedom.

28. The Treaty of Guadalupe Hidalgo ended the war between the United States and Mexico. The treaty ceded which of the following present-day states to the U. S.?
A. Texas, California, New Mexico, and parts of Utah
B. Texas California, New Mexico, and parts of Colorado and Nevada
C. Texas, California, New Mexico, Arizona, and parts of Colorado, Nevada, and Utah
D. Texas, California, New Mexico, and Arizona

29. Which statement best describes the significance of the Battle of Chapultepec during the U.S.-Mexican War?

A. General Zachary Taylor's performance gained him recognition as an American hero.
B. It was the first Mexican victory after a long string of Mexican defeats.
C. General Santa Ana narrowly escaped capture during the battle.
D. It was the last major U.S. assault prior to capturing Mexico City.

30. During the Civil War, General William T. Sherman led Union troops in a march from Atlanta to Savannah. Which is the best description of the goal of this March to the Sea?

A. Preventing Confederate access to Savannah
B. Distracting Robert E. Lee's troops from their engagement in Maryland
C. Breaking the will to fight among Southern civilians as well as soldiers
D. Freeing slaves who might otherwise contribute to the Confederate cause

31. After the Civil War, President Andrew Johnson disagreed with Congress over Reconstruction policies. Which action by President Johnson best describes the grounds for which he was impeached?

A. He dismissed a Cabinet member without congressional permission.
B. He refused to enforce the Fourteenth Amendment.
C. He sought to disenfranchise former Confederate officers.
D. He violated Constitution law in forming a third political party.

32. Which statement best describes how the Spanish-American War in 1898 shaped the international standing of the United States?

A. The United States gained new international respect through the strategic brilliance and efficiency of the U.S. Army.
B. The U.S. weakened its moral authority by being the first nation in the conflict to declare war.
C. The sinking of the U.S. Battleship Maine cast international doubts on the power of the U.S. Navy.
D. The United States gained new international power by acquiring Guam, Puerto Rico, and the Philippines.

33. United States Secretary of State Henry Kissinger most influenced the course of the Cold War by:

A. helping to slow the United States-Soviet Union arms race.
B. helping to establish a cease-fire in the Arab-Israeli War in 1973.
C. leaving the Soviet Union out of U.S. efforts to end the Vietnam War.
D. ordering a bombing campaign in Laos and Cambodia.

34. During the Cuban Missile Crisis, what did Soviet President Nikita Khrushchev demand in exchange for the removal of Soviet missile launching sites from Cuba?
A. A guarantee that the United States would not invade Cuba
B. The removal of U.S. missile launching sites from an island off the Soviet coast
C. An apology for the U.S. naval blockade that prevented Soviet access to Cuba
D. Negotiations regarding the production of nuclear weapons

35. How did isolationism most influence American society in the decade following World War I?
A. It shaped a temporarily strong economy as the U.S. avoided the troubled economies of postwar Europe.
B. It led to a system of admitting immigrants according to quotas based on their national origins.
C. It guided the U.S. government's decision to strengthen its navy as a safeguard against foreign attacks.
D. It influenced the collapse of trade deals, allowing U.S. companies access to oil in Colombia and in Middle Eastern countries.

36. The "sit-ins" of the civil rights movement during the 1960s were most important to which subsequent reform?
A. Integration of the United States armed forces
B. Banning of literacy tests as a requirement for voter registration
C. Integration of lunch counters, theaters, and other businesses
D. The Supreme Court decision outlawing "separate but equal" schools

37. Under President Franklin Roosevelt, New Deal legislation sought to restore faith in the banking system by:
A. creating a Public Works Administration to oversee banking institutions.
B. requiring banks to loan money at certain interest rates.
C. shifting ownership of prominent banks to the federal government.
D. establishing a corporation to insure bank deposits.

38. Martin Luther King, Jr. and Malcolm X were both important figures in the American civil rights movement. Which of the following statements best describes a difference between their respective approaches to civil rights?
A. Martin Luther King, Jr. advocated nonviolence; Malcolm X advocated self-defense against white aggression.
B. Martin Luther King, Jr. mobilized ordinary citizens; Malcolm X focused on working with local white political leaders.
C. Martin Luther King, Jr. related Christianity to civil rights; Malcolm X did not link religion to civil rights.
D. Martin Luther King, Jr. promoted Black Nationalism; Malcolm X did not.

39. The Populist Party most contributed to the prominence of which issue in the United States in the late 19th and early 20th centuries?
A. The rising cost of farm crops
B. The justification for the Electoral College
C. The basis for U.S. currency
D. The rights of organized labor

40. Which statement best describes how the 1944 passage of the G.I. Bill most influenced U.S. society?
A. It dramatically increased retention in the U.S. military.
B. It offered limited free housing for veterans.
C. It helped create a new middle class in U.S. society.
D. It transformed the work force by privileging veterans.

41. Water is continuously recycled in the hydrosphere. By which process does water return to the atmosphere after precipitation?
A. Percolation
B. Cohesion
C. Evaporation
D. Condensation

42. When the Northern Hemisphere of the Earth experiences summer, the Southern Hemisphere experiences winter. This is best explained by:
A. the changing distance of the Earth from the sun.
B. the angle of the Earth as it revolves around the sun.
C. the changing speed of the Earth's orbit.
D. the shape of the Earth relative to the sun.

43. The year-round warmth of tropical rainforests is best explained by:
A. their proximity to warm ocean currents.
B. the forest canopy's ability to trap heat.
C. the high humidity caused by frequent rainfall.
D. regular, intense solar energy.

44. In which environment would you most likely find animals that estivate, or sleep during the day?
A. Desert
B. Temperate forest
C. Tundra
D. Grasslands

45. Mecca is an important site for Muslims primarily because:
A. it is the birthplace of the prophet Muhammad.
B. according to the Koran, the Second Coming will occur in Mecca.
C. Muhammad fled to Mecca from Medina in 622 A.D,
D. it is home of the Ka'ba, a holy structure said to be built by Abraham.

46. What is the Noble Eightfold Path in Buddhism?
A. Samsara, the cycle of birth, death, and rebirth
B. Moral life as a means to end suffering
C. The Buddhist precepts of ethical conduct
D. The realization that self is an illusion

47. Which of the following statements best describes how Cubism reflected a changing world in the early 20th century?
A. It depicted subjects from multiple perspectives.
B. It portrayed the human body as sacrosanct.
C. It eschewed rationality in favor of emotion.
D. It used unusually vivid colors and color schemes.

48. Which of the following Roman numerals indicates the Colorado River in the figure below?
A. I
B. II
C. III
D. IV

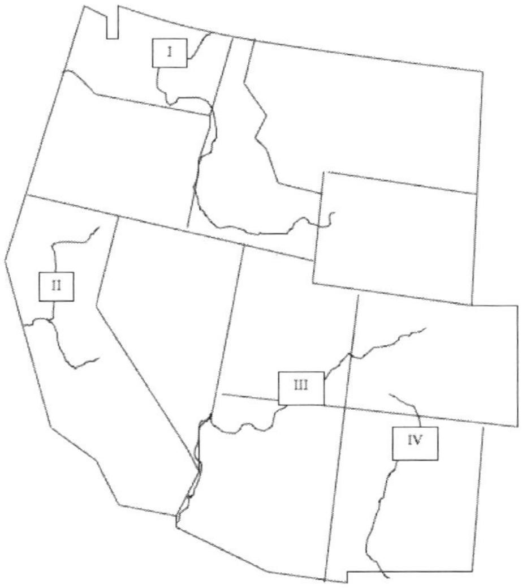

49. Which of the following statements best describes one effect of opening the Suez Canal?
A. It led to further European involvement and colonization of Asia.
B. It provided a trade route between the Mediterranean and Black Seas.
C. It led to more peaceful relations in the Middle East.
D. It served as a strategic route for military forces.

50. Which factor of the Neolithic Revolution most directly contributed to the practice of trade?
A. More freedom for people to choose where they lived
B. The rise of new religious practices
C. The ability of communities to stockpile surplus food
D. New advances in tools

51. Which of the following resources in the West Bank is the most significant motivation for Israel's continuing occupation of that territory?
A. The Mediterranean Sea
B. Oil reserves
C. Olive groves
D. Aquifers

52. World population growth has most significantly impacted which of the following aspects of Earth's physical environment?
A. Deforestation
B. Increased biodiversity
C. Shrinking ocean "dead zones"
D. Mass extinction events

53. Which is the best description for how cognitive psychologists seek to uncover and explain individual differences between humans?
A. By studying how society influences a person's beliefs
B. By studying the ways in which people know and think
C. By studying how people struggle with emotional conflicts
D. By studying human biology as it relates to behavior

54. The difficulty of discerning color in one's peripheral vision is best explained by:
A. the rods' slowness to react.
B. the cones' slowness to react.
C. the convergence of rods in the fovea.
D. the convergence of cones in the fovea.

55. A founder of modern psychology, Wilhelm Wundt studied the components of experience. Many philosophers had also done so. Which statement best describes why Wundt's studies helped found the specific study of psychology?

A. He collected data in an attempt to test his views.
B. He sought to explain experience in terms of publicly-observable behavior.
C. His written works outlined a single sophisticated theory of experience.
D. He pioneered modern psychology's method of introspection.

56. Consider the graphic below. Which sociological concept does the graphic best illustrate?

A. Assimilation
B. Stratification
C. Diffusion
D. Socialization

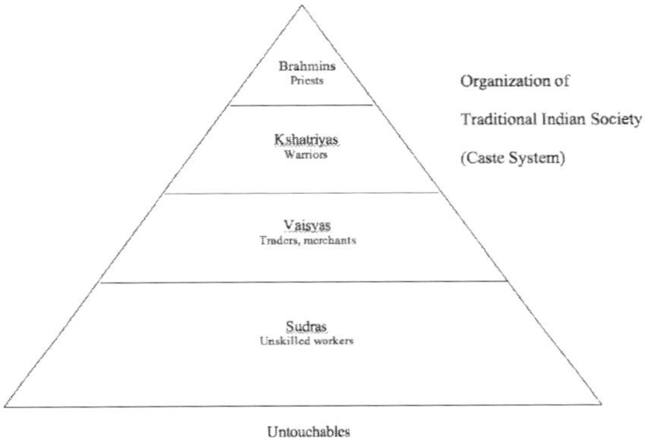

57. In 1973, the U.S. Congress passed the War Powers Act. How did the Act reassert congressional authority relative to that of the President?

A. It mandated congressional approval for funding war-related expenses.
B. It required the President to submit regular reports to Congress regarding conflicts lasting more than 60 days.
C. It restricted the power of the President to suspend key elements of the Constitution.
D. It limited the length of time the President could dispatch combat troops without congressional approval.

58. The Seventeenth Amendment to the U.S. Constitution made the U.S. government more democratic by:

A. requiring state governors to be selected by popular election rather than by state electoral colleges.
B. mandating a regular national census to reevaluate state representation in the House of Representatives.
C. requiring U.S. senators to be selected by popular election rather than by state legislatures.
D. mandating regular state censuses to determine appropriate representation in state Houses of Representatives.

59. Which statement best describes how the 1896 U.S. Supreme Court decision in Plessy v. Ferguson most influenced U.S. society?
A. It reinforced the rights of individual states.
B. It legalized poll taxes and similar measures.
C. It provided a legal basis for racial segregation.
D. It determined the legality of railway strikes.

60. The U.S. government is best understood as a federalist government because:
A. the legislative branch consists of two representative bodies.
B. it is a representative democracy rather than a direct democracy.
C. political power is divided between the federal government and the states.
D. a national Constitution shapes national legislation.

61. Which line of the chart below best lists the kinds of cases over which the U.S. federal court system has jurisdiction?
A. Line 1
B. Line 2
C. Line 3
D. Line 4

Jurisdiction of the Federal Court System

Line 1	Constitutional law	Bankruptcy	Most contract cases
Line 2	Constitutional law	Most contract cases	Most criminal cases
Line 3	Constitutional law	Bankruptcy	Disputes between states
Line 4	Constitutional law	Most personal injury cases	Disputes between states

62. Civic responsibility differs from personal responsibility in that the subject matter of civic responsibility is mainly:
A. fair reporting of government actions.
B. fair dealings between governments.
C. a person's responsibilities as a citizen.
D. a person's responsibilities as a government worker.

63. The concept of due process in the Fifth Amendment to the U.S. Constitution protects individuals by:
A. guaranteeing a citizen's right to a trial by jury within a reasonable timeframe.
B. restricting the government's ability to remove basic rights without following the law.
C. guaranteeing a citizen's right to equal protection under the law.
D. restricting the government's ability to remove basic rights without dire cause.

64. Elizabeth Cady Stanton most influenced the beginning of the women's suffrage movement in the United States by:

A. speaking at the World's Anti-Slavery Confederation in 1840.
B. serving as president of National American Woman Suffrage Association.
C. helping to organize the first women's right convention in the United States.
D. campaigning for both women's suffrage and African-American males' right to vote.

65. In the United States, the Electoral College elects the President and Vice President. The number of Electoral College members allowed to each state is equal to:

A. the state's number of U.S. Representatives plus counties.
B. the state's number of U.S. Senators plus Representatives.
C. the state's number of U.S. Representatives plus state Secretaries.
D. the state's number of U.S. Senators plus counties.

66. The link between female activists and the temperance movement in the 19th century is best explained by concerns regarding the relationship between alcohol and:

A. racial violence.
B. lost productivity.
C. domestic violence.
D. infertility.

67. According to John Locke's social contract theory, a central reason human beings enter social contracts is:

A. to delegate the right to punish to certain individuals.
B. because social contracts provide the basis for moral behavior.
C. to establish natural rights for citizens.
D. because the state of nature is nasty, brutish, and short.

68. Which statement best describes the significance of Hammurabi's Code?

A. It restructured Babylonian society.
B. It helped establish a precedent for codifying law.
C. It established the same penalties for all law-breakers.
D. It instituted penalties mainly in terms of fines.

69. How does the executive branch of a parliamentary democracy differ from that in the United States' form of government?

A. It appoints the legislative branch.
B. It is a committee of the judicial branch.
C. It is appointed by the judicial branch.
D. It is a committee of the legislative branch.

70. A historical antecedent of democracy is the government of ancient Athens. Which statement best describes a central feature of Athenian democracy?

A. Athenians practiced direct democracy, not representative democracy.
B. The right to vote depended on the wealth of a person's family.
C. Campaigns for political office traditionally involved religious leaders.
D. The right to vote could not be stripped from a citizen.

71. Which statement best describes the difference between a monopoly and an oligopoly?

A. A monopoly involves a single supplier of a good or service; an oligopoly involves a small number of suppliers of a good or service.
B. An oligopoly is a monopoly operating under price ceilings.
C. In a monopoly, one company owns a single plant that produces a given good; in an oligopoly, one company owns several plants that produce a given good.
D. An oligopoly is a legalized monopoly.

72. Which combination of factors is most likely to cause inflation?

A. High unemployment and reduced production
B. Credit restrictions and reduced production
C. An oversupply of currency and a relatively low number of available goods
D. An undersupply of currency and a relatively low number of available goods

73. The economic theories of John Maynard Keynes are most closely associated with:

A. the view that deficit spending leads to inflation.
B. advocating government action against monopolies.
C. the view that supply creates its own demand.
D. advocating government action to stimulate economic growth.

74. An action's opportunity cost is best explained in terms of:

A. the minimum amount a business must borrow for the action.
B. the opportunities given up in order to pursue that action.
C. the percentage of one's overall budget that the action requires.
D. the cost of a long-term action adjusted for inflation.

75. Which of the following is the most frequently used tool of the Federal Reserve to control monetary policy?

A. Changing the interest rate at which banks can borrow from the Federal Reserve
B. Buying and selling stock options to raise or reduce interest rates
C. Adjusting the percentage of deposits a bank is required to keep on hand
D. Buying and selling government bonds to raise or reduce interest rates

76. In 1890, the U.S. government passed the Sherman Antitrust Act. The Act has been most influential in restricting anticompetitive practices by:

A. outlawing acts that restrained interstate trade.
B. its use in dissolving the Standard Oil trust.
C. outlawing acts that restrained intrastate trade.
D. by its use in dissolving the AT&T monopoly.

77. A business can be a corporation, partnership, or sole proprietorship. For a business owner, what is one advantage of a running a corporation instead of a sole proprietorship?

A. Corporations offer limited liability protection.
B. Corporations avoid the "double tax" problem.
C. Corporations are more expensive to form.
D. Corporations are easier to dissolve.

78. The U.S. government seeks to reduce unemployment in part to prevent individuals from suffering hardship. How is unemployment also most likely to affect the economy?

A. By causing inflation
B. By leading to lost productivity
C. By increasing aggregate demand
D. By increasing aggregate supply

79. In his 1905 special theory of relativity, Albert Einstein postulated which of the following?

A. A unified field theory
B. A mathematical definition of gravity
C. The relativity of the speed of light
D. That there is no absolute simultaneity

80. How did Eli Whitney's invention of the cotton gin in 1973 most influence the U.S. economy?

A. It elevated cotton as a basis of the Southern economy.
B. It led to many smaller cotton plantations.
C. It reduced the U.S. need to import cotton.
D. It decreased the dependence of plantations on slave labor.

81. Arabic mathematics most contributed to the development of mathematics in the Western world by:

A. founding the mathematics of calculus.
B. using negative numbers in mathematical equations.
C. founding the mathematics of probability.
D. making important advances in algebra.

82. Which is the best description of how Jonas Salk's 1955 development of the polio vaccine most affected American society?

A. The invention drastically reduced the incidence of polio in the United States.
B. The vaccine caused polio in some people who received the vaccine.
C. The announcement of the vaccine sparked a debate regarding the media and science.
D. The vaccine ignited a vigorous search for a cancer vaccine.

83. In social sciences, reification is best understood as:

A. using qualitative data instead of quantitative data.
B. treating an abstraction as a concrete thing.
C. the use of heuristic devices.
D. mistaking subjectivity for objectivity.

84. Suppose that every time a cat hears a can opener, it is fed. The cat runs to the kitchen to be fed every time it hears a can opener. In psychology, this kind of association is called:

A. Operant conditioning
B. Habituation
C. Classical conditioning
D. Conformity

85. Which of the following best describes a main difference between anthropology and psychology?

A. Anthropology involves natural science; psychology does not.
B. Anthropology focuses on humans as a species; psychology focuses more on humans as individuals.
C. Anthropology uses primarily quantitative research methods; psychology does not.
D. Anthropology focuses only on the physical evolution of the human species; psychology focuses on human behavior.

86. Social studies education has many practical applications. Which of the following is the most direct application of teaching high school seniors the structure of the U.S. government?

A. Knowledge of the fundamentals of federalism
B. Informed participation in school elections
C. Knowledge of a system of checks and balances
D. Informed participation in U.S. political processes

87. What is one reason for using a secondary source over a primary source?

A. To understand an event through a first-hand account
B. Primary sources are text-only
C. To understand an event through accounts after the fact
D. Primary sources are only visual

88. Consider the map below. Shaded areas indicate water use, with darker areas indicating heavier use. On the basis of the map, which of the following is the best inference regarding the areas where there is no shading?

A. They are less inhabited.
B. They are more desert-like.
C. Residents are better at conservation.
D. Residents require less water per capita.

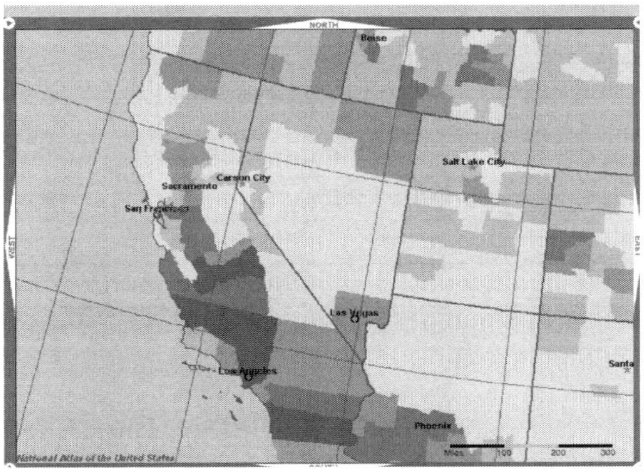

Map source: http://www.nationalatlas.gov/natlas/Natlasstart.asp

89. Consider the graph below. Which of the following is true?

A. The price has decreased with a shift in supply.
B. The equilibrium point has remained constant.
C. The price has risen with a shift in demand.
D. There a double coincidence of wants.

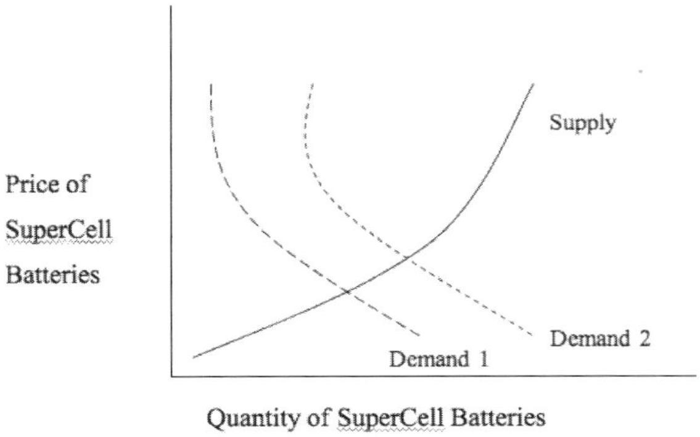

Questions 90 and 91 refer to the following passage:
I was very young, but I remember sitting in our living room watching the television the day of the first moon landing, in 1969. It was a black and white television—my family didn't have a color one till later—and we all gathered in the room and watched the pictures. I'm not sure how they got the pictures to us, but I think it involved satellites around the earth they'd made especially for that purpose. The satellites captured the pictures and somehow beamed them into our televisions, live. That just showed again how our technology, American technology, had become much more advanced than Russian technology. The moon was pocked and pitted, like a big pumice stone. Watching Neil Armstrong walk on the moon was like nothing I'd ever imagined, and because of that somehow it was less surprising; I'd never thought it was impossible. Afterwards I went outside with my parents and my brother and we just kind of stared at the moon and imagined that people were on it, all those miles away.

90. For which of the following lesson units would this primary source be most appropriate?
   A. Having students learn what it was like to witness the first moon landing
   B. Teaching students about the surface of the moon
   C. Teaching about the technology used to show the moon landing live on television
   D. Having students learn about changes in television use

91. Which of the following claims by the author is the claim most likely to be influenced by bias?
   A. The first moon landing occurred in 1969.
   B. The author's family watched the moon landing on a black and white TV.
   C. Satellites captured the live images from the moon landing.
   D. American technology was much more advanced than Russian technology.

92. A typical case study in the field of social studies primarily involves:
   A. gathering qualitative data.
   B. gathering quantitative data.
   C. statistical analysis.
   D. no researcher/subject contact.

Questions 93 and 94 refer to the following passage:

The U.S. decision to drop the atomic bomb on Japan during World War II is a complex one that has received little examination by most ordinary American citizens. Many citizens are under the impression that the decision to use the bomb on Japan was primarily based on a desire to prevent a bloody and prolonged war on Japanese soil, with the view that the use of the bomb thus saved many more American lives – perhaps many more American and Japanese lives – that would otherwise have been lost.

Much less considered, however, is the fact that prior to the bombing of Hiroshima and Nagasaki, the United States government believed not only that Japan was losing the war, but that Japan was considering how best to surrender. Note: Japan was considering not whether to surrender, but under what conditions Japan could surrender. Viewed in this light, the U.S. decision to drop the bomb seems to have rather less to do with bringing a swift end to World War II than with the looming Cold War: in dropping the bomb, the United States demonstrated its power to the Soviet Union and its willingness to use that power. This casts a rather different perspective on the bombing, a perspective we would do well to consider in this age of terrorist threats and weapons of mass destruction. Under what circumstances is the use of such deadly weapons on civilians justified?

93. Which of the following best describes the main idea of the passage?
   A. We should think carefully about what actually justifies the use of deadly weapons.
   B. The use of weapons of mass destruction on civilians is not justified.
   C. Many Americans are mistaken about why the United States uses deadly weapons.
   D. The United States used the atomic bomb on an enemy that was already defeated.

94. Which of the following is the best conclusion regarding the author's views about history?
   A. Popular culture ignores the views of historians.
   B. Cold War history matters more than World War II history.
   C. History is relevant to contemporary issues.
   D. Victors write history to make themselves look better.

Questions 95 and 96 refer to the following graph:

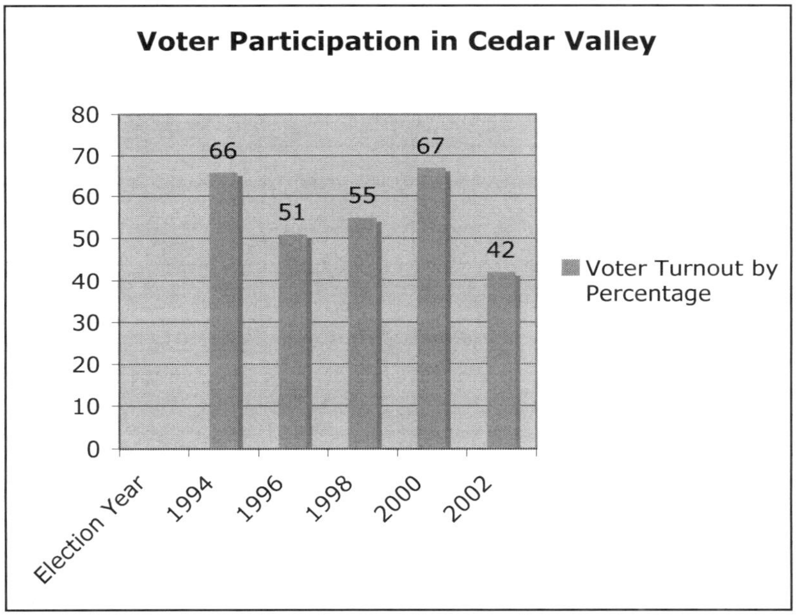

95. Applying generally-accepted principles of statistical analysis, what is the range of data for voter participation?
   A. 55
   B. 0-80
   C. 25
   D. 42-67

96. What is the median for voter participation?
A. 56.2%
B. 55%
C. 50%
D. 40%

97. Suppose you are teaching a unit on different forms of government. Which of the following is the best way to teach students to write critically in relation to this topic?
A. Ask the students to write an essay regarding why one form of government is better than another.
B. Have the students give organized, written descriptions of the different characteristics of each form of government.
C. Ask the students to write a creative work from the point of view of someone living under one of the forms of government.
D. Have the students write a report on a country that uses a specific form of government.

98. Which of the following is the most effective use of technology for showing a class of students the relationship between supply and demand?
A. Asking the students to maintain a class wiki listing those and other key economic terms
B. Having students look up definitions of "supply" and "demand" in an online dictionary
C. Using presentation software to show students different supply and demand curves
D. Using spreadsheet software to track the rise and fall of demand of a given product

99. High school students are expected to learn U.S. history from which of the following periods?
A. From the Civil War to the present
B. From Reconstruction to the present
C. From World War I to the present
D. From the Great Depression to the present

100. Which of the following assignments is the best means of assessing a student's ability to apply knowledge of the concepts of supply and demand?
A. Write detailed definitions of "supply" and "demand."
B. Write a detailed interpretation of a supply and demand curve.
C. Write a report on the history of a recession.
D. Write a compare/contrast essay on free-market systems versus others.

Answer Key

Number	Answer	Number	Answer	Number	Answer	Number	Answer
1	A	30	C	60	C	90	A
2	A	31	A	61	C	91	D
3	D	32	D	62	C	92	A
4	C	33	A	63	B	93	A
5	B	34	A	64	C	94	C
6	D	35	B	65	B	95	C
7	C	36	C	66	C	96	B
8	A	37	D	67	A	97	A
9	A	38	A	68	B	98	C
10	B	39	C	69	D	99	B
11	B	40	C	70	A	100	B
12	C	41	C	71	A		
13	A	42	B	72	C		
14	D	43	D	73	D		
15	A	44	A	74	B		
16	B	45	D	75	D		
17	D	46	B	76	A		
18	D	47	A	77	A		
19	C	48	C	78	B		
20	C	49	A	79	D		
21	B	50	C	80	A		
22	A	51	D	81	D		
23	A	52	A	82	A		
24	C	53	B	83	B		
25	D	54	D	84	C		
26	B	55	A	85	B		
27	A	56	B	86	D		
28	C	57	D	87	C		
29	D	58	C	88	A		
30	C	59	C	89	C		

Answer Explanations

1. A: According to Plato's Theory of Forms, nonphysical ideal forms are most good and real. The form of the Good has the highest degree of reality and goodness. Answer B can be rejected because Plato did not believe there was an ideal form of evil. Answer C can be rejected because Plato did not believe the Good formed a trinity with other forms. Answer D can be rejected because, though Plato advocated Socratic reasoning as a method for coming to know the forms, he did not believe such reasoning led to redemption from sin as Christian doctrine contemplates this notion.

2. A: The Nile River flooded regularly and reliably, irrigating the crops of the ancient Egyptians. This best explains the stability of Egyptian culture. Answer B can be rejected because though the Nile River is expansive; its size did not prevent the Egyptian people from settling elsewhere. Answer C can be rejected because the Valley of the Kings, an ancient Egyptian city, did not separate Upper and Lower Egypt. Answer D can be rejected because, even if true, interaction with other cultures is more likely to lead to a dynamic, changing culture than a stable, unchanging culture.

3. D: Ziggurats were towers dedicated to gods; their prevalence indicates the importance of religion in Mesopotamian culture. The other options can be rejected because they pair accurate facts about Mesopotamia with inaccurate summaries of the purposes of the ziggurats. For example, while rulers of Mesopotamian cities fought among themselves, ziggurats were not used as lookouts. This eliminates option A. Although astrology was practiced in Mesopotamia, ziggurats did not function as places for stargazing or observing the sky. Finally, Mesopotamian cities were ruled by kings, but the ziggurats were not dedicated to them. This eliminates options B and C.

4. C: Power was centralized in the Incan Empire. When the invading Spaniards imprisoned Incan ruler Atahualpa and killed other Incan military leaders, the Incas were unable to mount an effective military response. Incas of lesser status simply lacked the appropriate authority. Answers A and B may be eliminated because they are factually inaccurate. The Incas had built some functional roads, which allowed the invading to Spanish access some Incan cities. Also, Pizarro's soldiers did not outnumber the Incans. The final answer can be rejected because though the Spanish did introduce new diseases to Native Americans, such was not a significant factor in the defeat of the Incas. The introduction of disease did, however, greatly contribute to the overall European conquest of the Americas.

5. B: Although Charlemagne himself may not have believed his authority was conferred by the Pope, Charlemagne's successors sometimes used the title "Holy Roman Emperor" (given to them by the Pope) as a basis for their authority. Thus, the title "Holy Roman Emperor" strengthened the notion that political authority was conferred by the Pope. Charlemagne united much of Europe under a single ruler prior to being named Holy Roman Emperor. While Catholicism may have been the recognized religion, the naming of Charlemagne as Holy Roman Emperor did not

make it so. After being so named, Charlemagne did not renounce his conquests. This eliminates options A, C, and D respectively.

6. D: The Triple Alliance allowed the city-states to conquer city-states and land by combining forces against mutual enemies. The Triple Alliance and its conquered areas are commonly thought of as the Aztec Empire. While some conquered areas did rebel against the Aztec Empire at the time the Spanish conquistadores arrived, such rebellion did not specifically concern the city-states of the Triple Alliance. Texcoco and Tlacopan did not use the Alliance as a front against Tenochtitlan. The Triple Alliance had nothing to do with the number of annual human sacrifices. This eliminates options A, B, and C.

7. C: Under the Western European feudal system, rulers granted vassals land in exchange for military and political service. Although the right to use land would often pass from father to son, it was not on the basis of blood relations that a ruler granted land to a vassal; this eliminates option B. Religious institutions such as monasteries did indeed own land, but did not own most of it, eliminating option A. Finally, feudalism was a land-based economy that made a shift from a spice-based economy to a gold-based economy. Therefore, option D can be eliminated.

8. A: The Catholic Church was both powerful and wealthy in medieval Europe. It affected the lives of both the rich and poor; for example, wealthy families often donated to monasteries in exchange for prayers on the donors' behalf. This eliminates option B. Because of these donations, some monasteries became quite wealthy. Rather than being a neutral force, the Catholic Church wielded political power. In medieval times, some claimed that rulers derived their authority to rule from the Catholic Church itself. These facts eliminate options C D.

9. A: The Crusades' biggest impact upon Europe's Jewish population was that entire Jewish communities were killed during the First Crusade. This is the only option that accurately describes historical effects of the Crusades on the Jewish population. Rather than diminishing anti-Jewish sentiment, the Crusades seemed to inflame it, eliminating option B. One specific example of Crusades-era anti-Semitism is that many Jewish people were excluded from particular trades, and thus did not profit from the Crusades. This fact eliminates option C. Finally, there were no Jewish-only battalions during the Crusades, eliminating option D.

10. B: Johann Gutenberg's printing press led to increased scientific knowledge and advancement as scientific texts were printed and dispersed throughout Europe. Because the distribution of such texts extended outside of Germany, options C and D may be eliminated. Gutenberg Bibles were printed using Gutenberg's press, and thus Gutenberg's invention was likely a factor in the Reformation of the Catholic Church. In fact, Martin Luther's Ninety-Five Theses (against the Catholic Church) were printed using a printing press. However, this reformation occurred alongside, rather than in place of, the advancement of scientific knowledge. This eliminates option A.

11. B: Akbar allowed the practice of both Hinduism and Islam, despite pressure from Islamic religious leaders to do otherwise. Akbar specifically permitted the construction of Hindu temples, which freed Akbar from Hindu resistance that he might otherwise have faced. This fact

eliminates answer D. Breaking from some past practices, Akbar also used cash instead of land to pay empire officials, allowing him to control more land. Because of this, option A can be rejected. Option C can be rejected because Akbar allowed certain defeated princes to keep their lands.

12. C: With its emphasis on an individual's relationship with God and personal responsibility for salvation, the religious reformation sparked by Martin Luther in 1517 contributed to a rise in individualism. Rather than weakening the civil authorities in Europe, the Reformation served to strengthen many secular authorities by undermining the authority of the Catholic Church. This eliminates answer B. Although the Reformation deemphasized the Virgin Mary, it influenced improvements to education for women and girls, particularly in Germany. This eliminates answer A. Finally, option D can be rejected because the Catholic Church underwent its own internal reformation, in part due to Luther's Reformation.

13. A: In the 1780s, the French national debt was very high. The French nobility adamantly resisted attempts by King Louis XVI to reform tax laws, which led to a high tax burden on the French peasantry. The French government spent almost 50% of its national expenditures on debt-related payments during the 1780s; thus it could not and did not spend almost 60% to finance luxuries for the French nobility. This eliminates choice B. King Louis XVI temporarily banned the guild system to bolster, rather than stifle, free trade. Because this system gave skilled craftsmen economic advantages, journeymen opposed ending the system. This eliminates choice D. Regardless of the status of guilds before the French Revolution, French society did not offer many opportunities for upward social mobility. Few peasants were able to advance. This eliminates choice C.

14. D: In Charles Darwin's theory of evolution, natural selection is the mechanism by which species evolve. Darwin posited that there is a variation of characteristics in individual organisms within a species. Some characteristics better equip individual organisms to survive and reproduce. When these organisms reproduce, their offspring are likely to inherit those advantageous characteristics. Over time, the species itself may evolve based on the widespread inheritance of such characteristics with survival value. Therefore, natural selection is concerned with the evolution of species as a whole, rather than adaptation of individual organisms. This eliminates choice B. While environmental pressures can play a role in natural selection, natural selection does not describe the diversity of such pressures. This eliminates choice A. Answer C can be rejected because Darwin did not believe characteristics acquired during an organism's lifetime were inherited.

15. A: Russian's involvement in World War I brought social tension in Russia to a head. Contributing factors included military defeats and civilian suffering. Prior to Russia entering the war, Russian factory workers could legally strike, but during the war, it was illegal for them to act collectively. This eliminates answer C. Protests continued during World War I, and the Russian government was overthrown in 1917. This eliminates answer D. Answer B can be rejected because World War I did not go well for the Russian Army; Nicholas III, therefore, had no successes upon which to capitalize.

16. B: Many Americans migrated during World War II, seeking work in war-related factories; boomtowns sprang up as a result. Some Japanese-Americans served in the United States military during World War II; in fact, the all-Japanese 442nd Regimental Combat Team, was decorated by the U.S. government for its service. This eliminates choice D. Answer C can be rejected because Caucasian and African-American soldiers served in segregated units. Answer A can be eliminated because consumption actually increased in postwar American society, as production was high and returning U.S. soldiers had income to spend.

17. D: The Truman Doctrine was intended to prevent Greece and Turkey from becoming communist countries. However, its broad language had implications beyond those two nations, suggesting that U.S. policy generally should be to aid people who resisted outside forces attempting to impose communist rule. This doctrine led to U.S. involvement in Korea and Vietnam, where U.S. forces fought against communist forces in those nations. The United States did have a plan for assisting the European economies, but it was the Marshall Plan, not the Truman Doctrine. This eliminates choice B. While President Truman did establish a President's Committee on Civil Rights, it was not as a result of the Truman Doctrine. This eliminates answer A. Finally, when inflation plagued the postwar U.S. economy, the federal government took measures to address inflation and other economic issues, rather than steering clear of them. This eliminates choice C.

18. D: During the Vietnam War, a central aim of the United States was to prevent the spread of communism. At the time of the war, North Vietnamese communist forces threatened South Vietnam, and the United States came to the aid of the South Vietnamese government. The Domino Theory of communism held that one nation's conversion to communism was likely to lead to other nations in that region also converting to communism. The aim of the United States was essentially negative (to stop communism) rather than positive (to implement a specific kind of democracy). This eliminates option A. Option B and C can both be rejected because neither describes the primary aim of U.S. involvement in Vietnam in the 1960s and 1970s. While A, B, and C could have been incidental benefits obtained by fighting North Vietnam, none correctly state the primary goal of the U.S.

19. C: The male passengers of the Mayflower signed the Compact after a disagreement regarding where in the Americas they should establish a colony. The Compact served as a written basis for laws in their subsequent colony. Because the Mayflower Compact did not list particular rights, it is not best understood as a blueprint for the Bill of Rights. This eliminates choice B. Though the Compact did in part serve as a basis for government, it did not declare independence from King James; its last line, for example, specifically refers to King James as the writers' sovereign. This eliminates choice A. Finally, although the Mayflower Compact does include religious language, it is a brief document that does not detail, defend, or establish as official any particular religious doctrine, including Puritan religious doctrine. This eliminates choice D.

20. C: Pennsylvania is most closely associated with William Penn, a Quaker of the Society of Friends. Penn hoped to establish a colony where Quakers would be free to practice their religion. This colony offered religious tolerance toward many other religions as well; Dutch Mennonites and German Baptists were among those who came to Pennsylvania. The desire for freedom of

the press was not a salient concern in the motivation for colonizing Pennsylvania; this eliminates option A. Although some European colonists came to Pennsylvania for economic reasons, these are not best understood in terms of escaping high taxes or trade restrictions. This eliminates options B and D.

21. B: Peter Zenger was an 18th century journalist in New York who was charged with seditious libel after he published articles critical of New York governor William Cosby. His subsequent acquittal in 1735 established a precedent for American freedom of the press. Options A, C, and D can all be rejected because they do not accurately describe the historical significance of Peter Zenger's trial. Although these options name other important freedoms or rights in American history, these rights or freedoms were not central to Peter Zenger's trial. In particular, note that while answers B, C, and D all list rights contained in the First Amendment to the United States Constitution, only B contains the particular right at issue in the Zenger case.

22. A: The Iroquois Confederacy was a confederacy of originally five (and later six) Native American Tribes, founded in 1570. Many decisions involved compromise between two sets of Lords from different tribes, analogous to the compromise involved in decision-making between the U.S. House of Representatives and the U.S. Senate. For the Confederacy to accept a decision, Mohawk and Seneca Lords needed to come to an agreement with Oneida and Cayuga Lords. Option B can be rejected because there is no chief in the Iroquois Confederacy analogous to the U.S. President. Option C can be rejected because the Iroquois Confederacy did not involve representation based upon a tribe's population. Option D can be rejected because there was no judicial branch in the Iroquois Confederacy analogous to that of the U.S. government.

23. A: The Navigation Acts in the seventeenth and eighteenth centuries restricted commercial activity in the American colonies and resulted in the constraint of manufacturing. The Acts were a logical extension of British mercantilism, a view according to which the colonies existed primarily to benefit Great Britain. Answer B can be rejected because one Navigation Act forced the colonists to buy more expensive sugar from the British West Indies, rather than the French West Indies. Option C can be eliminated because a positive result of the Navigation Acts was giving the American colonists a monopoly on tobacco by restricting tobacco production in Great Britain itself. Option D can be eliminated because the Acts did not place a tax on shipping goods to Great Britain.

24. C: The Federalist Party advocated a pro-British foreign policy and therefore opposed the War of 1812. This made the Federalists unpopular with many Americans; this unpopularity deepened when the war ended with American victory. The Federalist Party did advocate a strong central government; however, this position was not a key factor in the Party's decline. This eliminates option D. Option A can be rejected because the Federalist Party did organize state political parties in states such as Connecticut, Delaware, and Maryland. Many members of the Federalist Party were pro-trade and pro-business, as many members were well-to-do businessmen. This eliminates option B.

25. D: After the American Revolution, the framers of the American government were concerned that a strong central government could lead to abuses of power. Accordingly, The Articles of

Confederation did not grant the federal government the ability to raise taxes. Another restriction was the inability to regulate interstate commerce. Options A, B, and C can all be eliminated because, though the federal government was generally weak under the Articles of Confederation, the Articles granted the federal government each of the powers given in those options.

26. B: The cost of the French and Indian War was high, and after the war, Great Britain sought to have the American colonies help pay for the war through measures such as higher taxes. This led to colonial resentment, in part because the colonists lacked representation in the British government. Option A can be rejected because, rather than limiting oversight on the American colonies, Great Britain reasserted its authority there. The Proclamation of 1763, although it did limit the location of new American colonies, was modified in response to colonial demands prior to the American Revolution. This eliminates choice C. Option D can be rejected because the French and Indian War (in which American colonists participated) actually decreased colonial dependence on the British military.

27. A: Central to the Manifest Destiny (the belief that it was the right and duty of the United States to expand its borders) was the belief that the United States had a duty to spread democracy, offering a democratic example to the rest of the world. Option B was much less significant; proponents of the Manifest Destiny were more interested in spreading what they regarded as civilization than in spreading material prosperity in particular. Option C can be rejected because the issue of slavery was controversial; some proponents of the Manifest Destiny were decided supporters of slavery, and others were not. Option D can be rejected because religious freedom was not a central issue for proponents of Manifest Destiny.

28. C: Under the Treaty of Guadalupe Hidalgo, the United States acquired modern-day Texas, California, New Mexico, and Arizona; in addition, the United States also acquired parts of present-day Colorado, Nevada, and Utah. Options A, B, and D can each be rejected because they leave out some part of land acquired by the United States through the treaty. Under the Treaty of Guadalupe Hidalgo, Mexico lost over half of its territory. The United States agreed to pay Mexico $15 million for damaged incurred in Mexico during the U.S.-Mexican War and to respect Mexican land grants; however, when the U.S. Congress ratified the treaty, it deleted the latter provision.

29. D: The Battle of Chapultepec, a citadel outside Mexico City, was the last major U.S. assault prior to the U.S. capture of Mexico City. When the United States won the battle, the Mexican defensive line collapsed, leaving the way open for U.S. troops to march on the Mexican capital. The assault on Chapultepec was organized by U.S. General Winfield Scott; although General Zachary Taylor was considered an American hero due in part to his performance during the U.S.-Mexican War, this was not because of any involvement with the Battle of Chapultepec. This eliminates option A. Because the U.S. won the battle, option B can be rejected. General Santa Ana was not personally involved in the battle, eliminating option C.

30. C: In his March to the Sea, General Sherman sought to make both civilians and soldiers experience the brutal hardships of war in order to weaken their will to fight, thereby undermining the Confederate war effort itself. Sherman accomplished this through burning crops and killing livestock. Option A does not describe a primary goal of the March and can be

rejected on that basis. Although a secondary motivation might have been to distract Lee, at the time of Sherman's march, Lee's troops were engaged with Grant's forces in Virginia, not Maryland. This eliminates option B. Option D can be eliminated because Sherman's primary intention was not to liberate slaves (although slaves were in fact liberated during the march).

31. A: After a series of disagreements over Reconstruction Policy, Congress passed the Tenure of Office Act, according to which the President needed congressional consent to dismiss from office anyone who had been confirmed by the Senate. President Johnson violated the Act by dismissing Secretary of War Edwin Stanton, whom radical Republicans wanted to keep in office. Congress accordingly impeached President Johnson. Regarding option B, Southern states did enact "Black Laws" to prevent African Americans from voting, but President Johnson was not impeached because he allowed such laws (and thus failed to enforce the Fourteenth Amendment). Johnson did seek to disenfranchise former Confederate officers, and he did attempt to form a third political party; but neither of these actions were grounds for his impeachment (with respect to the former action, radical Republicans were in agreement). This eliminates choices C and D respectively.

32. D: As a result of the Spanish-American War, the United States became a more powerful nation. At the war's end, Spain ceded Guam and Puerto Rico to the United States, and the United States purchased the Philippines for $20 million. Answer A can be rejected because, though the United States Navy represented itself very well throughout the war, the United States Army was plagued by inefficiency. Answer B can be rejected because Spain was the first nation in the conflict to issue a formal declaration of war. This is true in spite of the fact that Spain's declaration of war came in part as a response to American actions. Answer C can be rejected because the sinking of the Maine did not cast doubts on the U.S. Navy. Rather, the U.S. Navy defeated Spanish ships rather handily.

33. A: Henry Kissinger, U.S. Secretary of State from 1973-1977 and National Security Adviser from 1969-1965, helped negotiate two agreements related to the arms race between the United States and the Soviet Union. According to one such agreement, SALT I (from the Strategic Arms Limitation Talks), the U.S. and Soviet Union agreed to limit the number of offensive strategic missiles. Kissinger also helped to establish a cease-fire in the Arab-Israeli War in 1973, and he was also involved in a bombing campaign in Laos and Cambodia. However, neither of these events influenced the course of the Cold War to the degree to which the arms agreements did. Answers B and D respectively may thus be eliminated. Answer C can be rejected because Kissinger did attempt to involve the Soviet Union in U.S. efforts to end the Vietnam War.

34. A: In exchange for the removal of Soviet Cuban missile launching sites, which were under construction at the time of the crisis, President Khrushchev sought a pledge from the United States that the United States would not invade Cuba. Khrushchev also demanded that the United States close its missile launching sites located in Turkey, not on an island off the Soviet coast. This eliminates option B. The Soviet Union did not demand either an apology from the United States as a condition for the removal of the launching sites, or negotiations regarding the production of nuclear weapons. This eliminates options C and D.

35. B: After World War I, the United States passed the Immigration Act of 1924, which regulated the number of immigrants in part according to their national origin. The United States sought to avoid the problems of Europe and other nations by limiting the number of foreigners who entered the United States. Option A can be rejected because quite soon after World War I, both inflation and unemployment were significant problems in the United States. Option C can be rejected because in the years immediately following World War I, the United States did not built its navy even to the extent allowed by treaty. Finally, option D can be rejected because after World War I, the United States made arrangements for the U.S. to have access to oil in Colombia and in Middle Eastern countries.

36. C: Sit-ins were peaceful protests during which both African-American and Caucasian participants protested segregated, or "whites-only," businesses by sitting at such establishments and asking to be served. These protests led to the integration of lunch counters and other businesses. In 1954, the Supreme Court ruled in Brown versus the Board of Education that public schools could not be separate and equal; this ruling occurred independently of sit-ins. This eliminates choice D. The sit-ins did not focus on either integration of the armed forces, or on literacy tests as requirements for voter registration. Though reforms regarding these issues were passed, they were not directly a result of sit-ins. This eliminates choices A and B respectively.

37. D: Under the New Deal, the federal government created the Federal Deposit Insurance Corporation to insure bank deposits. Option A can be eliminated because, although the Public Works Administration was a component of the New Deal, it was concerned with providing work to Americans through projects such as the construction of dams and bridges. Answer B can be eliminated because Roosevelt did not require banks to loan money at certain interest rates, and option C can be rejected because Roosevelt did not attempt to shift ownership of prominent banks to the federal government.

38. A: While Martin Luther King is famous for his advocacy of nonviolence, Malcolm X defended self-defense against aggression by white people. In the course of his work, King did indeed mobilize ordinary citizens; however, Malcolm X did not focus on working with local white political leaders, but instead focused on black communities. This eliminates option B. Malcolm X also sometimes spoke against black citizens practicing Christianity, linking the practice of that religion in part to oppression; this eliminates option C. Finally, option D can be rejected because King did not promote Black Nationalism, while Malcolm X did.

39. C: A central plank in the platform of the Populist Party was free coinage of silver, which allowed citizens to exchange their silver at U.S. mints for U.S. currency. This platform was subsequently adopted by the Democratic Party and was a major domestic issue in the 1892 and 1896 presidential elections. The heart of the issue was the standard on which U.S. currency would be based. Option A can be rejected because the Populist Party was formed in part by farmers unhappy about the decreasing cost farm crops; the elevation of these costs contributed to the dissolution of the Populist Party. Options B and D can both be rejected because neither were influential planks in the platform of the Populist Party.

40. C: The 1944 G.I. Bill offered several significant benefits for U.S. U.S. veterans. These included economic assistance for veterans to attend college, mortgage subsidies, and unemployment benefits. Over a million veterans took advantage of the opportunity to attend college, and many homes were built with support provided by the G.I. Bill. This increase in home ownership and the availability of higher education contributed to the creation of a new middle class. The Bill did not offer veterans specific incentives for staying in the military after World War II; this eliminates option A. It did not offer free housing for veterans; this eliminates option B. Finally the Bill did not privilege veterans in the work force; this eliminates option D.

41. C: After precipitation, the heat of the sun causes evaporation, a process by which water molecules change from a liquid to a gas, ultimately returning to the atmosphere. The other options describe processes that pertain to properties of water, but not to water's return to the atmosphere. Percolation is the process by which water moves down through soil. Cohesion (specifically, structural cohesion) is the property of matter by which the molecules in a single substance stay together. Condensation is the process by which matter changes from a gas to a liquid; after evaporation, molecules of water form rain droplets through condensation.

42. B: The Southern Hemisphere of the Earth experiences winter when the Northern Hemisphere experiences summer because of the angle of the Earth. The Earth rotates on its tilted axis as it orbits the sun. At different positions in its orbit, the axis is tilted toward or away from the sun to varying degrees. The sun shines more brightly and directly on one hemisphere than the other, causing the difference in seasons. When a hemisphere is tilted toward the sun, that hemisphere experiences its summer season. Options A, C and D all fail to give a good explanation for the difference. It is neither the changing distance from the sun nor the changing speed of the Earth's orbit that causes the difference in seasons, though these attributes do fluctuate slightly. Also, the shape of the earth does not cause the difference in seasons.

43. D: Because tropical rainforests lie near the equator, they typically receive 12 hours of intense sunlight on a regular basis; as a result, they are typically warm year-round. None of the other options given describe the primary cause of the heat. Although a forest canopy might indeed help trap heat, for example, the canopy itself is not the actual source of the heat itself; this eliminates option B. Similarly, although humidity might make the heat seem more intense (due to chemical properties of water), humidity itself is not the cause of heat. This eliminates choice C. Option A can be rejected because it is the sun, not warm ocean currents, that are the principle cause of warmth in tropical rainforests.

44. A: In desert environments, where little rain falls, some animal species have adapted by estivating during the day, thus allowing the animals to escape the desert's searing daytime heat. The other answers can be eliminated because the associated climates are not nearly as hot, removing the impetus for an animal to avoid the daytime heat. The climate of a tundra, for example, is much cooler, and in that environment it would make much less sense for an animal to avoid daytime heat. This eliminates answer C. Options B and D can be rejected because the climates of the temperate forests and grasslands are not as hot as that of deserts, providing less reason for animals to adapt by estivating.

45. D: The Ka'ba is an ancient structure Muslims consider holy; it was purportedly built by Abraham. The Ka'ba's location in Mecca is the central reason for Mecca's importance to Muslims. Although Muhammad was born in Mecca, that fact is not the primary reason for Mecca's importance in Islam; the location of the Ka'ba is more important. This eliminates option A. Option C can be rejected because Muhammad fled from Mecca to Medina in 622 A.D., not the other way around. Option B can be rejected because Muslims believe the Second Coming will occur in Damascus, not Mecca.

46. B: According to Buddhism, life is full of suffering. However, by following the Noble Eightfold Path, the path of moral living, it is possible to end suffering. Samsara, the cycle of birth, death, and rebirth, is an important concept in Buddhism, but it is not the Noble Eightfold Path; therefore option A can be rejected. Regarding option C, there are Precepts in Buddhism that offer a guide to Buddhist ethical behavior; these are related to the Noble Eightfold Path, but they are not the same; this eliminates option C. Finally, while self is an illusion according to Buddhist doctrine, this view is not the substance of the Noble Eightfold Path. This eliminates option D.

47. A: In a departure from classical painting, Cubists painted their subjects as though from multiple perspectives rather than from a single perspective, as though to reflect the increasingly complex world of the 20th century. This approach to painting included paintings of the human body; the paintings therefore sometimes seemed to distort the human body rather than elevate it or regard it as sacrosanct. This eliminates option B. Cubism favored rationality over emotion in that it involved breaking up subjects along geometric planes; this eliminates option C. Finally, option D can be rejected because Cubist paintings often utilized tame, mild colors, rather than bright, vivid ones.

48. C: Roman numeral III indicates the Colorado River. The Colorado River begins in Colorado and journeys through Arizona, Utah, and Nevada along the border of California, and into Mexico. The Colorado River is a major river; it is responsible for carving out the Grand Canyon, and is important for agricultural use and other uses. Roman numeral I indicates the Snake River. Roman numeral II indicates the Sacramento River. Roman numeral IV indicates the Rio Grande River. Each of these rivers is a major river in the United States, but all are separate bodies of water from the Colorado River.

49. A: Built in the nineteenth century, the Suez Canal provided the shortest water route between Europe and Asia by connecting the Mediterranean Sea with the Gulf of Suez and the Red Sea (not the Black Sea; this eliminates option B). This had the effect of allowing Europeans greater access to Asia, which led to further trade between Europe and Asia, as well as European colonization of Asia. Option C can be rejected because the Suez Canal has been the specific focal point of violence in the Middle East, for example between Egypt and Israel. Option D can be rejected because the main significance of the Suez Canal is that of a trade route rather than a military route.

50. C: Although options A, B, and D all describe important factors in the Neolithic Revolution, option C—the ability of communities to stockpile surplus food—is the factor most directly responsibility for the rise of trade practices. Communities were thus able to trade surplus food for other goods and services, a societal feature not present in hunter-gatherer societies. Option

A, the ability of people to better choose where they lived (because they could carry the portable tools of agriculture with them to make a place habitable) contributed to the spread of agriculture, but less directly to the rise of trade practices. New advances in tools also contributed less directly to the rise of trade, as did the rise of new religious practices. These facts eliminate answers D and B, respectively.

51. D: The West Bank contains a number of significant natural water reserves (aquifers). These aquifers are an important source of water not only to the Palestinians living in the West Bank but to Israel as well. Access to these aquifers is a significant motivation to Israel's continuing control of the West Bank. The West Bank does not border the Mediterranean Sea; this eliminates option A. There are no significant oil reserves in the West Bank; this eliminates option B. Though there are olive groves in the West Bank, olives and olive products are far less important resources to Israel than water.

52. A: World population growth has significantly affected global deforestation, as forests have been cleared for agricultural use, livestock, and timber harvesting. World population growth has not lead to increased biodiversity. Global biodiversity has actually shrunk in response to humanity's exponential population growth; this eliminates option B. Similarly, ocean dead zones – regions featuring low concentrations of oxygen – have grown in the last decades rather than shrunk; this eliminates option C. Finally, although there have been mass extinction events throughout earth history (such as those involving dinosaurs), they are not linked to world population growth; this eliminates option D.

53. B: Cognitive psychologists seek to explain individual differences between humans by studying how people think and come to acquire knowledge. This is the best answer for the question. Regarding option A, although a cognitive psychologist might study how society influences a person's beliefs, this description is too narrow to constitute the best answer. In other words, a cognitive psychologist doesn't just look at the influence of society on an individual's thought processes, but studies those thought processes independent of such influence. This eliminates option A. Option C can be eliminated because it describes the approach of the clinical psychologist (not the cognitive psychologist), and option D can be rejected because it describes a biological approach (not that of the cognitive psychologist).

54. D: Rods and cones are visual receptors located in the eye. Cones allow us to see colors, see in the daylight, and have detailed visual experiences. Rods allow us to see in dim light. The central area of the retina is called the fovea, and it consists of cones. Because there are far fewer cones outside the fovea, it is more difficult to discern color in one's peripheral vision. This explanation eliminates option C, which identifies rods instead of cones as the receptors responsible for seeing color. Options A and B can both be rejected because they identify reaction times of rods and cones to stimuli as the key factors in seeing color. However, it is the type of visual receptor rather than the visual receptor's reaction time that is the determining factor.

55. A: Although some of Wundt's questions may have overlapped with those of philosophers, Wundt tried to test his views by collecting data. In doing so, he helped establish psychology as an empirical science. A central component of Wundt's methodology was asking subjects to report

their internal perceptions, or to introspect. However, modern psychology does not make use of this method; this eliminates option A. Wundt's method also eliminates option B; Wundt's views depended on reports of internal perception, rather than relying on publicly-observable behavior. Wundt wrote voluminously on many topics but often changed his mind; this eliminates option C.

56. B: the graphic best illustrates the concept of stratification. In sociology, stratification is the hierarchical structure or organization of human society. Because the chart indicates a hierarchical division of traditional Indian society (dividing society's members according to caste, with Brahmins occupying the most elevated position), the chart illustrates stratification. Assimilation is the process of an individual or group adopting the customs of another group; the graphic does not illustrate this process and option A can therefore be rejected. Diffusion occurs when a culture borrows ideas from another; socialization is the process by which an individual learns a culture. As the graphic illustrates neither of these processes, both options C and D can be rejected.

57. D: Under the War Powers Act of 1973, the President can send combat troops to battle (or to an area where hostilities are imminent) for only 60 days, with the possibility of extending this period of time to 90 days. In order to keep deployed troops in place (or to send additional troops) after this period of time has elapsed, the President must seek Congressional approval, either in the form of a mandate or in the form of a declaration of war. Option A can be eliminated because Congress was responsible for approving war-related funding prior to the War Powers Act, which did not affect this responsibility. Neither option B nor option C accurately describes the importance of the War Powers Act.

58. C: Prior to the Seventeenth Amendment, adopted in 1913, U.S. senators were chosen by state legislatures rather than by popular state elections. The former system caused problems beginning in the mid-nineteenth century, problems exacerbated by the fact that there was no consistent process among the states for just how state legislatures chose their U.S. Senators. The Seventeenth Amendment required that U.S. Senators be chosen by direct popular election by the citizens of the relevant state. The Seventeenth Amendment did not concern state senators (i.e., senators serving state Senates), governors, or censuses to determine the appropriate level of representation in a House of Representatives. This eliminates options A, B, and D.

59. C: The U.S. Supreme Court decision in Plessy v. Ferguson affirmed the state of Louisiana's constitutional right to offer "separate but equal" accommodations on railway lines within that state. The decision provided a legal basis for racial segregation in U.S. society, including segregation in education and other public services. Option A can be rejected because the primary importance of the ruling was less to reinforce state's rights than to affirm the supposed legality of segregation. The decision produced increasingly significant consequences as U.S. society continued to segregate. Plessy v. Ferguson did not address poll taxes or the legality of railway strikes; this eliminates options B and D.

60. C: A federalist system of government is a government under which power is shared by a central authority and sub-components of the federation. In the United States in particular, power is shared by the federal government and the individual states. Option A, that the legislative

branch consists of two representative bodies (the House of Representatives and the Senate) is true, of course, but does not describe a uniquely federalist structure. Rather, it describes the concept of bicameralism. Option A may thus be eliminated. Option B, likewise, describes different types of democracy but not federalism. B can thus be eliminated. Regarding option D, this statement is also true (the U.S. Constitution shapes national legislation) but it is not a descriptive statement of the federalist system because the statement makes no mention that power is shared by the states.

61. C: Line 3 best lists the kinds of cases over which the U.S. federal court system has jurisdiction. The U.S. federal court system has jurisdiction over cases involving constitutional law, bankruptcy, and disputes between states (the federal court system also has jurisdiction over cases concerning U.S. treaties and laws, among other types of cases). State courts have jurisdiction over most contract cases, most criminal cases, and most personal injury cases; this eliminates Line 1, Line 2, and Line 4, each of which list one of those kinds of cases as under the jurisdiction of the U.S. federal court system.

62. C: The main subject matter of civic responsibility is a person's responsibilities as a citizen. By contrast, the main subject matter of personal responsibility is one's responsibilities as a person. For example, keeping a promise to a friend is often a matter of personal responsibility because such a duty arises from the friendship. Serving on a jury when called to do so is an example of civic responsibility because such a duty arises from the person's citizenship. None of the other options given accurately describe the main subject matter of civic responsibility. For example, while a journalist might see accurate reporting of government actions as his or her civic responsibility, such reporting is not the main subject matter of civic responsibility, and is also a responsibility that arises from that journalist's employment. Similar reasoning applies to a person's responsibilities as a government worker. This eliminates options A and D. Civic responsibility does not primarily concern inter-government relations; this eliminates option B.

63. B: Under the Fifth Amendment to the U.S. Constitution, the government may not strip certain basic rights from citizens without following the law. In the language of the Fifth Amendment itself, a person shall not "be deprived of life, liberty, or property without due process of law." Of all the options, option C is the only one that accurately describes the concept of due process as understood in the Fifth Amendment. Because due process does not explicitly guarantee a trial by jury within a reasonable timeframe, nor equal protection under the law (concepts covered elsewhere in the Constitution), options A and C and be rejected. Option D can be rejected because the Constitution restricts the government's ability to take away certain rights without following the law, not without a "dire cause" (such as the threat of imminent attack).

64. C: Together with Lucretia Mott, women's rights advocate Elizabeth Cady Stanton organized the first women's rights convention in the United States. Historians often credit the convention with sparking the campaign for women's suffrage in the United States. Option A can be rejected because, though Stanton did attend the World's Anti-Slavery Confederation, women delegates were not officially recognized, and her attendance there did not carry the same weight regarding women's suffrage as Stanton's organization of the women's rights convention. Option B can be rejected because Stanton's service as president for the National American Woman Suffrage

Association occurred after the women's suffrage movement had already begun. Option D can be rejected because Stanton (with other activists) opposed the 15th Amendment giving African-American males the right to vote on the grounds that it was unjust, so long as the right to vote was still denied to women.

65. B: The Electoral College officially elects the President and the Vice President. The number of electors, or Electoral College members, allotted to a state is equal to that state's total number of U.S. Senators and U.S. Representatives. A state with two U.S. Senators and one U.S. Representative, for example, would have three electors in the Electoral College. Because every state has two U.S. Senators and at least one U.S. Representative, every state has at least 3 electors in the Electoral College. Option B is the only option that correctly describes how a state's number of Electoral College voters is determined; neither the number of counties in a state, nor the number of State Secretaries is relevant to this number.

66. C: Women, including notable women's rights activists such as Susan B. Anthony, figured importantly in the temperance movement of the 19th century in the United States. Many women were motivated not only by the association of saloons with gambling and prostitution, but by the association of alcohol and domestic violence. Lost productivity was a concern held by figures such as Henry Ford, but figured less prominently with respect to women's role in the temperance movement. This eliminates option B. Option D, infertility, was not a motivating factor. Regarding option A, some women's rights activists were also concerned about race relations and racial injustice, but a specific concern about racial violence was not a primary motivating factor behind the drive for temperance.

67. A: According to John Locke's version of social contract theory, when human beings are in the state of nature (prior to entering a social contract), each person has a right to punish another for breaking the moral law. Because it is not always feasible for someone to punish anyone else for such an offense, people form the social contract in part to delegate the right to punish to certain individuals. Option B can be rejected because Locke thought natural law provided a basis for moral behavior, and natural law was independent of a social contract. Option C is can be rejected because Locke believed that humans had natural rights inherently, i.e. that these rights were not conferred on them by a social contract. Finally, option D can be rejected because it describes Thomas Hobbes's view of the state of nature; Locke held a less pessimistic view.

68. B: Hammurabi's Code, a code by for ancient Babylonian society written by Hammurabi (king of Babylonia), is among the earliest written codes of law and helped establish a precedent for codifying law. Rather than restructuring Babylonian society, the Code described and codified many existing practices; this eliminates option A. Option C can be eliminated because Hammurabi's Code did not establish the same penalties for all law-breakers; rather, according to the Code, punishment depended in part upon the offender's social status, as well as that of the victim. Option D can be rejected because the Code included many punishments involving death or mutilation.

69. D: In a parliamentary form of government, the executive branch is essentially a committee of the legislative branch. This is the only answer that correctly describes the relation between the

executive branch and another branch of the government. The executive branch is neither a committee of the judicial branch, nor is it appointed by the judicial branch; this eliminates options B and C. The executive branch does not appoint members of the legislative branch; this eliminates option A. In the parliamentary government in Great Britain, for example, the legislature elects the Prime Minister, and the members of the Prime Minister's Cabinet are also selected from members of the legislative branch (either the House of Commons or the House of Lords).

70. A: Democracy of ancient Athens was direct rather than representative: citizens voted directly on issues rather than elected representatives doing it for them. Answer B can be rejected because the right to vote did not depend on a person's wealth or a on a person's family's wealth. However, voters did need to have Athenian parentage, and only free men could vote; women and slaves could not. Rather, Athens took pains to ensure that poor people could participate politically. Option C can be rejected because there were no political campaigns in Athens as they are understood today; many political positions were chosen by lot, i.e. men did not campaign for them. Finally, some actions could result in losing the right to vote; this eliminates option D.

71. A: When a company has a monopoly, it is the sole supplier of a good or service and therefore exercises great control over the price of that good or service. In an oligopoly, a small number of companies supply a given good or service (these companies might also act to control prices of that good or service). Because a monopoly differs from an oligopoly in this fundamental way, options B and D can each be rejected, as those answers describe an oligopoly as a kind of monopoly. Also, a monopoly might involve only one plant, but it could just as easily involve more than one; the distinguishing feature of a monopoly is its control over supply, not the number of plants or factories it uses in production. This eliminates option C.

72. C: Inflation is an overall increase in prices. Inflation commonly occurs when there is a large amount of printed currency circulating in an economy at a time when there are few available goods relative to that amount. Options A and B can be eliminated because each describe conditions under which deflation occurs (an overall falling of prices, the opposite of inflation). Option D can be rejected because when there is a relatively low amount of currency circulating within in an economy together with a relatively low number of available goods, prices are not apt to rise.

73. D: Keynes was an influential advocate of government intervention in a domestic economy for the purpose of stimulating economic growth. Keynes believed that appropriate government action could help end a recession more quickly; such measures might involve deficit spending. Because of this, and because Keynes is not associated with the view that deficit spending leads to inflation, option A can be eliminated. Additionally, Keynes is not closely associated with advocating government action to break up monopolies; this eliminates option A. Finally, option C can be eliminated because it describes Say's Law, which is in fact the opposite of Keynes's law: demand creates its own supply.

74. B: Economists understand the true cost of an action as not only its monetary cost but the cost of other opportunities missed as a result of pursuing that action. For example, if a person

chooses to go to school rather than working, the cost of the action involves not only tuition and other associated fees and expenses, but the money one would have earned working, as well as the time one could have spent pursuing other activities. The concept of opportunity cost is not described by options A, C, or D, each of which is concerned only with monetary costs. Each of these answers can be rejected on that basis.

75. D: The Federal Reserve has the power to buy and sell government bonds to or from banks, thereby raising or reducing interest rates. When banks buy government bonds, they have less money available to loan, and interest rates are higher; when banks sell bonds, they have more money available to loan, and interest rates are lower. Option A does accurately describe a tool of the Federal Reserve, but not a tool the Federal Reserve uses frequently; the same is true of option C, and therefore both options A and C can be rejected. Option D can be eliminated because the Federal Reserve does not buy or sell stock options to change interest rates.

76. A: The Sherman Antitrust Act outlawed "every contract, combination . . . or conspiracy in restraint of trade or commerce among the several States, or with foreign nations." Option C describes trade within states; because the Sherman Antitrust Act does not address such trade, option C can be rejected. Options B and D each describe a use of the Sherman Antitrust Act; i.e. the Act was instrumental in breaking up both the Standard Oil trust and the AT&T monopoly. However, neither of these particular uses are as influential as the general outlawing of acts restraining trade between states; rather, it was the general prohibition which made these particular applications (and others) possible. This eliminates options B and D.

77. A: Corporations offer limited liability protection, unlike sole proprietorships. For example, the person running a corporation is not personally liable for the debts of a corporation to the extent that a person running a sole proprietorship is for the debts of the proprietorship. In a sole proprietorship, the sole proprietor has unlimited liability for the debts of the business. Note that such debts include ordinary operating expenses, tax liability, liability from lawsuits, etc. Option B can be eliminated because corporations run afoul of the "double tax" problem, when the person running a corporation (who pays himself from the company earnings) pays tax on the company's earnings twice, first via the taxes assessed against corporation itself and second via his or her own personal income tax. Corporations are more expensive to form than sole proprietorships, but this is a disadvantage; this eliminates option C. Option D can be eliminated because corporations are more difficult to dissolve than sole proprietorships.

78. B: Unemployment leads to lost productivity because people who would be productive if employed (thus contributing to economic growth) are not economically productive when they do not have work. Option A can be rejected because high unemployment is not typically thought to be a central cause of inflation; rather, high levels of unemployment might instead contribute to deflation (an overall decrease in prices). Option C can be rejected because unemployment would tend to have the effect of decreasing aggregate demand rather than increasing it, simply because fewer people would have money with which to make purchases. Option D can be rejected because unemployment is less likely to increase aggregate supply than to reduce it (fewer people working means fewer people producing goods and services).

79. D: Einstein's special theory of relativity, which he proposed in 1905, postulated the relativity of simultaneity (also the relativity of motion), i.e. that there is no absolute simultaneity. What counts as simultaneous depends on one's frame of reference. Some of Einstein's later work, but not his 1905 special theory of relativity, pertained to constructing a unified field theory; this eliminates option A. Option B can rejected because Einstein's famous work on gravity occurred later, not in his special theory of relativity. Option C can be rejected because Einstein did not believe that the speed of light is relative; rather, it is constant no matter one's frame of reference.

80. A: Eli Whitney's invention of the cotton gin, a mechanism for quickly separating cotton seeds from cotton fiber, helped elevate cotton as a basis of the Southern economy. Option B can be rejected because, rather than leading to smaller plantations, the invention led to larger cotton plantations. Choice C can be rejected because the United States did not need to import cotton; rather, particularly after the invention of the cotton gin, the United States became a leading exporter of cotton. Finally, option D can be rejected because with larger plantations came an increased need for slaves: the cotton gin had the effect of increasing dependence on slave labor rather than decreasing it.

81. D: Arabic mathematicians, such as the ninth-century mathematician al-Khwarizmi, made important contributions to algebra; the term "algebra" itself derives from a work of al-Khwarizmi's. However, Arabic algebra did not recognize negative numbers; this eliminates option B. Option C can be rejected because probability was developed initially by French mathematicians Blaise Pascal and Pierre de Fermat. Option A can be rejected because modern calculus (building on earlier foundations) is usually taken to have begun (separately) in the works of Isaac Newton and Gottfried Leibniz.

82. A: Jonas Salk's polio vaccine prevented thousands of new cases of polio in a nation which had become accustomed to the ravages of the disease. The invention was a major innovation that affected Americans all over the United States, as children were vaccinated against the disease. Unfortunately, Salk's vaccine did cause polio in a small number of children; however, option B can be rejected because the impact of this was lesser than the impact than the near eradication of the disease in the United States. Option C can be rejected because, although Salk's manner of announcing the vaccine ruffled the feathers of some of his scientist peers, it did not ignite a widespread or public debate regarding the media and science. Finally, option D can be rejected because it is simply false.

83. B: Reification is the act of treating an abstraction as a real, concrete thing. For example, the concept of society might be useful, but it is not an actual, concrete thing separate from the components (such as people and infrastructure) that make up society. Options A, C, and D can all be rejected because none accurately capture the concept of reification. Social scientists might indeed be concerned with relative appropriateness of qualitative data and quantitative data, but using one over the other is not reification. Social scientists might use heuristic devices, but this is not simply reification (not all cases of reification are cases of using heuristic devices). Reification is not mistaking subjectivity for objectivity.

84. C: Learning such an association is classical conditioning. Generally, classical conditioning is the process of learning an association between two stimuli, one of which is neutral (in this instance, the sound of the can opener) and one to which an organism responds automatically (in this instance, food). Habituation occurs when an organism becomes desensitized to a repeated stimulus; this eliminates option B. Operant conditioning differs from classical conditioning in that, in the former, an organism changes its behavior in response to reinforcement (that is, an organism can change the outcome of an event by changing its behavior). This eliminates option A. Conformity is the process by which an organism changes its behavior to match others' behavior. This eliminates option D.

85. B: Anthropology is the study of the origin and development of human kind and is much less concerned than psychology with individual human behavior (psychology is the study of the human mind and behavior). Psychology and anthropology both involve natural sciences, for example information about how the brain works; option A can rejected on that basis. Anthropologists commonly use qualitative methods as well as quantitative methods; this eliminates option C. Finally, option D can be rejected because anthropology involves more than a study of physical human evolution; it also includes subjects such as culture and language, for example.

86. D: A practical application of content learned involves action, not merely knowledge. Options A and C, although they describe content that students would reasonably learn in a class or unit on the structure of the U.S. government, do not describe applications of content, or applications of a social studies education. Therefore options A and C can both be rejected. Option B does involve action and not merely the acquisition of knowledge. However, it is not as directly tied to learning the structure of the U.S. government as option D, informed participation in U.S. political processes. This is because informed participation in school elections is quite possible without knowing the structure of the U.S government. Informed participation in U.S. political processes requires knowledge of the structure of the U.S. government (i.e., voting on an issue requires an understanding of where a given candidate stands on that issue).

87. C: Primary sources are sources that were created at the time of the event in question. For examples, recordings of Martin Luther King's speeches, newspaper accounts of King's activities at the time of those activities, and King's written documents are all primary resources regarding Martin Luther King's work. Secondary sources, such as a history book that contains a subchapter on the work of MLK, are secondhand and are almost always created after the fact. This eliminates choice A. Secondary sources do not need to be text-only, nor visual only, as the example above illustrates; this eliminates both options B and D.

88. A: the most reasonable inference based on the data given by the map is that the areas with no shading (which represent areas of low water use) are less inhabited than areas with shading. Note that the areas with no shading also have no listed cities; cities on the map are surrounded by shaded areas. Because the map does not give any information regarding how much water is required per capita, option D can be rejected. The map gives no indication regarding residents' prowess at conservation efforts (positive or negative). This eliminates option C. Additionally,

there is no indication from the map that any land is more desert-like. In fact, some of the lightly-shaded are is adjacent to the ocean. Therefore, option B can be rejected.

89. C: The graph shows a shift in demand, with a corresponding increase in the price of SuperCell Batteries. The shift is illustrated by the two demand curves, with Demand 2 curve illustrating an increase in price. Because the price has increased, not decreased, this eliminates option A. The equilibrium point is the point at which the quantity demanded equals the quantity supplied. The graph shows two equilibrium points, the first where Demand 1 meets the supply curve, and the second where Demand 2 meets the supply curve. Because equilibrium has shifted, option B can eliminated. Regarding option D, a double coincidence of wants occurs when two people each have a good or service the other wants, giving rise to the possibility of trade (without money). The graph does not illustrate anything regarding a double coincidence of wants, so option D can rejected on that basis.

90. A: The passage is a firsthand account of witnessing, via television, the first moon landing, and is best suited for teaching students what that experience was like. Although the source does briefly describe the surface of the moon, this description is not the main idea of the passage and is too brief to be well-suited for a unit on this topic. This eliminates option B. Option C can be eliminated because the author of the passage makes clear that he or she was very young at the time of the landing, and the author explicitly states that he or she is not clear how it was possible to show the moon landing live on earth. Finally, option D can be rejected because although the author does describe a change the author's family's own television, the passage makes no general claims about changes in television use.

91. D: A claim is biased when it is not objective but instead tilted in favor of a perspective. In this case, the author's use of "our" in the sentence, "That just showed again how our technology, American technology, had become much more advanced than Russian technology," shows that the author is American and identifies with American achievements. This in and of itself does not demonstrate that the author's claim is biased but illustrates that the author reasonably has a motivation for making a claim biased in favor of American technology. Further, because the author was young when he or she had the thought about technology, and because there is no indication that the author had been to Russia or studied technology, there is no foundation to show that the author used any objective criteria when rendering his or her opinion. There seems to be no similar motivation for the claims in the other options to be biased.

92. A: Case studies typically involve gathering qualitative data, such as data acquired through personal observations of the subjects of the case study, or by interviewing the subjects of the case study. Less common in case studies is the gathering of quantitative data. Because a typical case study does not gather quantitative data, it also does not involve statistical analysis. This eliminates options B and C. Finally, option D can be eliminated because common research methods in case studies, such as interviews, do not involve an absence of contact between a researcher and the subjects of the study.

93. A: The author's main point in the passage is that people should consider what justifies the use of deadly weapons on civilians, both in the historical case of the bombing of Hiroshima and

Nagasaki, as well as in the present. Both the opening and concluding sentences concern citizens and reflection, or examination, while the middle of the passage offers historical facts to illustrate an alternative and lesser-known reason for the bombing. All this suggests that A correctly describes the main idea of the passage. Option B can be rejected because the author, rather than stating that the use of such weapons is not justified, instead raises the question of when it is and urges the importance of asking this question. Options C can be rejected because the author does not make that general claim; option D describes a more minor idea expressed in the passage.

94. C: In the final sentences of the passage, the author explicitly draws a connection between the historical events of the bombings of Hiroshima and Nagasaki and the contemporary issue of terrorism; relevant to both, the author suggests, is the issue of when it is justified to use deadly weapons on civilians. Option A can be rejected because the author does not claim that popular culture ignores the views of historians. Option B can be eliminated because the author does not make a general claim about the importance of one historical event over the other. Option D can be eliminated because the author does not make a claim that history is written by the victors; nowhere in the passage, for example, is the claim that the U.S. government or U.S. citizens attempted to give a deceptive account of the bombings of Hiroshima and Nagasaki.

95. C: 25%. In statistical analysis, the range is the difference between the highest value and the smallest value within a given set of data. Here, the highest value for voter participation in Cedar Valley is 67%, and the smallest value is 42%. The difference between these two is 25, so the range here is 25. Option C is the only answer that correctly gives the range for this set of data; options B and D express a span of numbers but not the range in the statistical sense; they can therefore be rejected. Option D does not give a difference between the largest and smallest values and can therefore be rejected.

96. B: according to the chart, the median for voter participation in Cedar Valley is 55%. In general, the median is the value in the "center" – it is the middle value within a set of values that are arranged in ascending or descending order. For example, in a set of values consisting of 2, 4, 6, 8, and 10, the median is 6. Option A gives the mean (or average) for voter participation, not the median. Options C and D do not give the median, either, and can therefore be rejected.

97. A: Critical writing involves evaluation, not merely the reporting of information. Because option A asks students to make a claim and defend it, it requires students to practice their critical writing skills. Options B and D can be rejected because they do not involve this sort of evaluation or judgment, but merely the reporting of information. Option C is not the best choice because creative work does not necessarily involve making arguments or giving reasons, i.e. does not necessarily involve explicit argumentation in the way that critical writing does.

98. C: A key to the question is the relation between supply and demand. The use of graphics in presentation software can be used effectively to show supply and demand curves, which effectively show the relation between supply and demand. Neither options A and B explain the relation between supply and demand; option A merely involves listing such terms, and B merely involves understanding the terms in isolation, but not the relation between them. Option C can be rejected because it concerns only demand, not supply and demand.

99. B: According to TEKS, students in high school, having previously studied earlier periods of U.S. history, must learn U.S. history from Reconstruction to the present. Required content specifically includes (but is not limited to) an understanding of significant eras in the United States during that time, U.S. involvement in conflicts such as World Wars I and II, various social and political issues, and more. Option B is the only option that correctly answers this question; options A, C, and D each wrongly identify the earliest era of U.S. history school students study.

100. B: Only option B requires a student to take knowledge of supply and demand and consider how each component interacts with the other, i.e. to analyze the concepts. To interpret a supply curve is to consider how supply affects demand and vice versa in a particular case. Option A requires the giving of information of supply and demand, but not the application of it; A can therefore be eliminated. Options C and D, though related perhaps to supply and demand, do not explicitly call for the application of particular knowledge of supply and demand. Options C and D, then, can both be rejected.

Constructed Response

The Great Depression was a sudden turning point for U.S. culture. Under President Franklin D. Roosevelt's "New Deal" legislation, programs and departments like the Works Progress Administration, Civilian Conservation Corps, Social Security System, and Securities and Exchange Commission, among others, were born. Discuss the impact the Great Depression and subsequent New Deal legislation had on U.S. history, focusing on how these effects can still be seen in the current culture, economy, and political ideology of the United States.

Special Report: What Your Test Score Will Tell You About Your IQ

Did you know that most standardized tests correlate very strongly with IQ? In fact, your general intelligence is a better predictor of your success than any other factor, and most tests intentionally measure this trait to some degree to ensure that those selected by the test are truly qualified for the test's purposes.

Before we can delve into the relation between your test score and IQ, I will first have to explain what exactly is IQ. Here's the formula:

Your IQ = 100 + (Number of standard deviations below or above the average)*15

Now, let's define standard deviations by using an example. If we have 5 people with 5 different heights, then first we calculate the average. Let's say the average was 65 inches. The standard deviation is the "average distance" away from the average of each of the members. It is a direct measure of variability - if the 5 people included Jackie Chan and Shaquille O'Neal, obviously there's a lot more variability in that group than a group of 5 sisters who are all within 6 inches in height of each other. The standard deviation uses a number to characterize the average range of difference within a group.

A convenient feature of most groups is that they have a "normal" distribution- makes sense that most things would be normal, right? Without getting into a bunch of statistical mumbo-jumbo, you just need to know that if you know the average of the group and the standard deviation, you can successfully predict someone's percentile rank in the group.

Confused? Let me give you an example. If instead of 5 people's heights, we had 100 people, we could figure out their rank in height JUST by knowing the average, standard deviation, and their height. We wouldn't need to know each person's height and manually rank them, we could just predict their rank based on three numbers.

What this means is that you can take your PERCENTILE rank that is often given with your test and relate this to your RELATIVE IQ of people taking the test - that is, your IQ relative to the people taking the test. Obviously, there's no way to know your actual IQ because the people taking a standardized test are usually not very good samples of the general population- many of those with extremely low IQ's never achieve a level of success or competency necessary to complete a typical standardized test. In fact, professional psychologists who measure IQ actually have to use non-written tests that can fairly measure the IQ of those not able to complete a traditional test.

The bottom line is to not take your test score too seriously, but it is fun to compute your "relative IQ" among the people who took the test with you. I've done the calculations below. Just look up your percentile rank in the left and then you'll see your "relative IQ" for your test in the right hand column-

Percentile Rank	Your Relative IQ		Percentile Rank	Your Relative IQ
99	135		59	103
98	131		58	103
97	128		57	103
96	126		56	102
95	125		55	102
94	123		54	102
93	122		53	101
92	121		52	101
91	120		51	100
90	119		50	100
89	118		49	100
88	118		48	99
87	117		47	99
86	116		46	98
85	116		45	98
84	115		44	98
83	114		43	97
82	114		42	97
81	113		41	97
80	113		40	96
79	112		39	96
78	112		38	95
77	111		37	95
76	111		36	95
75	110		35	94
74	110		34	94
73	109		33	93
72	109		32	93
71	108		31	93
70	108		30	92
69	107		29	92
68	107		28	91
67	107		27	91
66	106		26	90
65	106		25	90
64	105		24	89
63	105		23	89
62	105		22	88
61	104		21	88
60	104		20	87

Special Report: What is Test Anxiety and How to Overcome It?

The very nature of tests caters to some level of anxiety, nervousness or tension, just as we feel for any important event that occurs in our lives. A little bit of anxiety or nervousness can be a good thing. It helps us with motivation, and makes achievement just that much sweeter. However, too much anxiety can be a problem; especially if it hinders our ability to function and perform.

"Test anxiety," is the term that refers to the emotional reactions that some test-takers experience when faced with a test or exam. Having a fear of testing and exams is based upon a rational fear, since the test-taker's performance can shape the course of an academic career. Nevertheless, experiencing excessive fear of examinations will only interfere with the test-takers ability to perform, and his/her chances to be successful.

There are a large variety of causes that can contribute to the development and sensation of test anxiety. These include, but are not limited to lack of performance and worrying about issues surrounding the test.

Lack of Preparation

Lack of preparation can be identified by the following behaviors or situations:

Not scheduling enough time to study, and therefore cramming the night before the test or exam
Managing time poorly, to create the sensation that there is not enough time to do everything
Failing to organize the text information in advance, so that the study material consists of the entire text and not simply the pertinent information
Poor overall studying habits

Worrying, on the other hand, can be related to both the test taker, or many other factors around him/her that will be affected by the results of the test. These include worrying about:

Previous performances on similar exams, or exams in general
How friends and other students are achieving
The negative consequences that will result from a poor grade or failure

There are three primary elements to test anxiety. Physical components, which involve the same typical bodily reactions as those to acute anxiety (to be discussed below). Emotional factors have to do with fear or panic. Mental or cognitive issues concerning attention spans and memory abilities.

Physical Signals

There are many different symptoms of test anxiety, and these are not limited to mental and emotional strain. Frequently there are a range of physical signals that will let a test taker know that he/she is suffering from test anxiety. These bodily changes can include the following:

Perspiring
Sweaty palms
Wet, trembling hands
Nausea
Dry mouth
A knot in the stomach
Headache
Faintness
Muscle tension
Aching shoulders, back and neck
Rapid heart beat
Feeling too hot/cold

To recognize the sensation of test anxiety, a test-taker should monitor him/herself for the following sensations:

The physical distress symptoms as listed above
Emotional sensitivity, expressing emotional feelings such as the need to cry or laugh too much, or a sensation of anger or helplessness
A decreased ability to think, causing the test-taker to blank out or have racing thoughts that are hard to organize or control.

Though most students will feel some level of anxiety when faced with a test or exam, the majority can cope with that anxiety and maintain it at a manageable level. However, those who cannot are faced with a very real and very serious condition, which can and should be controlled for the immeasurable benefit of this sufferer.

Naturally, these sensations lead to negative results for the testing experience. The most common effects of test anxiety have to do with nervousness and mental blocking.

Nervousness

Nervousness can appear in several different levels:

The test-taker's difficulty, or even inability to read and understand the questions on the test
The difficulty or inability to organize thoughts to a coherent form
The difficulty or inability to recall key words and concepts relating to the testing questions (especially essays)
The receipt of poor grades on a test, though the test material was well known by the test taker

Conversely, a person may also experience mental blocking, which involves:

Blanking out on test questions
Only remembering the correct answers to the questions when the test has already finished.

Fortunately for test anxiety sufferers, beating these feelings, to a large degree, has to do with proper preparation. When a test taker has a feeling of preparedness, then anxiety will be dramatically lessened.

The first step to resolving anxiety issues is to distinguish which of the two types of anxiety are being suffered. If the anxiety is a direct result of a lack of preparation, this should be considered a normal reaction, and the anxiety level (as opposed to the test results) shouldn't be anything to worry about. However, if, when adequately prepared, the test-taker still panics, blanks out, or seems to overreact, this is not a fully rational reaction. While this can be considered normal too, there are many ways to combat and overcome these effects.

Remember that anxiety cannot be entirely eliminated, however, there are ways to minimize it, to make the anxiety easier to manage. Preparation is one of the best ways to minimize test anxiety. Therefore the following techniques are wise in order to best fight off any anxiety that may want to build.

To begin with, try to avoid cramming before a test, whenever it is possible. By trying to memorize an entire term's worth of information in one day, you'll be shocking your system, and not giving yourself a very good chance to absorb the information. This is an easy path to anxiety, so for those who suffer from test anxiety, cramming should not even be considered an option.

Instead of cramming, work throughout the semester to combine all of the material which is presented throughout the semester, and work on it gradually as the course goes by, making sure to master the main concepts first, leaving minor details for a week or so before the test.

To study for the upcoming exam, be sure to pose questions that may be on the examination, to gauge the ability to answer them by integrating the ideas from your texts, notes and lectures, as well as any supplementary readings.
If it is truly impossible to cover all of the information that was covered in that particular term, concentrate on the most important portions, that can be covered very well. Learn these concepts as best as possible, so that when the test comes, a goal can be made to use these concepts as presentations of your knowledge.

In addition to study habits, changes in attitude are critical to beating a struggle with test anxiety. In fact, an improvement of the perspective over the entire test-taking experience can actually help a test taker to enjoy studying and therefore improve the overall experience. Be certain not to overemphasize the significance of the grade - know that the result of the test is neither a reflection of self worth, nor is it a measure of intelligence; one grade will not predict a person's future success.

To improve an overall testing outlook, the following steps should be tried:

Keeping in mind that the most reasonable expectation for taking a test is to expect to try to demonstrate as much of what you know as you possibly can.
Reminding ourselves that a test is only one test; this is not the only one, and there will be others.
The thought of thinking of oneself in an irrational, all-or-nothing term should be avoided at all costs.
A reward should be designated for after the test, so there's something to look forward to. Whether it be going to a movie, going out to eat, or simply visiting friends, schedule it in advance, and do it no matter what result is expected on the exam.

Test-takers should also keep in mind that the basics are some of the most important things, even beyond anti-anxiety techniques and studying. Never neglect the basic social, emotional and biological needs, in order to try to absorb information. In order to best achieve, these three factors must be held as just as important as the studying itself.

Study Steps

Remember the following important steps for studying:

Maintain healthy nutrition and exercise habits. Continue both your recreational activities and social pass times. These both contribute to your physical and emotional well being.
Be certain to get a good amount of sleep, especially the night before the test, because when you're overtired you are not able to perform to the best of your best ability.
Keep the studying pace to a moderate level by taking breaks when they are needed, and varying the work whenever possible, to keep the mind fresh instead of getting bored.
When enough studying has been done that all the material that can be learned has been learned, and the test taker is prepared for the test, stop studying and do something relaxing such as listening to music, watching a movie, or taking a warm bubble bath.

There are also many other techniques to minimize the uneasiness or apprehension that is experienced along with test anxiety before, during, or even after the examination. In fact, there are a great deal of things that can be done to stop anxiety from interfering with lifestyle and performance. Again, remember that anxiety will not be eliminated entirely, and it shouldn't be. Otherwise that "up" feeling for exams would not exist, and most of us depend on that sensation to perform better than usual. However, this anxiety has to be at a level that is manageable.

Of course, as we have just discussed, being prepared for the exam is half the battle right away. Attending all classes, finding out what knowledge will be expected on the exam, and knowing the exam schedules are easy steps to lowering anxiety. Keeping up with work will remove the need to cram, and efficient study habits will eliminate wasted time. Studying should be done in an ideal location for concentration, so that it is simple to become interested in the material and give it complete attention. A method such as SQ3R (Survey, Question, Read, Recite, Review) is a wonderful key to follow to make sure that the study habits are as effective as possible, especially in the case of learning from a textbook. Flashcards are great techniques for memorization. Learning to take good notes will mean that notes will be full of useful information, so that less sifting will need to be done to seek out what is pertinent for studying. Reviewing notes after class and then again on occasion will keep the information fresh in the mind. From notes that have been taken summary sheets and outlines can be made for simpler reviewing.

A study group can also be a very motivational and helpful place to study, as there will be a sharing of ideas, all of the minds can work together, to make sure that everyone understands, and the studying will be made more interesting because it will be a social occasion.

Basically, though, as long as the test-taker remains organized and self confident, with efficient study habits, less time will need to be spent studying, and higher grades will be achieved.

To become self confident, there are many useful steps. The first of these is "self talk." It has been shown through extensive research, that self-talk for students who suffer from test anxiety, should be well monitored, in order to make sure that it contributes to self confidence as opposed to sinking the student. Frequently the self talk of test-anxious students is negative or self-defeating, thinking that everyone else is smarter and faster, that they always mess up, and that if they don't do well, they'll fail the entire course. It is important to decreasing anxiety that awareness is made of self talk. Try writing any negative self thoughts and then disputing them with a positive statement instead. Begin self-encouragement as though it was a friend speaking. Repeat positive statements to help reprogram the mind to believing in successes instead of failures.

Helpful Techniques

Other extremely helpful techniques include:

Self-visualization of doing well and reaching goals
While aiming for an "A" level of understanding, don't try to "overprotect" by setting your expectations lower. This will only convince the mind to stop studying in order to meet the lower expectations.
Don't make comparisons with the results or habits of other students. These are individual factors, and different things work for different people, causing different results.
Strive to become an expert in learning what works well, and what can be done in order to improve. Consider collecting this data in a journal.
Create rewards for after studying instead of doing things before studying that will only turn into avoidance behaviors.
Make a practice of relaxing - by using methods such as progressive relaxation, self-hypnosis, guided imagery, etc - in order to make relaxation an automatic sensation.
Work on creating a state of relaxed concentration so that concentrating will take on the focus of the mind, so that none will be wasted on worrying.
Take good care of the physical self by eating well and getting enough sleep.
Plan in time for exercise and stick to this plan.

Beyond these techniques, there are other methods to be used before, during and after the test that will help the test-taker perform well in addition to overcoming anxiety.

Before the exam comes the academic preparation. This involves establishing a study schedule and beginning at least one week before the actual date of the test. By doing this, the anxiety of not having enough time to study for the test will be automatically eliminated. Moreover, this will make the studying a much more effective experience, ensuring that the learning will be an easier process. This relieves much undue pressure on the test-taker.

Summary sheets, note cards, and flash cards with the main concepts and examples of these main concepts should be prepared in advance of the actual studying time. A topic should never be eliminated from this process. By omitting a topic because it isn't expected to be on the test is only setting up the test-taker for anxiety should it actually appear on the exam. Utilize the course syllabus for laying out the topics that should be studied. Carefully go over the notes that were made in class, paying special attention to any of the issues that the professor took special care to emphasize while lecturing in class. In the textbooks, use the chapter review, or if possible, the chapter tests, to begin your review.

It may even be possible to ask the instructor what information will be covered on the exam, or what the format of the exam will be (for example, multiple choice, essay, free form, true-false). Additionally, see if it is possible to find out how many questions will be on the test. If a review sheet or sample test has been offered by the professor, make good use of it, above anything else, for the preparation for the test. Another great resource for getting to know the examination is reviewing tests from previous semesters. Use these tests to review, and aim to achieve a 100% score on each of the possible topics. With a few exceptions, the goal that you set for yourself is the highest one that you will reach.

Take all of the questions that were assigned as homework, and rework them to any other possible course material. The more problems reworked, the more skill and confidence will form as a result. When forming the solution to a problem, write out each of the steps. Don't simply do head work. By doing as many steps on paper as possible, much clarification and therefore confidence will be formed. Do this with as many homework problems as possible, before checking the answers. By checking the answer after each problem, a reinforcement will exist, that will not be on the exam. Study situations should be as exam-like as possible, to prime the test-taker's system for the experience. By waiting to check the answers at the end, a psychological advantage will be formed, to decrease the stress factor.

Another fantastic reason for not cramming is the avoidance of confusion in concepts, especially when it comes to mathematics. 8-10 hours of study will become one hundred percent more effective if it is spread out over a week or at least several days, instead of doing it all in one sitting. Recognize that the human brain requires time in order to assimilate new material, so frequent breaks and a span of study time over several days will be much more beneficial.

Additionally, don't study right up until the point of the exam. Studying should stop a minimum of one hour before the exam begins. This allows the brain to rest and put things in their proper order. This will also provide the time to become as relaxed as possible when going into the examination room. The test-taker will also have time to eat well and eat sensibly. Know that the brain needs food as much as the rest of the body. With enough food and enough sleep, as well as a relaxed attitude, the body and the mind are primed for success.

Avoid any anxious classmates who are talking about the exam. These students only spread anxiety, and are not worth sharing the anxious sentimentalities.

Before the test also involves creating a positive attitude, so mental preparation should also be a point of concentration. There are many keys to creating a positive attitude. Should fears become rushing in, make a visualization of taking the exam, doing well, and seeing an A written on the paper. Write out a list of affirmations that will bring a feeling of confidence, such as "I am doing well in my English class," "I studied well and know my material," "I enjoy this class." Even if the affirmations aren't believed at first, it sends a positive message to the subconscious which will result in an alteration of the overall belief system, which is the system that creates reality.

If a sensation of panic begins, work with the fear and imagine the very worst! Work through the entire scenario of not passing the test, failing the entire course, and dropping out of school, followed by not getting a job, and pushing a shopping cart through the dark alley where you'll live. This will place things into perspective! Then, practice deep breathing and create a visualization of the opposite situation - achieving an "A" on the exam, passing the entire course, receiving the degree at a graduation ceremony.

On the day of the test, there are many things to be done to ensure the best results, as well as the most calm outlook. The following stages are suggested in order to maximize test-taking potential:

Begin the examination day with a moderate breakfast, and avoid any coffee or beverages with caffeine if the test taker is prone to jitters. Even people who are used to managing caffeine can feel jittery or light-headed when it is taken on a test day.

Attempt to do something that is relaxing before the examination begins. As last minute cramming clouds the mastering of overall concepts, it is better to use this time to create a calming outlook.
Be certain to arrive at the test location well in advance, in order to provide time to select a location that is away from doors, windows and other distractions, as well as giving enough time to relax before the test begins.

Keep away from anxiety generating classmates who will upset the sensation of stability and relaxation that is being attempted before the exam.

Should the waiting period before the exam begins cause anxiety, create a self-distraction by reading a light magazine or something else that is relaxing and simple.

During the exam itself, read the entire exam from beginning to end, and find out how much time should be allotted to each individual problem. Once writing the exam, should more time be taken for a problem, it should be abandoned, in order to begin another problem. If there is time at the end, the unfinished problem can always be returned to and completed.

Read the instructions very carefully - twice - so that unpleasant surprises won't follow during or after the exam has ended.

When writing the exam, pretend that the situation is actually simply the completion of homework within a library, or at home. This will assist in forming a relaxed atmosphere, and will allow the brain extra focus for the complex thinking function.

Begin the exam with all of the questions with which the most confidence is felt. This will build the confidence level regarding the entire exam and will begin a quality momentum. This will also create encouragement for trying the problems where uncertainty resides.

Going with the "gut instinct" is always the way to go when solving a problem. Second guessing should be avoided at all costs. Have confidence in the ability to do well.

For essay questions, create an outline in advance that will keep the mind organized and make certain that all of the points are remembered. For multiple choice, read every answer, even if the correct one has been spotted - a better one may exist.

Continue at a pace that is reasonable and not rushed, in order to be able to work carefully. Provide enough time to go over the answers at the end, to check for small errors that can be corrected.

Should a feeling of panic begin, breathe deeply, and think of the feeling of the body releasing sand through its pores. Visualize a calm, peaceful place, and include all of the sights, sounds and sensations of this image. Continue the deep breathing, and take a few minutes to continue this with closed eyes. When all is well again, return to the test.

If a "blanking" occurs for a certain question, skip it and move on to the next question. There will be time to return to the other question later. Get everything done that can be done, first, to guarantee all the grades that can be compiled, and to build all of the confidence possible. Then return to the weaker questions to build the marks from there.

Remember, one's own reality can be created, so as long as the belief is there, success will follow. And remember: anxiety can happen later, right now, there's an exam to be written!

After the examination is complete, whether there is a feeling for a good grade or a bad grade, don't dwell on the exam, and be certain to follow through on the reward that was promised...and enjoy it! Don't dwell on any mistakes that have been made, as there is nothing that can be done at this point anyway.

Additionally, don't begin to study for the next test right away. Do something relaxing for a while, and let the mind relax and prepare itself to begin absorbing information again.

From the results of the exam - both the grade and the entire experience, be certain to learn from what has gone on. Perfect studying habits and work some more on confidence in order to make the next examination experience even better than the last one.

Learn to avoid places where openings occurred for laziness, procrastination and day dreaming.

Use the time between this exam and the next one to better learn to relax, even learning to relax on cue, so that any anxiety can be controlled during the next exam. Learn how to relax the body. Slouch in your chair if that helps. Tighten and then relax all of the different muscle groups, one group at a time, beginning with the feet and then working all the way up to the neck and face. This will ultimately relax the muscles more than they were to begin with. Learn how to breathe deeply and comfortably, and focus on this breathing going in and out as a relaxing thought. With every exhale, repeat the word "relax."

As common as test anxiety is, it is very possible to overcome it. Make yourself one of the test-takers who overcome this frustrating hindrance.

Special Report: Retaking the Test: What Are Your Chances at Improving Your Score?

After going through the experience of taking a major test, many test takers feel that once is enough. The test usually comes during a period of transition in the test taker's life, and taking the test is only one of a series of important events. With so many distractions and conflicting recommendations, it may be difficult for a test taker to rationally determine whether or not he should retake the test after viewing his scores.

The importance of the test usually only adds to the burden of the retake decision. However, don't be swayed by emotion. There a few simple questions that you can ask yourself to guide you as you try to determine whether a retake would improve your score:

1. What went wrong? Why wasn't your score what you expected?

Can you point to a single factor or problem that you feel caused the low score? Were you sick on test day? Was there an emotional upheaval in your life that caused a distraction? Were you late for the test or not able to use the full time allotment? If you can point to any of these specific, individual problems, then a retake should definitely be considered.

2. Is there enough time to improve?

Many problems that may show up in your score report may take a lot of time for improvement. A deficiency in a particular math skill may require weeks or months of tutoring and studying to improve. If you have enough time to improve an identified weakness, then a retake should definitely be considered.

3. How will additional scores be used? Will a score average, highest score, or most recent score be used?

Different test scores may be handled completely differently. If you've taken the test multiple times, sometimes your highest score is used, sometimes your average score is computed and used, and sometimes your most recent score is used. Make sure you understand what method will be used to evaluate your scores, and use that to help you determine whether a retake should be considered.

4. Are my practice test scores significantly higher than my actual test score?

If you have taken a lot of practice tests and are consistently scoring at a much higher level than your actual test score, then you should consider a retake. However, if you've taken five practice tests and only one of your scores was higher than your actual test score, or if your practice test scores were only slightly higher than your actual test score, then it is unlikely that you will significantly increase your score.

5. Do I need perfect scores or will I be able to live with this score? Will this score still allow me to follow my dreams?

What kind of score is acceptable to you? Is your current score "good enough?" Do you have to have a certain score in order to pursue the future of your dreams? If you won't be happy with your current score, and there's no way that you could live with it, then you should consider a retake. However, don't get your hopes up. If you are looking for significant improvement, that may or may not be possible. But if you won't be happy otherwise, it is at least worth the effort.
Remember that there are other considerations. To achieve your dream, it is likely that your grades may also be taken into account. A great test score is usually not the only thing necessary to succeed. Make sure that you aren't overemphasizing the importance of a high test score.

Furthermore, a retake does not always result in a higher score. Some test takers will score lower on a retake, rather than higher. One study shows that one-fourth of test takers will achieve a significant improvement in test score, while one-sixth of test takers will actually show a decrease. While this shows that most test takers will improve, the majority will only improve their scores a little and a retake may not be worth the test taker's effort.

Finally, if a test is taken only once and is considered in the added context of good grades on the part of a test taker, the person reviewing the grades and scores may be tempted to assume that the test taker just had a bad day while taking the test, and may discount the low test score in favor of the high grades. But if the test is retaken and the scores are approximately the same, then the validity of the low scores are only confirmed. Therefore, a retake could actually hurt a test taker by definitely bracketing a test taker's score ability to a limited range.

Special Report: Additional Bonus Material

Due to our efforts to try to keep this book to a manageable length, we've created a link that will give you access to all of your additional bonus material.

Please visit http://www.mometrix.com/bonus948/priisocstped to access the information.